PENGUIN BOOKS

# A TREASURY OF DECEPTION

Michael Farquhar is the author of *A Treasury of Royal Scandals: The Shocking True Stories of History's Wickedest, Weirdest, Most Wanton Kings, Queens, Tsars, Popes, and Emperors* and *A Treasury of Great American Scandals: Tantalizing True Tales of Historic Misbehavior by the Founding Fathers and Others Who Let Freedom Swing*. A writer and editor at *The Washington Post* specializing in history, he is coauthor of *The Century: History as It Happened on the Front Page of the Capital's Newspaper*. His work has been published in *The Chicago Sun-Times, Chicago Tribune, The Dallas Morning News, Reader's Digest,* and Discovery Online. He appeared on the History Channel's programs *Russia: The Land of the Tsars* and *The French Revolution*.

# A
# *Treasury of*
# DECEPTION

Liars, Misleaders,

Hoodwinkers, and the Extraordinary

True Stories of History's Greatest

Hoaxes, Fakes, and Frauds

## Michael Farquhar

PENGUIN BOOKS

PENGUIN BOOKS

Published by the Penguin Group

Penguin Group (USA) Inc., 375 Hudson Street, New York, New York 10014, U.S.A.
Penguin Group (Canada), 10 Alcorn Avenue, Toronto, Ontario, Canada M4V 3B2
(a division of Pearson Penguin Canada Inc.)
Penguin Books Ltd, 80 Strand, London WC2R 0RL, England
Penguin Ireland, 25 St Stephen's Green, Dublin 2, Ireland (a division of Penguin Books Ltd)
Penguin Group (Australia), 250 Camberwell Road, Camberwell, Victoria 3124, Australia
(a division of Pearson Australia Group Pty Ltd)
Penguin Books India Pvt Ltd, 11 Community Centre, Panchsheel Park, New Delhi–
110 017, India
Penguin Group (NZ), cnr Airborne and Rosedale Roads, Albany, Auckland 1310,
New Zealand (a division of Pearson New Zealand Ltd)
Penguin Books (South Africa) (Pty) Ltd, 24 Sturdee Avenue, Rosebank, Johannesburg 2196,
South Africa

Penguin Books Ltd, Registered Offices: 80 Strand, London WC2R 0RL, England

First published in Penguin Books 2005

Illustration credits
Frontispiece: Patterson Clark
Page 140: Copyright © Nick Galifianakis, 2005
All other illustrations: The Granger Collection, New York

LIBRARY OF CONGRESS CATALOGING IN PUBLICATION DATA
Farquhar, Michael.
A treasury of deception : liars, misleaders, hoodwinkers, and the extraordinary true
stories of history's greatest hoaxes, fakes, and frauds / Michael Farquhar.
p.   cm.
Includes bibliographical references.
ISBN 0 14 30.3544 4
ISBN 978-0-143-03544-2 (international)
1. Impostors and imposture—History—Case studies.   2. Deception—History—
Case studies.   I. Title.
HV6751.F37 2005
000.19'5—dc22      2004063314

Set in Bembo
Designed by Kathryn Parise

146028962

*For my mom and dad,*
*who (except about Santa Claus)*
*have always told me the truth.*

*"All that deceives may be said to enchant."*

—PLATO

# Contents

～

## Part III
### The Wars of the Ruses
55

## Part IV
### State-Sponsored Deceptions
77

## Part VIII
## The Great Pretenders
### 197

## Part IX
## Escapes Hatched
### 223

## Part X
## Gotcha!
### 241

# Contents

# Introduction

～

"Beauty is truth," Keats wrote, "truth beauty." History, however, is blemished, disfigured even, by deception. The quest for truth, mankind's greatest ambition, has forever been compromised in favor of more immediate considerations—not all of them ignoble, by the way. The hoodwinking of Hitler, for example, may very well have saved civilization. The frequent sacrifice of our ideals is a fundamental part of being human, and the great lies perpetrated throughout history are as varied and nuanced as humanity itself.

For centuries the Vatican laid claim to much of Europe because of a preposterously forged document known as the *Donation of Constantine.* In 1915 renowned scientists declared the so-called Piltdown Man irrefutable evidence of the missing link between man and ape, even though it turned out to be a clumsy concoction made from the skull of a medieval Englishman and the jawbone of an orangutan. Hitler never wrote his diaries. Anastasia never escaped the Bolsheviks. Nostradamus didn't have a clue about the future. And Bill Clinton really did have sexual relations with that woman, Miss Lewinsky.

Call this a historical treasury of imposters, charlatans, and liars. Or call it a hoax: a bogus excuse for a book of no actual value, other than the gleeful celebration of the art of deceit. Some of the stories may be familiar. Pardon the retelling, but no collection of deception would be complete without them. Many are culled from the annals of Western civilization, a reflection of the author's woeful ignorance of the Eastern world. And, most important, though this is an anthology of lies, every story is true!

Nostradamus: Fraud of the "Centuries"

# Part 1

~≈~

# SUPER-DUPERS

All of the characters in this treasury of deception could rightly be called "super-dupers," but those featured in this part of the book don't fit neatly into categories as the others do. Sure, they were all con men of sorts, but each had a unique flair for mendacity.

# 1

## Charlatan's Web

If Nostradamus was such a know-it-all, why didn't he clue in his beloved king that it might be a good idea to sit out the tournament that would kill him in 1559? Instead, the famed sixteenth-century "seer," born Michel de Nostredame, wrote a dedicatory epistle to Henri II in his book of prophesies, *Centuries,* predicting great things for the French monarch. He even went so far as to call the king "invincible." Soon after, Henri was dead, the victim of a freak jousting accident. Subsequently, however, Nostradamus flourished under the patronage of King Henri's widow, Catherine de Médicis. And, thanks to four centuries' worth of credulous disciples, he is still flourishing.

Through the nearly one thousand quatrains that constitute *Centuries,* Nostradamus has been credited with predicting a wide range of calamities, from the Great Fire of London to the rise of Hitler. The methods he used to write his predictions, and the way his believers have interpreted them, are a marvel of systematic deception and unwavering faith. The trick, perhaps best articulated by noted debunker James "The Amazing" Randi, is to make lots of pronouncements, cage them in ambiguous language, and use as much symbolism and allegory as possible. Those who are desperate to believe can then cram into them an almost infinite amount of meaning and truth.

John Hogue, for example, marvels over Nostradamus's remarkable abilities in a number of books. He has a field day with this quatrain:

> *The religion of the name of the seas will win,*
> *Against the sect of the son of Adaluncatif,*
> *The obstinate deplored sect will be afraid*
> *Of the two who are wounded by A & A.*

This of course refers to Libyan despot Mu'ammar Gadhafi, Hogue gushes. "Adaluncatif" is obviously an anagram for Cadafi Luna (even if there is no place for that extra *t*), which he translates into "Gadhafi Moon." The moon features a crescent, which happens to be a symbol of Islam. Then there's this quatrain, used to prove the master's foreknowledge of the Beast of Berlin:

> *Beasts mad with hunger will swim across rivers,*
> *Most of the army will be against the Lower Danube.*
> *The great one shall be dragged in an iron cage*
> *When the child brother will observe nothing.*

The old Latin word for the Lower Danube, used on Roman maps of the area, is Hister, which sounds so much like Hitler that Nostradamians have been in ecstasy ever since they made the (tenuous) connection. Before then, the verse was applied to a Turkish invasion of the region, an event that conveniently occurred before Nostradamus wrote *Centuries*. This was a sure way to guarantee a successful prophecy.

Cataclysmic events being his forte, Nostradamus predicted the end of the world. Interpretations of when that would be, however, vary between 1999 and 7000. It is impossible to determine an exact date because Nostradamus knew the greatest rule of prophecy: avoid specifics at all costs.

# 2

## A Taste for Trickery

His real name is unknown to this day, but the man calling himself George Psalmanazar created one of the most impressive and successful hoaxes in history. He arrived in London in 1704, billing himself as the "Native of Formosa." Although he had never been near the island (present-day Taiwan, which at that time was largely unexplored), he told excited audiences that he was a member of a princely Formosan family who had made his way to Japan and then to the outside world. His book, *An Historical and Geographic Description of Formosa,* presented elaborate details and drawings of Formosan clothing, culture, religion, and manners—all entirely fabricated. It even had a Formosan alphabet chart.

Psalmanazar became a European sensation. His book was a bestseller, and was translated into a number of languages. Scientific societies sat spellbound at his lectures. The Formosa he described was a strange and brutal society, where a man had only to declare his wife an adulteress in order to behead and eat her. Each year, he said, eighteen thousand boys under the age of nine were sacrificed to the Formosan god, and cannibalism was lustily practiced. The consumption of the blood of snakes, he said, allowed most Formosans to live well past one hundred years.

If anyone ever disputed Psalmanazar on his facts, he held firm to a strategy of stubbornness. "What ever I had once affirmed in conversation," he later wrote, "tho' to ever so few people, and tho' ever so improbable, or even absurd, should never be amended or contradicted in the narrative. Thus having once, inadvertently in conversation, made the yearly number of sacrificed infants to amount to eighteen thousand, I could never be persuaded to lessen it, though I had been often made sensible of the impossibility of so small an island losing so many inhabitants every year, without becoming at length quite depopulated, supposing the inhabitants to have been so stupid as to comply."

Psalmanazar's ruse was so successful that the Bishop of London sent him to Oxford, where he was to study and lecture on Formosan history, and the Anglican Church commissioned him to translate the Old and New Testaments into his native language. Within a few years, though, the charade began to crumble and its perpetrator was increasingly burdened by guilt, as well as a wicked opium addiction. His tortured memoirs, published two years after his death in 1763, revealed the deception—but never his true identity.

# 3

## "Prince of Humbugs"

It was 1842, a year of great scientific advances. Joseph Henry discovered the oscillatory character of the electrical discharge, while Christian Doppler lent his name to the effect of a moving source on sound waves. The first law of thermodynamics was introduced, and ether was used for the first time as a surgical anesthetic. Steam-powered ships plied America's waterways, a feat unimaginable to most just a few years before, and Queen Victoria gave the royal stamp of approval to a new method of transportation when she took her first train ride.

Science and technology certainly seemed to rule in 1842, but in that very same year of stunning human achievement, P. T. Barnum, the self-styled "Prince of Humbugs," put on display a blatant fraud he called "the Feejee Mermaid." People lined up by the thousands to see what amounted to the head and torso of a dead monkey attached to the tail of a dried-out fish. They were, it seemed, as eager as ever to swallow any heap of bunk fed to them. What was wrong? Shouldn't folks living in such an enlightened era have been just a bit more sophisticated? Well, not necessarily.

Some historians say it was precisely because of the dizzying rate of progress that people were left so credulous. The onslaught of new discoveries made almost anything seem possible. It was this dynamic that made the New York *Sun*'s bogus accounts of life on the moon so believable (see Part II, Chapter 4). And it's what buttered P. T. Barnum's bread. "Every crowd has a silver lining," he reportedly said, and it was his life's mission to relieve them of it.

The legendary showman and humbug artist made his debut in 1835 with an exhibition of what he called "the most astonishing and interesting curiosity in the world," an elderly black woman named Joice Heth. She was 161 years old, Barnum trumpeted, and had served as a nurse to none other than George Washington when he was just a baby. A master of publicity, Barnum corralled huge audiences in New York with handbills, posters, and paid newspaper features announcing the "most ancient specimen of mortality" Americans were ever likely to encounter, the first person "to put clothes" on the father of the nation.

So successful was the New York exhibition of Joice Heth that Barnum put her on a tour of New England to regale the public with tales of little George and the Washington family. When interest began to wane, Barnum was prepared. He planted a letter in a Boston newspaper that claimed Joice Heth was a fraud, "a curiously constructed automaton, made up of whalebone, india-rubber, and numberless springs, ingeniously put together and made to move at the slightest touch, according to the will of the operator." It was a brilliant ploy. Now people paid to see whether Joice Heth was real, or some kind of robot.[1]

With his career launched, Barnum began to assemble other curiosities to display at his new American Museum in New York City. Many of the objects were of dubious origin, like a wooden leg said to have belonged to General Santa Anna, but few items excited the masses like the Feejee Mermaid. Barnum described it to an associate: "The animal was an ugly, dried-up, black-looking, and diminutive specimen, about three feet long. Its mouth was open, its tail turned over, and its arms thrown up, giving it the appearance of

1. An autopsy performed on Joice Heth after her death in 1836 indicated that she was at least half the age Barnum claimed she was. The New York *Sun* excoriated Barnum for the fraud, but his associate Levi Lyman planted a story in the New York *Herald* that the autopsy itself was a fraud and that Joice Heth was alive and well.

having died in great agony." Unappealing as it may have been, Barnum was determined to make his "mermaid" a real money maker.

Before it was ever put on display, letters secretly written by Barnum were sent to New York newspapers from various southern cities mentioning that a British naturalist named Dr. Griffin (who was in reality his associate Levi Lyman) had in his possession a mermaid supposedly captured near the "Feejee Islands." Barnum then set up "Dr. Griffin" in a New York hotel and arranged for reporters to come and see for themselves this remarkable specimen. Meanwhile, Barnum wrote, "while Lyman was preparing public opinion on mermaids at the Pacific Hotel, I was industriously at work (though of course privately) in getting up wood-cuts and transparencies, as well as a pamphlet, proving the authenticity of mermaids."

Barnum took a mermaid woodcut to each of the New York newspapers and offered it to them for free. Most printed it on July 17, 1842. He also distributed ten thousand copies of the mermaid pamphlet throughout the city. Then, with the public's interest aroused, Lyman, posing as "Dr. Griffin," exhibited the bogus specimen at Concert Hall on Broadway and discoursed on its rare place in nature. A week later, the "mermaid" was transferred over to Barnum's museum with great fanfare and presented "without extra charge." Paid attendance at the museum nearly tripled.

After many years of success with other entertaining hoaxes, in the fall of 1869 the "Prince of Humbugs" discovered someone competing for his crown. His name was George Hull, and the fraud he perpetrated rivaled any Barnum had ever produced. Hull buried a huge figure of a man carved out of gypsum on his cousin's farm in upstate New York. He was inspired, he said, by an argument he had with an evangelical preacher who maintained that giant men once roamed the earth because the Bible said they did. The statue was a sensation when Hull arranged for its "discovery" a year after its burial. Huge crowds came to see the "Cardiff Giant," as it was called, and paid handsomely for the privilege. "As one looked upon it he could not help feeling that he was in the presence of a great and superior being," wrote one reporter. "The crowd as they gathered around it seemed almost spellbound. There was no levity." But there was controversy. Some said the figure was a fossilized human thousands of years old. Others claimed that it was an ancient statue. Then there were those who dismissed it as a total fraud.

Word of the discovery quickly reached Barnum, who was always on the lookout for curiosities that generated cash. He knew the Cardiff Giant was a winner, and offered a generous sum to buy it. (Hull had by then sold the giant to new owners.) He was rebuffed, but not deterred. Instead of walking away from such a potential bonanza, Barnum simply had another statue carved and called it the *real* Cardiff Giant. He displayed it at Wood's Museum in New York at the same time the original was in town, and often outdrew his competitors.[2] They filed for an injunction, but a circuit court judge refused to stop Barnum from essentially out–hoaxing his rivals. When one of the investors in the original fraud observed the lines of people waiting to see Barnum's copy, he reportedly remarked, "There's a sucker born every minute." Ironically enough, Barnum stole credit for that memorable line, too.

2. The two giants are still on display. The original is at the New York Historical Society's Farmer's Museum in Cooperstown, New York, and Barnum's knockoff is at Marvin's Marvelous Mechanical Museum in Farmington Hills, Michigan.

# 4

∼

# Unreal Estate

Unlike P. T. Barnum, who essentially tricked people in order to entertain them, confidence men like Oscar Hartzell sought only to fleece the unwary with their schemes. Although few today would recognize his name, Hartzell remains one of history's greatest scam artists. Early in the twentieth century, he convinced as many as one hundred thousand of his fellow midwesterners to hand over millions with the promise of enormous profits from the imaginary estate of the famed British buccaneer Sir Francis Drake. So convincing was his ruse that even after his arrest and conviction many of his investors refused to believe he was a fraud. Instead, they made him their hero.

Hartzell didn't originate the Drake estate fraud. In fact, he was first conned by two hucksters who convinced him the Drake venture was legitimate. A true believer, he worked for them, in exchange for bogus shares, until he got wise and eventually stole their scheme right out from under them. He made it his own, with bold flourishes impossible to believe—almost. The gist of it was this: Drake, who had made a fortune during the Elizabethan era by robbing Spanish ships of their treasure, left a vast estate of property, gold, and other valuable assets when he died in 1596. There were said to be irregularities in his will, however, which formed the foundation of the con. While other schemers merely found Drakes in

the phone book and advised them they were potential beneficiaries
of a rich estate that could be recovered only with their contributions, Hartzell actually claimed that *he* was the sole heir of the fortune, having been assigned that right by a Drake descendant,
"Colonel Drexel Drake." He was engaged to the colonel's niece, he
explained, and was assigned all rights as heir because of the colonel's
desire to keep the estate in the family. Investors, Hartzell wrote from
England, stood to earn staggering returns once the Drake estate was
turned over to him:

> Figure up all the land in Missouri, Kansas, and Iowa at an average of
> $125 an acre, and all of the stocks, and all the bank deposits, all the
> railroads and cities in those three states and add them together and
> the combined amount would not be as large as the Sir Francis
> Drake estate here in England, of which I am the sole owner, and to
> which I hold the sole title, which the British parliament is now
> conveying to me in cash, and which I am going to bring to Amer-
> ica to distribute among the men and women who have advanced
> me money with which to carry on the [effort] to win this es-
> tate. . . . I will put it to you in another form: it has been said by
> people of high finance here in London that the amount I am to re-
> ceive from the sale of the Drake [estate] is considerably more than
> the combined debt of Britain to the United States, and the debts of
> all other countries to Great Britain, and that, as you can read for
> yourselves, is over four and a half billion pounds sterling, or some
> 20 billion dollars, a stake worth fighting for and working for and
> waiting for.

As the money poured in from the American heartland, Hartzell
lived lavishly in London, from where he ran the con safely isolated
from eager investors and U.S. law alike. Once bankrupt, the failed
farmer and rancher now dressed in the finest suits, dined in the
most expensive restaurants, and mingled with the English elite. He
even styled himself the Baron of Buckland, a title he said became
his when "Colonel Drake" assigned him his rights as Sir Francis's
heir. This, along with all other rights, had been confirmed by the
"King & Crown Commission," which, though it didn't actually ex-

ist, was described by Hartzell as Britain's highest court. Investors ate it right up.

Of course, without an actual Drake estate, it was impossible for Hartzell to give his backers anything but hope. He kept them at bay with promises that the great fortune was almost ready to be distributed. First, though, there were complex audits and accounting procedures that had to be completed. The estate was enormous, after all, with properties that extended all the way from central London to South America. And three centuries' worth of income and interest couldn't be sorted through overnight. As time went on, Hartzell, out of necessity, became more and more inventive with his excuses.

"The King of England has been working upon the transfer of these titles to me until he has been stricken down with sickness," he wrote to his U.S. agents in 1926, "and we must wait until he recovers to resume work, and this waiting takes money, so tell our people in the West who have so nobly contributed of their funds in the past that the machinery must not stop over here now, but they must send more money, and keep on sending it, until the transfers are made. I must have $6,000 more by the end of the month, without fail."

Amazingly enough, the money kept coming, in ever increasing amounts. Hartzell's biographer Richard Rayner believes a number of factors contributed to his subject's extraordinary success. "Like all great con men he was creating theater," Rayner writes, "a believable yet entirely illusory world, and he plucked its dominant imaginative fabric—the contingency, the chance event—from the air around him." He heard King George V was sick, for example, and wove that into his deception. Furthermore, Rayner continues, Hartzell was operating at a time in history when Americans were especially receptive to outrageous schemes. "America presupposes an optimistic view of itself and life's possibilities," he writes, "especially the possibility of getting rich, and in the 1920s that boisterous self-belief reached a dizzy new height of delusion." President Calvin Coolidge said at the time, "The business of America is business." And business was booming. With vast fortunes being made almost overnight, nothing seemed impossible. Sir Francis Drake's estate appeared to be a safe investment to midwesterners wary of Wall Street, and the stock market crash of 1929 seemed only to deepen their faith. "They now believe in Hartzell with the fire of the most rabid religious fanatics," an observer wrote.

As he collected a fortune from his worshipful dupes, Hartzell seemed invincible, consistently frustrating the efforts of U.S. officials to stop him. "The swindle was on its face absurd and yet absurdly difficult to disprove," writes Rayner, "hence its genius." Nevertheless, there was one man more persistent than most, an inspector for the United States Postal Service named John Sparks. Sparks was eventually able to collect enough evidence of mail fraud to get Hartzell deported from Britain and arrested upon his return to the United States.

During the subsequent trial, which began in Sioux City, Iowa, on October 23, 1933, Hartzell's flock remained intensely loyal. Woe to anyone who opposed the venerated heir of the fortune that he still promised to share with them. "Hartzell's campaign had reached evangelistic proportions," wrote Harry Reed, the U.S. attorney who prosecuted the case. "It was like the Crusades in the Middle Ages. One church fired the preacher because he opposed a contribution. If you did not believe in Oscar Hartzell, you better keep your mouth shut. I talked to hundreds of people who had contributed before, during, and after the trial and I never found anyone who did not think he had made a good investment."

Hartzell was eventually found guilty, yet no sooner was he out on bail pending appeal than the swindle started anew. Thousands of dollars were raised within days. "The whole Drake deal would have been fixed up by now if it weren't for that bunch of racketeers they sent over from Washington," said one disciple. "Those men at the trial are just sore because they can't get in on it."

After the conviction was upheld and an appeal to the U.S. Supreme Court rejected, Hartzell was hauled off to Leavenworth Prison. His agents, however, continued to solicit funds from the faithful, who happily provided them. As a result, Hartzell was taken from prison and tried again, this time in Chicago along with a number of his accomplices. By now, though, a certain madness seemed to have settled upon the great swindler. He was sent to a prison hospital where he died in 1943, reportedly convinced that he really was the Baron of Buckland and worth billions.

# 5

~~~

# Imposter on a Role

Like James Thurber's fictional character Walter Mitty, Stanley Clifford Weyman sought refuge from his own oppressively ordinary existence by inhabiting other, more interesting lives. Yet what Mitty did only in his daydreams—becoming, by turns, a naval commander, a celebrated surgeon, a criminal attorney, and an ace fighter pilot—Weyman did in reality. This low-level clerk from Brooklyn, born Stephen Weinberg, was a serial imposter, and a very skilled one at that.[3]

In one of his early acts of imposture, Weyman (the name he always used) became a Romanian army officer serving as his nation's consul general in New York. One day in 1915, he decided a battleship inspection was in order, so he called the U.S. Navy to arrange it. Queen Marie of Romania had instructed him to pay his respects, he claimed, and, as no one questioned his credentials, he was ushered aboard the USS *Wyoming,* which was anchored in the Hudson River. Sporting a light-blue uniform, decorated with gold braid, and an admiral's hat, Weyman was escorted by the ship's captain past rows of sailors standing at attention. Periodically he would pause to

---

3. There are a number of other imposters in this collection (see Part VIII), but they all posed as royalty. Weyman, on the other hand, took on a number of different guises.

reprimand a sailor for smudge on his shoe or for an incorrect stance, never once breaking character.

After the inspection, Weyman announced that he wanted to throw a dinner for the officers at the Astor Hotel in Times Square. Still dressed in his spiffy uniform, he arranged a lavish banquet at the hotel. The bill, he told the manager, was to be sent to the Romanian consulate in Washington, D.C. As Weyman and the officers celebrated, however, the party was interrupted by two detectives who had read an announcement of the event in *The New York Times* and recognized Weyman's name from other impostures he had pulled. He was immediately dragged out of the party and arrested. "All I can say," the captain of the *Wyoming* later told a reporter, "is the little guy put on one hell of a tour of inspection."

Weyman served some time in prison before his next caper, which was inspired by an advertisement he saw in the *Times* seeking a physician to travel to Lima, Peru, to oversee sanitation conditions there for a New York development company. Bolstered by phony credentials and supreme self-confidence, he got the job. Life in Peru was luxurious for "Doctor Weyman." He rented an estate with a large staff of servants, and spent lavishly on parties and other extravagances—all added to his expense account and sent to New York. When it came to actual work, Weyman got by pretending to know what a sanitation specialist ought to have known, usually nodding in agreement at suggestions made by others that seemed to make sense. Eventually, though, his expense account raised suspicions.

After his ruse in Peru was revealed, Weyman was sent home and in 1921 adopted the role of an official of the U.S. State Department. It was in this guise that he came to the rescue of Princess Fatima of Afghanistan, whose visit to the United States, he read, had not been given any official recognition. Determined to give the princess her due, he swept into her suite at the Waldorf-Astoria Hotel and, on behalf of Secretary of State Charles Evans Hughes, apologized for the poor reception she had received in America. He promised to take Her Royal Highness to Washington to meet the secretary and the president. All he would need from her was

$10,000 to pay for the gifts he said foreign dignitaries traditionally gave to officials in the nation's capital.

Weyman took part of the money and rented a private railroad car to escort Princess Fatima and her party to Washington. When they arrived, he dropped the Afghans off at the Willard Hotel and hurried over to the State Department, dressed as a naval officer. He told an official there that he had been sent by several senators, whom he named, to arrange a visit for the princess with Secretary of State Hughes. Her Highness was accorded all the diplomatic niceties, and during the encounter Weyman took Hughes aside and told him that the princess also wished to meet President Warren Harding. A phone call was made to the White House and a meeting hastily arranged. There Weyman chatted familiarly with the president, something a naval officer would never do, and nudged his way into the photographs Harding took with the princess. This of course raised suspicions, but Weyman had slipped away before his fraud was uncovered.

He next emerged as personal physician to the actress Pola Negri, who was distraught over the recent death of her lover Rudolph Valentino. As poor Pola grieved at the Ambassador Hotel, Weyman announced himself as a doctor and friend of the late screen idol, who, he said, would have wished for him to take care of her. He then proceeded to take her temperature, gave her some sedatives, and suggested he stay with her in an adjoining room. The bereaved actress was most grateful, and as she rested, he issued regular reports of her condition to the press. Then he accompanied her to Valentino's funeral, which was a scene of chaos as thousands lined up to get a glimpse of the great star in repose. Weyman sensed an opportunity to expand his role. After he returned Pola Negri to her hotel room, he came back to the funeral home, now dressed in full doctor garb, and administered smelling salts and other treatments to Valentino's swooning fans.

During World War II, "Doctor" Weyman opened a school for draft-dodgers. There he taught cowards how to fake stupidity or simulate deafness. If he found that a guy was too dumb to fake being deaf, Weyman simply punctured his eardrum. It was a lucrative business, until an FBI agent posing as a dodger got in the way. Weyman was arrested and sent to prison. After his release in 1948, the great imposter redeemed himself in 1960 when he tried to stop two armed thieves from robbing the motel where he worked. Weyman was shot and killed. Ironically enough, he died a hero just being himself.

# 6

*CHIN*canery

The two Mafia bosses could not have appeared more unalike. John Gotti, the "Dapper Don" of the Gambino organization, strutted around town in expensive suits and flashy jewelry with perfectly coiffed hair, while Vincent "the Chin" Gigante, the so-called "Oddfather" of the Genovese crime family, was often seen shuffling around Greenwich Village in his bathrobe, unkempt and babbling in apparent dementia. Yet though Gigante seemed like a harmless flake to the rest of the world, Gotti was terrified of him. He knew the Chin only feigned madness to fool the authorities; that beneath the dirty bathrobe was a ruthless killer who had already ordered one hit on him, and who could strike again at any time.[4]

Gigante's insanity charade served him well for three decades before it finally ended in 2003 when he admitted his ruse as part of a plea agreement with the U.S. government. It started around 1970. The Chin was still a Genovese capo then and faced bribery charges in New Jersey. Psychiatrists told the court that he was delusional, a paranoid schizophrenic whose condition was rapidly deteriorating. The charges were eventually dropped, but not the crazy act. Gigante had discovered a great way to keep the law away. He periodically

---

4. Gigante was infuriated by Gotti's unsanctioned hit on a fellow don, Gambino boss Paul Castellano.

checked into a psychiatric hospital, and also performed little acts of lunacy to enhance the image. One time, for example, FBI agents burst into his apartment and found him in the shower, under an umbrella. "Vincent is a paranoid schizophrenic," his brother, a Roman Catholic priest, told reporters. "He hallucinates. He's been that way since 1968 or 1969."

After he became boss of the Genovese family, Gigante continued the deception to help disguise his new position. Soldiers were instructed never to use his name, but to point to their chin when they referred to him. He conducted much of the family's business in the wee hours of the morning when he believed the FBI was less vigilant. The rest of the day was spent drooling and sputtering to himself. "The guy acts like a fruitcake 23 hours a day," noted one investigator who had tracked the Chin for years, "but he finds one hour someplace each day to run the biggest Mafia family in the United States. Is he crazy? He's the only one not in jail. Maybe he's a genius."

In 1990, Gigante was arrested at his mother's home on a variety of murder conspiracy and racketeering charges. Mrs. Chin seemed surprised by the accusations (or at least pretended to be), especially about his leadership position in the Genovese organization. "Vincenzo?" she exclaimed. "He's the boss of the toilet!" For the next seven years, the Chin delayed his day of reckoning as his mental competence was evaluated and debated. When his case finally came to trial in 1997, a number of prominent psychiatrists testified on his behalf. "Mr. Gigante currently has moderate to severe dementia which reflects significant underlying central nervous system dysfunction," opined Dr. Wilfred G. van Gorp, director of neuropsychology at Columbia University Medical School. The jury was unimpressed, and Gigante was convicted and sentenced to a minimum of ten years in prison.

Behind bars, the Chin apparently felt free to drop the crazy act. He was captured on tape directing Genovese business in "a coherent, careful, and intelligent manner," according to prosecutors, and once told a prison guard, "Nobody fucks with me." Rather than face another trial for running a criminal enterprise from jail, Gigante agreed to plead guilty to obstruction of justice for his seven-year con on the legal system before his 1997 trial. "The jig is up," announced U.S. Attorney Roslynn R. Mauskopf. "Vincent Gigante was a cunning faker, and those of us in law enforcement always knew that this was an act." And it only took three decades for them to prove it.

"Batmen" of the moon, inspired by the Sun

## Part 11

### ALL THE NEWS THAT'S SLIPPED TO PRINT

Thomas Jefferson's declaration that "advertisements contain the only truths to be relied upon in a newspaper" may have been a bit cynical. But given all the lies, misrepresentations, and distortions that have been printed over the years, his wariness of the Fourth Estate seems well founded.

# 1

## What Janet Cooked Up

It was what's called in newspaper parlance a "holy shit" story—a drop-your-spoon-in-your-cereal type of exposé that journalists drool over. "Jimmy is 8 years old and a third generation heroin addict," began reporter Janet Cooke's breathtaking account of a young drug user on the front page of *The Washington Post,* "a precocious little boy with sandy hair, velvety brown eyes and needle marks freckling the baby-smooth skin of his thin brown arms."

"Jimmy's World," as the story was titled, caused an immediate sensation when it ran on September 28, 1980. What was the world coming to, readers wanted to know, when a mother could stand by and allow her live-in boyfriend to inject her child with high-grade heroin? And how could the *Post,* which had agreed to keep identities confidential, possibly justify protecting these people? Washington's police chief launched an intensive search for the little boy, while Mayor Marion Barry declared that the city knew who "Jimmy" was and that help was on the way. The following April, the account that so vividly illustrated the depths of the urban drug culture won a Pulitzer Prize. Only problem was, as the *Post* was mortified to discover, not one word of "Jimmy's World" was true. Janet Cooke had invented the entire story.

So how could a newspaper as prestigious as *The Washington Post*—still basking in the glory of its Watergate investigations—have been so thoroughly suckered? The answer was disarmingly simple. All it took were a few lapses in editorial quality control, and "a one-in-a-million liar," as *Post* executive editor Benjamin C. Bradlee called the young woman who had invented "Jimmy." Less than a week after Cooke won the Pulitzer, which was subsequently returned, the *Post*'s independent ombudsman Bill Green gave readers the whole story of her epic deception in an exhaustive report of nearly fifteen thousand words that ran in the paper's front section.

For a newspaper striving for diversity, Janet Cooke was like an answered prayer—bright, ambitious, and black, a 1976 Phi Beta Kappa graduate of Vassar, and an immensely talented writer. The *Post* snatched her away from the *Toledo Blade* in 1979, convinced they had found a rising star reporter. Cooke did not disappoint. She wrote fifty-two well-received stories in her first nine months of employment. "She was a conspicuous member of the newsroom staff," Bill Green wrote in his report. "When she walked, she pranced. When she smiled, she dazzled. Her wardrobe seemed always new, impeccable and limitless." But there was something else. "She was consumed by blind and raw ambition," noted her first editor Vivian Aplin-Brownlee. "It was obvious, but it doesn't deny the talent."

Cooke was assigned to investigate a new type of heroin on the streets of Washington and came back with extensive notes and taped interviews. Among her discoveries was a report she had heard of a young heroin addict. "That's the story," City editor Milton Coleman told her. "Go after it. It's a front-page story." After a two-week search Cooke told Coleman that she could not find the boy, but a week later she claimed to have found another young user—the soon-to-be infamous "Jimmy." Because he had promised confidentiality to his reporter for her sources, Coleman did not ask for names or an address. Thus, wrote Green, "The jugular of journalism lay exposed—the faith an editor has to place in a reporter."

Coleman had little reason to doubt Cooke. For one thing, she had included so many telling details about "Jimmy" in a thirteen-page memo that outlined her story. "[He] wears a blue and green Izod T-shirt," Cooke wrote in the memo, " 'Bad, ain't it. I got six of these.' " She meticulously described the imaginary child's living room, down to a rubber tree plant, fake bamboo blinds, a brown shag rug, two lamps, and a chrome-and-glass coffee table. She also included the elementary school "Jimmy" attended, as well as the general neighborhood in which he lived. There was even a supposed real name, "Tyronne," which reassured Coleman further.

As "Jimmy's World" made its way closer to print, other editors up the chain of command put their trust in Cooke too. "Janet had written a great piece," said Metro editor Bob Woodward, who had earlier gained prominence for his Watergate reporting with Carl Bernstein. "In a way, both she and the story were almost too good to be true. I had seen her go out on a complicated story and an hour later turn in a beautifully written piece. This story was so well-written and tied together so well that my alarm bells simply didn't go off. My skepticism left me. I was personally negligent." Ben Bradlee read "Jimmy's World" the week before it ran and thought it was "a helluva job," worthy of the front page that coming Sunday— a day when the *Post*'s circulation is highest. With Bradlee, as Bill Green wrote in his report, "The story, colors flying, had passed its last and most powerful filter."

Almost as soon as "Jimmy's World" appeared in the paper, doubts about its veracity began rumbling through the newsroom. Coleman was concerned that the police were unable to find the child after several days of searching. Reporter Courtland Milloy grew suspicious when Cooke was unable to locate "Jimmy's" home as they drove around looking for it. Cooke's first editor Vivian Aplin-Brownlee was among the most skeptical. "I never believed it," she told Bill Green, "and I told Milton [Coleman] that. I knew her so well and the depth of her. In her eagerness to make a name she would write further than the truth would allow." Even outside the newsroom skepticism mounted. "I've been told the story is part myth, part reality," said Mayor Barry. "We all have agreed that we don't believe that the mother or the pusher would allow a reporter to see them shoot up."

Yet despite the growing doubts, the *Post* submitted "Jimmy's World" for a Pulitzer Prize. "I have used the phrase 'in for a dime, in for a dollar' to describe my overall conclusion about submitting the Cooke story for a Pulitzer or any other prize," Woodward told

Green. "I believed it, we published it. Official questions had been raised, but we stood by the story and her." Then, on April 13, 1981, as Bradlee wrote in his memoirs, "the worst happened: 'Jimmy's World' won a Pulitzer." With that great journalistic honor, the whole fabricated story began to crumble. As various news organizations prepared reports on Cooke and her Pulitzer win, discrepancies in her background repeatedly cropped up. They were quickly brought to the attention of the *Post.*

It soon became apparent that Janet Cooke had lied extensively on the résumé she gave the paper when she applied there in 1979, and on the biography she provided the Pulitzer committee when her story was submitted. Among other falsehoods, she claimed to speak or read four languages, to have graduated magna cum laude from Vassar in 1976, attended the Sorbonne in 1975, and received a master's degree from the University of Toledo in 1977. None of it was true, as *Post* editors discovered. She had left Vassar after only one year, never attended the Sorbonne or the University of Toledo, and was dumbfounded when Ben Bradlee began peppering her with questions in French, a language she purported to understand. "You're just like Richard Nixon," Bradlee fumed, "you're trying to cover up." It was only a matter of time before the "Jimmy" story unraveled along with her résumé. Woodward bluntly accused her of making up the whole thing, and, he declared, "I'm going to prove it if it's the last thing I do."

Eventually Janet Cooke was forced to confess. " 'Jimmy's World' was in essence a fabrication," she admitted in a handwritten statement. "I never encountered or interviewed an 8-year-old heroin addict. The September 28, 1980, article in *The Washington Post* was a serious misrepresentation which I deeply regret. I apologize to my newspaper, my profession, the Pulitzer board and all seekers of the truth. Today, in facing up to the truth, I have submitted my resignation."

The fallout from Cooke's massive fraud, which Ben Bradlee later called "the darkest chapter in my newspaper life," was fierce. The credibility of a great newspaper had been battered, and many of its detractors reacted with glee. Other readers were simply stunned. "In truth," read a *Post* editorial, "just as readers may feel maltreated by publication of the 'Jimmy' tale and all the subsequent hullabaloo it created, so we at this newspaper feel at once angry, chagrined, mis-used ourselves, determined to continue the kind of aggressive re-porting Miss Cooke's story purported to be and determined also to maintain and honor the highest standards of straight and fair report-ing. . . . One of these episodes is one too many."

Yet the Janet Cooke episode was just one of a hurricane of hoaxes that have blown across newspaper history.

# 2

## Ben Franklin:
## The Devil Made Him Do It

It's hard to imagine what a fraud like Janet Cooke could possibly have in common with the great founding father Benjamin Franklin. Not much, it turns out, other than the fact that they both worked for newspapers and wrote complete fabrications. Yet while Cooke was fueling her ambition with her lies, Franklin simply wanted to make a point. He did it by poking fun at stupid people—stupid people who, for example, still believed in witches nearly forty years after the madness at Salem.[1]

On October 22, 1730, a story appeared in the *Pennsylvania Gazette,* which Franklin owned, that detailed a witch hunt at Mount Holly, New Jersey. A man and a woman were accused of being in league with the devil, the story (written anonymously by Franklin) reported, charged with "making the Neighbours Sheep dance in an uncommon Manner, and with causing Hogs to speak and sing Psalms, etc., to the great terror and Amazement of the King's good and peaceable subjects in this Province." To ascertain the truth of the charges, several tests were applied. In the first, a

---

1. Shameless Plug #1: For a detailed account of the Salem witch trials, see the author's brilliant book *A Treasury of Great American Scandals: Tantalizing True Tales of Historic Misbehavior by the Founding Fathers and Others Who Let Freedom Swing.*

large Bible would be weighed on a scale against the weight of the accused. If the Bible tipped the scale, it would be certain proof of witchcraft.

The man and woman agreed to undergo the tests, but only if their most vocal accusers, another man and woman, underwent the trials as well. This being agreed upon, an enormous Bible was produced. The alleged wizard was the first to be weighed, but "to the great Surprise of the Spectators, Flesh and Bones came down plump, and outweighed that good Book by abundance." Then, the phony story continued, each of the others were put on the scale with the same result: "their Lumps of Mortality . . . were too heavy for *Moses* and all the Prophets and Apostles."

With barely disguised glee, Franklin took his readers further away from reality with the next test, a medieval chestnut in which the accused were bound up and tossed into a pond. Those who floated were surely witches, it was said, while those who sank—and sometimes drowned—were declared innocent.

The problem at Mount Holly was *everyone* flunked the test, accused and accusers alike. When to her horror the righteous woman found herself floating, she demanded to be dunked again. Yet still she wouldn't sink. This, she sputtered, was obviously witchcraft at work. The accused were keeping her buoyant with an evil spell, but "she would be duck'd again a Hundred Times" to get the devil out of her.

Franklin reported that some of the more reasonable voices among the spectators decided that it was perfectly natural for the two men to stay afloat. It was simply the instinct to swim and survive. In the case of the women, however, it was obvious that their dresses were keeping them from going under. The only solution, the article concluded, was to wait for warmer weather and have the women dunked again. Nude.

# 3

~~

# A Poe Excuse for a Hoax

Ben Franklin made up a number of satiric tales disguised as truth, and he wasn't the only famous American to do so. Mark Twain wrote quite a few doozies designed to fool the public, as did Edgar Allan Poe. Poor Poe, however, never found much of an audience for most of the tales of science and exploration he concocted, bogged down as they often were with mind-numbing detail. His first attempted hoax, "The Unparalleled Adventures of One Hans Pfaall," appeared in a magazine called the *Southern Literary Messenger* in 1835. It told of a man who flew to the moon in a balloon and lived among its inhabitants for five years. Alas, "Hans Pfaall" was a flop. Considering typical passages like this one, in which Poe describes the view of earth from the balloon, it's little wonder why:

"I had, thoughtlessly enough, expected to see [earth's] real *convexity* become evident as I ascended; but a very little reflection sufficed to explain the discrepancy. A line, dropped from my position perpendicularly to the earth, would have formed the perpendicular of a right-angled triangle, of which the base would have extended from the right-angle to the horizon, and the hypothenuse from the horizon to my position." Perhaps Poe would have been better off keeping it simple, like, *"Wow! What a view!"*

Then, adding to the sting of his failure, soon after the first installment of Poe's story appeared, the New York *Sun* published an equally untrue but far more popular moon account. Dispirited, the hard-drinking writer decided against continuing his serial, leaving his hero stuck on the moon. "I did not think it advisable even to bring my voyager back to his parent Earth," Poe said. "He remains where I left him, and is still, I believe, 'the man in the moon.'"

# 4

~

# The *Sun* Promises the Moon

The New York *Sun*'s six-part moon series was a sensation, perhaps the most successful hoax in newspaper history. Thousands
were lured in by the paper's fantastic tale of exotic life on earth's
nearest neighbor, and the *Sun*'s circulation became the largest in the
world.

The series, which began in August 1835, was relatively restrained
at first, setting a tone of pseudoscientific credibility. It was reported
that Sir John Herschel, son of the great astronomer Sir William
Herschel (the first to observe Neptune), had sailed to South Africa
with a newly developed telescope capable of focusing on the moon
with incredible clarity. The mechanics of the huge instrument were
described in academic detail, almost lulling the reader into believing
the bombshells that were to follow. The story, invented by *Sun*
staffer Richard Adams Locke, then went on to explain how the
mass-market "penny" newspaper managed to get the scoop of the
century. Herschel, Locke wrote, had sent a report of his lunar discoveries to the Royal Society in London, while his assistant, Dr. Andrew Grant, wrote a report of his own for the prestigious *Edinburgh
Journal of Science* that was published in a special supplement brought
to the *Sun* by a gentleman returning from Scotland. That Herschel
was actually in South Africa making well-publicized astronomical
observations only lent more credibility to Locke's tale.

Having stirred reader interest with this introductory article, Locke further tantalized them in the next installment with glimpses of the lunar landscape and its inhabitants. There were beaches with brilliant white sand, rocks of green marble, and forests like none seen on earth. Buffalo-like creatures roamed vast plains, and another strange animal that "would be classed on Earth as a monster" was spotted as well, bluish in color, with a head and beard like a goat, and a single horn.

The images became more and more vivid in subsequent installments. Locke, as if quoting from Dr. Grant's imaginary report, described vast lakes and oceans, abandoned temples of emerald, and a strange beaverlike creature with no tail that walked upright on two feet. "It carries its young in its arms like a human being," it was reported, "and moves with an easy gliding motion. Its huts are constructed better and higher than those of many tribes of human savages, and from the appearance of smoke in nearly all of them, there is no doubt of its being acquainted with the use of fire."

Having seduced readers thus far, the paper revealed the most sensational discovery of all: the moon was inhabited by several species of humanlike creatures with wings—batmen of sorts. Their wings were semitransparent and extended from their shoulders to their legs. Some, observed bathing in a lake, spread their wings out and "waved them as ducks do theirs to shake off the water." Others politely shared fruit, passing the choicest pieces to their friends. The bat people apparently enjoyed vigorous sex lives, although the *Sun* only implied this by noting that Dr. Grant had requested certain portions of his report be censored for the sake of decency. The society of these startling creatures seemed remarkably peaceful and idyllic. "As far as we could judge," the *Sun* "quoted" Grant, "they spend their happy hours in collecting various fruits in the woods, in eating, flying, bathing, and loitering about." This in addition to the "improper behavior" the paper said "would ill comport with our terrestrial notions of decorum."

The *Sun*'s moon hoax was a smash. New Yorkers devoured the story, snatching up installments as fast as they were printed. The presses were run at full capacity for ten hours a day and still the demand could not be satisfied. Some of New York's more respectable papers picked up the story. *The New York Times* called the revelations "probable and plausible." Genuine belief in Herschel's moon discoveries was widespread, even in academic circles. "Yale College was alive with staunch supporters," a reporter wrote years later. "The literati—students and professors, doctors in divinity and law—and all the rest of the reading community, looked daily for the arrival of the New York mail with unexampled avidity and implicit faith. Have you seen the accounts of Sir John Herschel's wonderful discoveries? Have you read the *Sun?* Have you heard the news of the man in the Moon? These were the questions that met you everywhere. It was the absorbing topic of the day. Nobody expressed or entertained a doubt as to the truth of the story."

Edgar Allan Poe was understandably steamed over the success of the moon hoax that had eclipsed his own. He did his best to discredit the *Sun*'s story, but to no avail. People were determined to be deceived, he concluded in a huff. Almost ten years later, however, Poe had his own hoax published in the *Sun*. He reported that a balloon had been successfully piloted across the Atlantic Ocean for the very first time. Though no trip to the moon, it was a most successful ruse that delighted the normally dejected and morose writer. Poe noted happily that he "never witnessed more intense excitement to get possession of a paper." People had finally swallowed one of his stories.

# 5

## The Hoax That Roared

Rivaling the success of the *Sun*'s moon sham was a New York *Herald* fable with a more local angle. The city was swarming with hordes of vicious, snarling beasts, the headlines screamed—escaped animals from the Central Park Zoo. Scores of people had already been trampled, clawed, and bitten to death, according to the *Herald*'s dramatic account that filled the entire front page on November 9, 1874, and a number of dangerous animals were still on the loose.

An unidentified *Herald* reporter claimed to have been at the scene when the chaos erupted. A zookeeper had been tormenting a caged rhinoceros named Pete, the story went, poking him with a stick until the frustrated animal finally exploded. In a rage, Pete smashed apart his cage, charged the keeper, and stomped him into pulp before finishing him off with his horn. The rhino, his anger unsated, then began smashing open the cages of the other animals housed with him. Another zookeeper fired a bullet at the crazed beast, but it practically bounced off Pete's tough hide. With a snort, the rhino turned on the shooter. "The horrid horn impaled him against a corner cage and killed him instantly," the *Herald* breathlessly reported, "tearing the cage to pieces and releasing the panther." The big cat immediately started to make a meal out of the impaled zookeeper.

One by one the cages of other dangerous creatures were torn open, including that of Lincoln the lion. As horrified spectators looked on, Lincoln crashed through a window and escaped outside. The king of the beasts, paw planted on the corpse of an onlooker crushed under his weight, then let out a mighty roar. A bullet fired by a zookeeper missed the lion, which then leapt into the middle of a gathered throng. Women fainted and children screamed as Lincoln pounced on one man and tore him to pieces. Meanwhile, Pete the rhino continued to smash open cages and release even more creatures. As he emerged from the animal house, a small army of policemen and armed civilians that had rushed to the scene started shooting at him. The rhino, unscathed by the volley of bullets, turned and headed back inside. But, the *Herald* noted, it was almost as if Pete was deliberately setting up an ambush rather than retreating, for as the men followed him inside, a puma sprang up and attacked. "Almost on the heels of the puma came the black and spotted leopard, followed by the jaguar, the African lioness, and tiger."

Already the *Herald* story was stretching the limits of credibility, but it was merely a preview of more scenes of terror. Dangerous animals bolted from Central Park, including Pete, who attacked a party of young girls and killed one of them before moving on to destroy a shanty in which a family was having supper. All escaped, the paper reported, "except a child in the cradle, which was burned to a crisp." The animals attacked not only New Yorkers, but one another as well. In one instance, a tiger "buried his teeth in the lion's neck until the King of the Beasts howled with the keenest anguish. . . . Blood covered the avenue and, in the distance, awestruck spectators looked on in breathless fear."

Horrific events were reported throughout the city, with screaming citizens running for their lives as wild creatures chased after them. One "witness" told of a tiger entering the Church of St. Thomas: "Men and women rushed in all directions away from the beast, who sprang upon the shoulders of an aged lady, burying his fangs in her neck, and carrying her to the ground." At the 23rd Street ferry, one unidentified animal bounded onto the vessel. Terrified horses hitched to wagons plunged into the river, taking with them the wagons and all their occupants.

Armed New Yorkers, including Governor John A. Dix, tried to subdue the rampaging beasts in their midst. They fired wildly in all directions, including out of tenement windows. "There is no instance reported of any animals being hit," the *Herald* noted, "while it is believed many citizens were struck by the missiles. One policeman, Officer Lannigan of the Seventh Precinct, was wounded in the foot near Grand Street by a shot from a window during a chase after the striped hyena, which was mistaken by the crowd for a panther. This cowardly brute was finally killed by a bartender armed with a club."

The litany of horrors continued. The *Herald* actually printed a list of many of the supposed dead and wounded, and announced that some of the escaped animals were still at large. "There is a sharp lookout for the black wolf," the paper warned. "He has escaped into the city but looks so much like a Dutchman's dog he may evade detection until he has committed some lamentable tragedy." The mayor had issued a proclamation, the report continued, enjoining all citizens, except for the National Guard, to stay inside until all the escaped beasts were killed or captured.

The story then concluded with a paragraph headlined THE MORAL OF THE WHOLE. It was a frank admission that the entire report had been fabricated. "Not one word of it is true. Not a single act or incident described has taken place. It is a huge hoax, a wild romance, or whatever epithet of utter untrustworthiness our readers may choose to apply to it. It is simply a fancy picture which crowded upon the mind of the writer a few days ago while he was gazing through the iron bars of the cages of the wild animals in the menagerie at Central Park."

What the *Herald*'s editors failed to foresee, however, was that many panicked readers of the popular newspaper would never get to the last paragraph. People all over the city were utterly fooled, terrified by the menace supposedly lurking among them. "There was a public school in our street," the writer of the hoax, I. C. Clarke, later recalled, "and one after another I saw mothers come round the corner, make a dash for the school, and presently come forth with one or more children and dash homeward, dragging little ones after them. By George! It scared me. I went some half mile up to my mother's home through almost empty streets. I found the family around the lunch table in consternation. My cousin, Jennie, was reading my story in a broken voice, and my mother and sister were in tears. They rose as I came in, 'Thank God you are safe.'"

Some of those drawn in by the hoax were not amused. *The New York Times* was one of several newspapers that condemned it, publishing a number of letters from indignant readers. "My children had started for school about 10 minutes before we saw this monstrous joke," one irate father wrote. "A carriage was sent for at once to go after them, my wife trembling lest they should be already killed. I had read aloud part of this long rigmarole when glancing at the last paragraph, I saw the explanation. My wife said she will not have such a paper in the house again, and has ordered it stopped."

Despite the tempest it caused, the *Herald,* like the *Sun,* actually benefited from the fraud. Managing editor Thomas B. Connery, who had conceived the hoax and defended it as an entertaining way to alert readers to the careless way he had observed animals being handled at the zoo, claimed the paper's circulation "did not drop by so much as one subscriber." Instead, sales actually increased. Besides, Connery speculated, the reason *The New York Times* had been so critical of the story was because its editor had fallen for it, leaving his home "with a brace of pistols, prepared to shoot the first animals that would cross his path."

# 6

~~

# Extra! Greed All About It!

Abraham Lincoln was not a man given to fits of rage or rash decisions, but one day in May 1864 the normally placid president blew his stovepipe top. Two newspapers, the New York *World* and the *Journal of Commerce,* printed a proclamation, said to be from Lincoln, that detailed recent Union setbacks in the Civil War and announced the draft of an additional four hundred thousand men. The president was furious when he heard of the bogus announcement. He ordered the two newspapers shuttered and a number of their editors and reporters arrested.

It was soon discovered, however, that the *World* and the *Journal* had been duped into printing the false proclamation by a wily newspaperman named Joseph Howard, editor of the Brooklyn *Eagle.* Described in one account as "dashing and somewhat reckless in his way, ready to supply on short notice any sort of sensation that might be desired," Howard came up with a plan to profit from the Civil War. As a seasoned editor, he knew bad news about the war tended to drive up the price of gold, a stable commodity in uncertain times. Accordingly, he set out to create some bad news and buy up some gold. He enlisted the help of one of his reporters at the *Eagle,* Francis A. Mallison, and together they forged copies of an Associated Press dispatch with the dire proclamation supposedly issued by the president. Then they had it sent to a number of newspapers.

The *World* and the *Journal* were the only two that ran the announcement, but it was enough. The price of gold rose, and Howard pock-
eted a tidy profit.

But suspicions rose just as quickly as the price of gold. People
wondered why only two papers had printed the proclamation, and
crowds gathered at the *World* and the *Journal* to try to find out what
was happening. Major General John A. Dix, commander of the Department of the East, telegraphed Secretary of War Edwin Stanton
as soon as he saw the papers to verify the proclamation. Stanton
wired back, "this paper is an absolute forgery," and went to the
White House to confer with Lincoln.

The president had a particular loathing for those who sought to
profit from the war. "I wish every one of them had his *devilish* head
shot off!" he fumed. In a rage he issued the order that the offending
newspapers be closed, a controversial act that marred his reputation.
Given the constitutional implications, and the fact that he believed
the newspapers had been tricked, Dix was reluctant to carry out
Lincoln's order. He advised Stanton that he would start an investigation, which displeased the secretary tremendously. "A great national
crime has been committed by the publication," Stanton replied to
Dix. "The editors, proprietors, and publishers, responsible and irre-
sponsible, are in law guilty of that crime. You were not directed to
make an investigation but to execute the President's orders. . . .
How you can excuse or justify delay in executing the President's order until you make an investigation is not for me to determine!"

Dix had no choice but to do as the president demanded. The
doors of the two newspapers were padlocked and members of their
staffs arrested. Even the office of the Independent Telegraph Line
was seized for allegedly sending the false dispatch. It "was hasty,
rash, inconsiderate, and wrong and cannot be defended," Secretary
of the Navy Gideon Welles wrote in his diary. Such acts, he concluded, "weaken the Administration and strengthen its enemies."
And with the 1864 elections looming, Lincoln's decision gave his
political opponents ample fodder. "Will the people see the danger
of entrusting power again to a man who dares use it in the wanton
invasions of private rights?" editorialized the New York *Herald*.

The fact that the culprit was apprehended just days after the newspapers were forced to close only made the administration appear all the more reactionary. Howard was incarcerated in the New York military prison Fort Lafayette, where he served less than three months. Henry Ward Beecher, the renowned abolitionist preacher (and brother of *Uncle Tom's Cabin* author Harriet Beecher Stowe), interceded with Lincoln on Howard's behalf, and the president, apparently back to his more sanguine self, showed mercy.

# 7

~~

# False Alarm

Freedom of speech precludes yelling "Fire!" in a crowded theater, but what about a newspaper that *reports* a devastating theater fire that never happened? That's just what the *Chicago Times* did on February 13, 1875. BURNED ALIVE, screamed the top headline, followed by a number of smaller headlines outlining the calamity: "The Angel of Death Brings Terrible Mourning to Chicago," "Burning of a Theater Last Night—Hundreds Perish in the Flames." The eleventh headline above the story should have given it away: "Description of a Supposititious Holocaust Likely to Occur Any Night." But for people anxious to read exactly what had happened, the point of this subtle revelation was lost.

The story that followed had enough horrific detail to make it seem all too real. The fire started on the stage of an unnamed theater, the *Times* reported, and became a "roaring, seething, curling mass of flame, which lit up the interior of the theater with an awful glare and blistered and burned the unfortunate people who stood nearest to it." As the flames spread, so did the panic. "Timid females raised their hands to heaven, shrieked wild, despairing cries, and fell trampled into eternity by the heavy heels of the maddened, rushing throng. Mothers pleaded piteously, in the turmoil and the roar, that their darling little daughters might be spared." But, according to the *Times*, few were. When at last firemen were able to douse the flames and enter the ruined building, a gruesome scene conceived by an imaginative writer awaited them: "There were blackened corpses covered with the grime of the conflagration; and bloody corpses trampled to death and mutilated. There were corpses crisp and hideous, and hair burned off, the white teeth grinning, the hands fleshless. There were others that sat in their seats, who had evidently been seized with a fright and rendered incapable of moving." To make the story all the more realistic, a list of some of the dead and injured was published. Initials and common names were used, which made thousands believe that their loved ones had been among the many lost souls.

Finally, after delivering more gory details and castigating the theater owners for their negligence, the *Times* admitted the story was entirely fictitious. It was not a prank, but a public service designed to warn readers of the extremely dangerous conditions that actually existed in most Chicago theaters. Yet despite the paper's pretensions of civic mindedness, the false report was widely condemned. The rival *Chicago Tribune* published its own bit of fiction, reporting that a woman had been driven insane by the belief that her husband had perished in the flames, and that the woman's mother collapsed and died after reading the account in the *Times*. "She was as really murdered as though the assassin had sent a bullet through her heart," the *Tribune* opined in its own fake story, which concluded: "Whether anything of the kind has resulted from the publication of the hoax, we do not know. If there has not, no thanks are due to the editor of the *Times*, for it was calculated to accomplish just such calamities as we have imagined, and no amount of subterfuge or specious argument can justify such violations of journalistic decency."

# 8

## Mencken Up History

There was nothing at all remarkable about what famed journalist H. L. Mencken wrote in his *New York Evening Mail* column on December 28, 1917—no tales of life on the moon or wild beasts roaming New York—just a restrained, somewhat whimsical tribute to the bathtub. Perhaps that's why it became one of the most enduring of all media hoaxes, a perpetual source of misinformation that has fooled journalists, historians, and even the president of the United States. The simple, nonsensational quality of the story made it utterly believable. Who would ever suspect that something as benign as the bathtub might be the subject of a hoax?

The column, titled "A Neglected Anniversary," began: "On December 20, there flitted past us, absolutely without public notice, one of the most important profane anniversaries in American history—to wit: the 75th anniversary of the introduction of the bathtub into these states. Not a plumber fired a salute or hung out a flag. Not a governor proclaimed a day of prayer. Not a newspaper called attention to the day."

Mencken then went on to deliver his "history" of the tub. The first was installed on December 20, 1842, at the home of a Cincinnati merchant named Adam Thompson. It was an immediate sensation, Mencken wrote, that plunged Cincinnati into controversy. Critics condemned it as an elitist contrivance, an "obnoxious toy from England, designed to corrupt the democratic simplicity," while doctors warned that bathing might be dangerous, a possible cause of "phthisic, rheumatic fevers, inflammation of the lungs, and a whole category of zymotic diseases." Soon the controversy spread, the columnist continued, with various jurisdictions taxing bathtubs, charging exorbitant water rates for those who installed them, or attempting to ban them altogether. It was not until 1851, when President Millard Fillmore installed a bathtub in the White House, that the new contraption started to gain acceptance and respectability.

To his astonishment, Mencken's hoax—intended, he said, to amuse readers during the dreary days of World War I—started to weave its way into the culture as fact. Finally, in 1926, he felt compelled to admit his bathtub story was a fake, "a tissue of absurdities, all of them deliberate and most of them obvious." In the confession, published in his nationally syndicated column, Mencken wrote: "Pretty soon I began to encounter my preposterous 'facts' in the writings of other men. . . . They got into learned journals. They were alluded to on the floor of Congress. They crossed the ocean and were discussed solemnly in England, and on the continent. Finally, I began to find them in standard works of reference. Today, I believe, they are accepted as gospel everywhere on Earth."

Perhaps Mencken, never one for modesty, gave himself a bit too much credit. Still, his story was regularly passed on to the unquestioning public he contemptuously called the "booboisie." Two months after his first confession was published, Mencken wrote another. In it he noted that people are generally far more interested in a good story than the truth. And, once again, his gargantuan ego was abundantly evident. His hoax, he said, was superior to the "string of banalities" that probably constituted the true story of the bathtub. "There were heroes in it, and villains. I revealed a conflict, with virtue winning. So it was embraced by mankind, precisely as the story of George Washington and the cherry tree was embraced." Well, not quite. This was about bathtubs, after all. Nevertheless, the "facts" were often repeated, even by President Harry Truman, who responded to critics of his plan to add a balcony to the White House by reminding them that President Fillmore had earlier met resistance when he installed the tub. Even in recent years the White

House bathtub has been cited in the media as one of the few accomplishments of the Fillmore administration. As *The Washington Post* predicted in a 1977 story, the attempt to expose the truth of H. L. Mencken's hoax "will not even slow it up, any more than a single grape placed on the railroad tracks would slow up a freight train."

# 9

## Khmer Ruse

The *New York Times* had just over a year to gloat over the humiliation suffered by its rival *The Washington Post* after the Janet Cooke debacle before being shamed itself by an unscrupulous reporter with a tall tale of his own to tell. In December 1981, *The New York Times Magazine* published "In the Land of the Khmer Rouge," a dramatic account of a dangerous visit to Khmer Rouge territory in Cambodia by freelance writer Christopher Jones. As it turned out, Jones never left the comfort of a Spanish villa to report the story (though he did file a fake expense report). It was *The Washington Post* who first exposed the sham, which no doubt compounded the humiliation felt at the *Times.*

Two months after the article appeared, the *Post* reported that Khmer Rouge officials denied Jones had been to Cambodia the previous fall, nor had he interviewed the people quoted in his story. The quotes, in fact, were almost identical to those Jones had used in another dubious dispatch from Cambodia published the year before in the Asian edition of *Time* magazine. Furthermore, Jones had lifted passages almost verbatim from André Malraux's 1930 novel about Cambodia, *The Royal Way.* Then there was this glaring inconsistency caught by the *Post:* Jones wrote of a firefight that supposedly took place at night. When the fighting ended, "I stood up and peered through my field glasses." Having apparently forgotten that it was supposed to be dark outside, Jones continued: "Just then, on the summit of a distant hillside, I saw a figure that made me catch my breath: a pudgy Cambodian, with field glasses hanging from his neck. The eyes in his head looked dead and stony. I could not make him out in any detail, but I had seen enough pictures of the supreme leader to convince me, at that precise second, that I was staring at Pol Pot."

Asked to comment on the revelations about Jones, *Times* executive editor A. M. Rosenthal was defiant, at first: "As far as I'm concerned, the man, until somebody proves otherwise, is totally honest." Nevertheless, a *Times* editor and two correspondents were immediately dispatched to Spain to confront the twenty-four-year-old writer. For two days Jones stubbornly insisted his story was true before he finally broke down and confessed. "Shaken by the unraveling of his story, Jones fell mute," the *Times* reported in its own account of the deception. "Then, urged on by his questioners, he confirmed the hoax. 'I wanted to do the job, but I couldn't,' he said. 'I had to do my best from what I had, and consequently reconstructed it.' " As for plagiarizing Malraux (among several other previously published sources), Jones was succinct: "I needed a piece of color."

# 10

## *Times* Bomb

The embarrassment felt at the *Times* over the Khmer Rouge debacle was but a blush compared to the seismic mortification that shook the venerable newspaper in 2003 when it was revealed—again by the *Post*—that a twenty-seven-year-old reporter named Jayson Blair had filled its pages with fabrications, distortions, and material stolen from other sources. The journalistic fraud he perpetuated in at least thirty-six articles was acknowledged by the *Times* as "a low point in the 152-year history of the newspaper." Or as publisher Arthur Ochs Sulzberger Jr. put it, "It's a huge black eye."

For a number of stories Blair was supposed to have filed from various places across the country, he never left New York. Instead, he falsified expense accounts to cover his tracks—or, more accurately, his *lack* of tracks. In one instance, Blair faked an interview in West Virginia with the father of Jessica Lynch, a POW rescued in April 2003 during the Second Gulf War. The Lynch family was amused to read in the *Times* that there were tobacco fields and grazing cattle near their home—a pastoral setting completely imagined by Blair. Another story described two wounded Marines lying side by side at the Bethesda Naval Medical Center, even though Blair himself never saw them there.

While covering the detainment of two snipers who had terrorized the Washington, D.C., region in 2002, Blair made up
facts that upset and angered local officials. After one story ran,
Fairfax County Commonwealth Attorney Robert Horan called
a press conference and called Blair's account "dead wrong."
*Times* executive editor Howell Raines, however, seemed pleased
with his reporter. He even sent Blair a note praising his "great
shoe-leather reporting" on one sniper story. Raines, who later
lost his job because of the Blair fiasco, said he had no idea he was
dealing with "a pathological pattern of misrepresentation, fabricating and deceiving." Perhaps not. But there were warning
signs.

Blair could hardly be called an ace reporter. His shoddy reporting
during a three-and-a-half-year period resulted in fifty published
corrections, an abysmal record. "We have to stop Jayson from writing for the *Times*. Right now," Metropolitan editor Jonathan Land-
man wrote in a memo to newsroom executives. No one listened.
Blair was given the high-profile sniper case to cover. Little wonder he
later called his editors "idiots" in an interview with the New York
*Observer.*

The disgraced reporter was defiant in that interview, and appeared rather annoyed that his fabrications weren't better appreciated: "I don't understand why I am the bumbling affirmative-action
hire [Blair is African American] when Stephen Glass[2] is this brilliant
whiz kid, when from my perspective—and I know I shouldn't be
saying this—I fooled some of the most brilliant people in journalism. . . . They're all so smart, but I was sitting right under their nose

---

2. Glass, an associate editor at the *New Republic,* was fired in 1998 for fabricating
scores of stories, including "The First Church of George Herbert Walker
Christ," about people who supposedly worshipped the forty-first president, and
"Spring Breakdown," about the debauchery at a conservative political conference. An excerpt: "In the get-naked room, everyone disrobes immediately, without a hint of embarrassment. One couple fondles each other in the corner. A
muscular man, apparently hallucinating, prances around the room like a ballet
dancer. A woman locks herself in the bathroom, crying and shouting out the
name Samuel."

fooling them. If they're all so brilliant and I'm such an affirmative-action hire, how come they didn't catch me?"

Perhaps Blair's wounded feelings were soothed somewhat by the big, fat book advance he received for writing his side of the story.

The Trojan Horse

# Part III

~

# THE WARS OF THE RUSES

"All warfare is based on deception," the classical Chinese military strategist and philosopher Sun-tzu wrote in *The Art of War* more than two thousand five hundred years ago. He had a point. Some of history's most ingenious tricks have been played in battle. Perhaps the best known of these is the Trojan Horse. According to legend, after months of failed attempts to sack Troy, the Greeks constructed a giant wooden horse and left it outside the city's gates as a peace offering. It was filled with Greek warriors. When the horse was pulled inside the walls of Troy, the soldiers slipped out at night, opened the city's gates, and commenced a slaughter of Trojans. The story might be apocryphal, but its spirit has been revived in many great conflicts through the ages.

# 1

## The Agony of Deceit

Supreme sacrifices have always been made in times of war, though few quite as drastic as the one a Persian named Zopyrus reportedly made of himself, and seven thousand others, in the sixth century BC. It was part of his devious plan to conquer Babylon, one of the most stubborn of Persia's rebellious provinces, when Darius the Great came to the throne in 521. The Babylonians mocked the new monarch with the boast that he would rule over them when mules, which are sterile, bore foals. According to the Greek historian Herodotus—the source for this story—one of Zopyrus's mules actually did reproduce, which he took as a sign that it was time to crush Babylon. His plan to defeat the enemy was to become one of them.

The method Zopyrus chose to infiltrate their ranks was inventive, if somewhat deranged. He sliced off his own nose and ears, shaved himself bald, and had himself whipped. He then went to Darius and requested that seven thousand soldiers, marked for death, be put at his disposal. The king, stunned by his subject's extreme loyalty, could hardly refuse. Zopyrus next allowed himself to be captured by the Babylonians. He told them he had been mutilated by his capricious king and wanted to avenge himself by fighting for them. "And now," he declared, "here I am, men of Babylon; and my coming will be gain to you, but loss—and that the severest—to Darius and his army. He little knows me if he thinks he can get away with the foul things he has done me—moreover, I know all the ins and outs of his plans." The Babylonians had only to look at their hideously maimed guest to believe he was telling the truth. Zopyrus was given a military command.

As prearranged with Darius, one thousand of the sacrificial Persian soldiers were placed outside Babylon armed only with daggers. They were quickly slaughtered by the Babylonian forces led by Zopyrus. A week later, two thousand more soldiers were similarly killed. Zopyrus was becoming a valued warrior. His position was clinched three weeks after that when the last four thousand Persian soldiers were massacred. Now trust in Zopyrus was complete. He was given the ultimate reward for his services, which was complete control over Babylon's defenses. This was what he had planned for all along. And though, now noseless, he could not actually smell victory, it was within his grasp at last. Zopyrus threw open the gates of Babylon and in rushed a Persian horde. A grateful King Darius gave his loyal subject the kingdom he had conquered to rule—tax free—for the rest of his life.

# 2

## Sun's Burn

The ancient Chinese tactician Sun Bin, reportedly a direct descendant of Sun-tzu, proved that missing feet were no impediment to kicking ass. He defeated his mortal enemy Pang Juan with a little guile and his ancestor's famous maxim, "Know enemy, know self; one hundred battles, one hundred victories."

Sun Bin, whose name means Sun the Mutilated, lost his feet courtesy of Pang Juan. Both men had studied warfare under a mysterious sage known as the Master of Demon Valley, but the experience hardly bonded them. Pang Juan was bitterly jealous of his more talented classmate and set out to destroy him. He found the perfect opportunity after he became a general in the army of the Chinese state of Wei. Pang Juan lured Sun Bin to Wei, as if to consult with him on a military matter. But when he arrived, Pang had him arrested on bogus charges, the penalty for which was mutilation. Both of Sun Bin's feet were cut off and his face was branded.

It was in this pitiful state that Sun Bin encountered the ambassador from the neighboring state of Qi. The diplomat was impressed by Sun's extensive knowledge of strategy in warfare and sought to utilize it. He smuggled Sun out of Wei and brought him to Qi. There Sun was offered the rank of general in the Qi army, which he turned down because, as a strategist, he knew missing feet could be a rather significant handicap in battle. Instead, Sun Bin became a consultant to the great Qi general Tian Ji. It was the perfect position for this military genius, also known as Sun-tzu II, to exact his revenge on Pang Juan.

Sun Bin rose to prominence during a period in Chinese history known as the Era of the Warring States, which ran from about 475 BC to 221 BC. "Usurpers set themselves up as lords and kings," it was recorded in a traditional anthology known as *Strategies of the Warring States;* "states that were run by pretenders and plotters established armies to make themselves into major powers. . . . Fathers and sons were alienated, brothers were at odds, husbands and wives were estranged. No one could safeguard his or her life. Integrity disappeared. . . . This all happened because the warring states were shamelessly greedy, struggling insatiably to get ahead."

It was during these chaotic times that the army of Wei, headed by Sun Bin's old enemy Pang Juan, joined forces with the state of Zhao to attack the state of Han, which appealed to Sun's adopted state of Qi for help. As Qi's resident strategist, Sun Bin observed a characteristic of Pang's army which would ultimately defeat them. "The aggressor armies are fierce and think little of your army, which they regard as cowardly," Sun told Qi's general. "A good warrior would take advantage of this tendency and lead them on with prospects of gain."

Sun came up with a brilliantly deceptive battle plan that took full advantage of the enemy's prejudice. He instructed the army of Qi to light one hundred thousand campfires on the first night of occupation. The next night only fifty thousand fires were to be lit, then half of that on the third night. The illusion thus produced was that of an ever dwindling force. "I knew the soldiers of Qi were cowards," Pang Juan crowed triumphantly in the belief that the warriors of Qi were defecting—"they've only been in our territory for three days now, and more than half their army has run away!"

Pang Juan was so convinced of Qi's cowardly retreat that he left his own infantry behind and gave chase with nothing but a small force. It was a fatal error that played right into Sun Bin's plan. He ordered an ambush set up at a narrow gorge. When Pang and his little group arrived at the spot, they came across a felled tree with a message carved into it. "The general of Wei will die at this tree," it read. Sure enough, when Pang's soldiers lit a torch to read the message, a hail of Qi arrows fell on them. Those that weren't killed scattered, while Pang was left with nothing but the agonizing awareness that he had been tricked. He killed himself on the spot. Sun the Mutilated had been avenged.

# 3

~~~

# A Bridge Too Far?

Sure, all's fair in love and war, but there are still a few deceptions that strike a bit below the belt—like tricking an enemy with the promise of peace. It's the wartime equivalent of shaking a guy's hand then sucker punching him in the face. Indecorous as it may be, though, the ploy has worked well in a number of instances, perhaps most notably in 1805, just before the Battle of Austerlitz.

The large wooden bridge over the Danube River on the road to Vienna was of great strategic importance to Napoleon as his army marched to confront the combined forces of Austria and Russia. The Austrians knew this, of course, and kept the bridge well guarded. They also rigged it with explosives should a French approach make its destruction necessary. Confronted with this obstacle, two of Napoleon's top marshals, Jean Lannes and Joachim Murat, devised a scheme to take the bridge intact. Dressed in their full ceremonial uniforms and accompanied by a group of German-speaking officers, they approached the bridge.

"Armistice! Armistice!" they called as they calmly walked across. The Austrians, unsure what to do, called for the local commander, General Auersperg. Murat and Lannes told the elderly, and not too bright, general that the French and Austrian emperors had come to terms. As the leaders of each side conferred, French troops quietly advanced on the bridge and disabled the explosives. No one fired at them for fear of breaking what was believed to be a truce. There's a scene in Tolstoy's *War and Peace* in which an Austrian soldier warns General Auersperg that he is being deceived by the French. Murat responds to the accusation with a challenge to the general: "I don't recognize the world-famous Austrian discipline if you allow a subordinate to address you like that!"

Whether or not such an exchange actually occurred is unclear, but General Auersperg did give up the bridge in the belief that an armistice was in effect. The poor old guy was court-martialed for his folly and died in disgrace. Napoleon, meanwhile, went on to defeat the combined Austrian and Russian forces at Austerlitz, a battle he described as the greatest he ever fought. The emperor's private secretary called Lannes and Murat's trick preceding it an "act of courage and presence of mind, which had so great an influence on the events of the campaign." But another French officer, General Baron de Marbot, had a different opinion. "I know that in war one eases one's conscience," he wrote in his *Memoirs,* "and that any means may be employed to ensure victory and reduce loss of life, but in spite of these weighty considerations, I do not think that one can approve of the method used to seize the bridge . . . and for my part I would not care to do the same in similar circumstances."

# 4

≈

# Stretching the Troops

A few years before he became one of the Ku Klux Klan's charter members, Nathan Bedford Forrest was among the Confederacy's craftiest generals. On a number of occasions during the Civil War, Forrest successfully demanded the surrender of much larger Union forces by use of a ploy as old as scripture.

The Book of Judges records Gideon's defeat of a vast army of Midianites with only trumpets and torches, the latter hidden in clay jars. After he had surrounded the Midianite camp at dark with his tiny force of three hundred men, Gideon ordered his soldiers to blare their trumpets and smash open the clay pots with the torches inside at his signal. When they did, the resulting flash and din convinced the Midianites that they were surrounded by a massive force. They scattered and fled in a blind panic.

Forrest adopted a similar tactic in 1863. He called for the surrender of the Union troops of Colonel Abel Streight near Rome, Georgia, after a long march that had exhausted both sides. Though he was significantly outnumbered, Forrest created an illusion of strength. He had only two artillery pieces, for example, but he ordered them passed back and forth across Streight's line of vision as the two parlayed. "Name of God!" Streight exclaimed after watching this demonstration for a while. "How many guns have you got? There's fifteen I've counted already!" Forrest glanced in the direction the Union commander was looking and replied nonchalantly, "I reckon that's all that has kept up."

As the discussion with Streight continued, Forrest periodically issued fake orders for the movement of troops that did not in fact exist. The few Confederates that were there marched back and forth across Streight's line of sight, just as the artillery men had done with the two guns. It was a simple ploy, but it was enough to fool the Union commander. Streight ordered the surrender of fifteen hundred Federals to a rebel force half that size. It was, declared George W. Adair, editor of the *Southern Confederacy,* "the boldest game of bluff on record. . . . For cool audacity, it excels all history or imagination." Adair exaggerated slightly, but less than two years later his old friend Forrest pulled a similar stunt with even more remarkable results.

Union forces held a fort in Athens, Alabama, that defended the Central Alabama Railroad. The structure was "one of the best works of the kind I ever saw," noted a federal inspector of such defenses. Forrest wanted it surrendered. "Knowing it would cost heavily to storm and capture the enemy's works, and wishing to prevent the effusion of blood I knew would follow a successful assault, I determined to see if anything could be accomplished by negotiations," Forrest later reported. "Accordingly, I sent Major Strange, of my staff, with a flag of truce, demanding the surrender of the fort and garrison."

Union colonel Wallace Campbell, who had already been fed misleading information about the enemy's strength by two Confederate prisoners, agreed to a personal interview with Forrest. "[I] immediately met General Forrest," reported Campbell, "[who] told me he was determined to take the place; that his force was sufficiently large, and have it he would, and if he was compelled to storm the works it would result in the massacre of the entire garrison. He told me what his force was, and said myself and one officer could have the privilege of reviewing [it]."

Forrest gave Campbell a guided tour of his troops, the relatively small size of which was cleverly concealed. Dismounted cavalry were identified as infantry; horse-holders as cavalry. The same elements were then dispersed to other parts of the field to play different roles until, wrote one Confederate, "the whole place seemed to be swarming with enthusiastic troops and bristling with guns." Campbell, convinced, as he later wrote, "that there were at least 10,000 men and nine pieces of artillery," duly surrendered the fort.

The audacious trick only added to the luster of Forrest, respectfully known in the South as "the Wizard of the Saddle." Of course in the North, the epithets were somewhat less laudatory. General William Tecumseh Sherman called him "the very devil," but later acknowledged, "He had a genius which was to me incomprehensible."

# 5

~

# Warning: Smoking May Be Hazardous to Your Success

Captain Richard Meinertzhagen discovered one sure way to end a stalemate during World War I. He tricked the enemy into getting stoned. That and a few other deceptions allowed British forces under General Edmund Allenby to break through a line in the Gaza desert that had been stubbornly defended by Turkish and German troops and take the Holy Land.

The first step was to convince the enemy that the British planned an attack on heavily fortified Gaza, and that troop movement around the true target of Beersheba, some thirty miles east of Gaza and significantly less defended, was only a feint. Captain Meinertzhagen helped to give this impression by planting on the Turks a staff officer's notebook filled, as he later wrote, with "all sorts of nonsense about our plans and difficulties." The dummy notebook was stuffed into a canvas sack, along with an amount of cash large enough to indicate that the bag had not been lost intentionally. Other authenticating items were added as well, like a letter supposedly written by the wife of the nonexistent officer, and a valuable cipher of British secret codes.

Meinertzhagen then rode into the no-man's-land between the British and Turco-German lines in search of a patrol. When one fired on him, he dropped the sack—previously stained with horse's blood—and, pretending to be wounded, retreated back to his own line. The Turks retrieved the sack, which was then sent to German headquarters for analysis, while the British made a show of searching for it. Under the assumption that the enemy would use the cipher discovered in the bag, along with the dummy notebook, Meinertzhagen began to feed them false information from the British radio station in Egypt. One of the most significant bits of false data was that the supposed attack on Gaza would not occur before November 14 because British commander Edmund Allenby would be on leave until November 7. Meanwhile, the real assault on Beersheba was set for October 30.

British intelligence indicated that the enemy believed the ruse and had planned accordingly. It was then that Meinertzhagen launched the last phase of his plan. As British forces moved quietly from Gaza to Beersheba, leaving behind a "cavalry" of straw horses, he had one hundred and twenty thousand packs of cigarettes dropped over enemy lines. Whereas before the cigarette packages always contained propaganda messages, these smokes were laced with opium. What seemed like manna from heaven to the tobacco-starved Turks turned out to be a plague that paralyzed them. On October 30, 1917, the attack on Beersheba began. The city's defenders were sound asleep, too stoned to repel the invasion. From Beersheba, the British moved on to Gaza and then the rest of Palestine, leaving the Ottoman Empire crushed like a cigarette butt. "Meinertzhagen's device won the battle," Prime Minister David Lloyd George later wrote. He was "one of the ablest and most successful brains I had met in any army. . . . Needless to say he never rose in the war above the rank of Colonel."

# 6

~~~

# Drowned and Dirty:
# The Man Who Never Was

Doped cigarettes and bloodied knapsacks seem almost primitive next to the masterly deceptions executed during World War II. One of the most successful came on the eve of the Allied invasion of southern Europe in 1943. It's the story of the man who never was.

The Allies wanted Hitler to believe that they were going to invade by descending on the islands of Sardinia and Pelopónnisos, not Sicily as was actually planned. Any ruse capable of making the Germans believe there would be two invasions, eight hundred miles apart, had to be breathtaking. The British decided a dead man would carry the false message, and dubbed the plan Operation Mincemeat. The corpse, carrying phony invasion strategies in a briefcase chained to its wrist, would be floated off the coast of Spain, which teemed with German spies and operatives. If all went well, the body would be recovered and its false secrets revealed.

To help ensure the plan's success, scrupulous attention was devoted to detail. The perfect body had to look as though it had been in an air crash and then drowned. After an exhaustive search, the corpse of a man who had died from exposure and pneumonia was discovered and recruited. The lungs were already filled with fluid. With the body in cold storage, operatives devised a name, service, and rank for it. He was to be called Major William Martin. They were, however, unable to use a photograph of the corpse for a fake identity card. "It is impossible to describe how utterly and hope-lessly dead any photograph of the body looked," one operative wrote. The situation was saved when an officer who resembled the dead man posed for the picture.

The corpse's clothes were stuffed with everyday props—theater ticket stubs, an invitation to a London nightclub, notice of an over-drawn bank account, a picture of his fiancée, love letters, and a cranky letter from his father complaining about fuel rationing. Lord Louis Mountbatten added a touch of his own to explain why a rel-atively junior officer would have in his possession such important invasion documents. He wrote a personal letter to the British com-mander in the Mediterranean that said Major Martin was an expert in the employment of landing craft. "He is quite shy at first," Mountbatten wrote in the phony missive, "but he really knows his stuff. . . . Let me have him back, please, as soon as the assault is over."

All was now ready. After the conspirators selected the ideal spot in terms of winds and tides, "Major Martin" was launched. The plan was an evident success. After the major's body had been recov-ered, his effects were shipped back to London and scientific analysis indicated that the secret letters had been opened and carefully re-sealed. While conferring with President Roosevelt in Washington, British prime minister Winston Churchill received a succinct mes-sage: "Mincemeat swallowed whole." The success of the venture be-came evident several weeks later when Allied forces met little resistance at Sicily. The enemy had moved. To this day, the true identity of the operation's dead hero has never been revealed.

# 7

~~~

# Phantom Force

As much as Churchill savored the success of Mincemeat, it was merely an appetizer for the smorgasbord of deception that surrounded the Allied invasion of France in 1944. Never in the history of warfare had there been such a staggering challenge—to smash through the Nazi fortress of Europe from the sea. And never had secrecy and surprise been more imperative. If Hitler learned that the Allied assault was to be centered in Normandy, he would mass his forces there and shred the invaders as they landed. The expedition would be doomed, hundreds of thousands of lives lost, and the war effort gravely compromised. It was critical, therefore, that Allied intentions be carefully hidden from Hitler and his Wehrmacht—a task for which the British had proven themselves fully qualified. (See previous two chapters.)

"In warfare," Churchill once remarked, "truth is so precious that she should always be attended by a bodyguard of lies." The great prime minister certainly appreciated the value of this most subversive form of fighting, and from his comment emerged the code name for all cover and deception operations surrounding the invasion of Europe: Plan Bodyguard. Some of the kingdom's craftiest minds devised brilliant schemes to trick the Nazis. The goal was to make them believe the invasion of Europe could come anywhere— as far north as Norway, all the way down to the Mediterranean—

and thus cause them to stretch their forces thin in defense of the entire continent. There were misleading radio reports that were designed to be intercepted by the enemy. Captured German spies were
compelled to feed their masters false information, while bogus reconnaissance missions were sent to potential landing sites. And of
invaluable help in all the deceptive operations was the intelligence
derived from the Nazis' secret Enigma codes that had been cracked
at the beginning of the war—a fact the Allies took drastic measures
to keep concealed from the enemy.[1]

Perhaps the most elaborate in the Allied bodyguard of lies was
the First United States Army Group (FUSAG), an almost entirely
fictitious fighting force. What appeared to be a massive buildup of
fifty divisions and a million men in southeastern England was in reality a masterful illusion. The object of Quicksilver, the code name
of this particular element of Plan Bodyguard, was to make Hitler
think the Allies intended to invade France at the Pas-de-Calais, and
that Normandy was only a diversion to lure German forces away
from the prime landing sight. Hitler was already inclined to believe
that the Pas-de-Calais would be the center of attack, and kept one
of his strongest divisions there to defend it. The Allies intended to
keep it that way while they stormed Normandy.

The creation of the imaginary FUSAG turned a swath of southeastern England into something like a giant film set that dwarfed any
spectacle Cecil B. DeMille ever produced. From the air it was to appear that a mighty force was gathering. Rivers and lakes around the
region were filled with fake landing ships made of tubular scaffolding
and canvas and floated on oil drums. Smoke that coiled from the
"ship" funnels added to the illusion, as did oil patches in the water
around them. Other elements of FUSAG were also fabricated, in-

---

1. A startling example of these drastic measures may have come in 1940. Although
the evidence is inconclusive, some historians believe Churchill, from intelligence
derived from Enigma, had advance knowledge that Hitler intended a fierce aerial
assault on the English city of Coventry, and that he declined to give warning of the
impeding attack for fear that any measures taken by the populace to defend themselves might reveal to the Germans that their secret codes had been penetrated, thus
prompting them to switch to a new cipher system. As a result, Coventry became
what the London *Times* called "a martyred city."

cluding ammunition dumps, field kitchens, hospitals, troop encampments, and fuel lines. One morning a local farmer awoke to find a mass of tanks assembled in his fields. A bull charged one of them, and, rather than being knocked unconscious, walked away as the "tank" hissed and slowly deflated. It was, like all the others, inflatable.

Sporadic radio noises, meant to simulate a large army group, were periodically sent out into the ether, while planted newspaper reports described life around the ever expanding military base. One story described a local vicar who was livid over the moral collapse that accompanied the vast number of foreign troops assembling in the region, and another concerned "the immense numbers of rubber contraceptives" found around American paratroop bases.

One of the more clever illusions was a fake oil dock from which a pipeline under the English Channel would supposedly supply the invading armies at the Pas-de-Calais. The dock, made almost entirely of camouflaged scaffolding, fiberboard, and old sewage pipes, occupied nearly three miles of the English shoreline. Wind machines blew up dust to make it appear that construction was moving apace and to disguise the fact that there were only a few people working on the project. King George VI came to "inspect" the dock, while the Royal Air Force flew fighter patrols as if to protect the vital installation. German reconnaissance aircraft were allowed to fly overhead, but only after the fighter patrols made a show of engaging them. And when the Germans shelled the artificial dock with long-range missiles, massive sodium flares were lit to mimic the raging fires that accompanied direct hits.

To give FUSAG even more credibility, General George C. Patton was sent to Britain to head the phantom force. Though the famed American general was less than thrilled with the prospect of leading an army that didn't exist, he was an inspired choice. The Germans knew him and respected him, and his assignment to FUSAG could only underscore for them how important this force was to the Allies.

No matter how cleverly the elements of Quicksilver were executed, the Allies knew it would take more than rubber tanks and cardboard docks to trick the Germans into believing FUSAG existed as a true fighting force. Even Patton wasn't enough. The enemy needed details surreptitiously fed to them, like the location and identity of various formations. That's where German spies under Allied control were utilized. False information about FUSAG was relayed by a group of double agents believed by the Nazis to be reliable. And though there were some perilous episodes in which Quicksilver was almost exposed, this part of the ruse was most successful. After one particularly newsy dispatch, for example, a German intelligence officer informed the führer that valuable information about Allied plans for the invasion of France at Calais had been obtained. "The authenticity of the report was checked and proved," the officer stated. "It contains information about three armies, three army corps, and twenty-three [divisions] among which the location of only one need be regarded as questionable. The report confirms our operational picture."

One highly decorated German officer was the unwitting source of further misinformation. General Hans Cramer, who had been captured by the Allies in Tunisia, was in failing health and was to be sent back to Germany as part of a repatriation program run by the Swedish Red Cross. Before he left, however, he was to be given a glimpse of FUSAG to take home with him. On the journey from his prison camp in Wales to London, Cramer was driven through an area where an immense buildup of armor, shipping, and aircraft was taking place. He was told it was FUSAG in southeastern England, although what Cramer really saw were the actual preparations being made elsewhere in England for the invasion of Normandy. Cramer had no way of knowing where he was because all signposts and other identifying markers throughout Britain had been removed earlier in the war. So, like a good Nazi, Cramer dutifully informed his superiors of what he had seen and heard. Thus, FUSAG was officially verified by one of Germany's top generals.

On June 6, 1944—D-Day—the largest invasion force ever assembled hit Normandy. Though fighting was fierce, and many lives were lost, the Allies were able to gain a foothold on the continent. To maintain it, however, the fiction of FUSAG had to be maintained. Hitler had to remain convinced that this imaginary force was still poised to strike at Calais. Otherwise, he would send the defenders there to Normandy, which would have devastating consequences. Here Churchill played a part in the grand deception. He announced in the House of Commons that the D-Day assault at

Normandy had commenced, but he broadly suggested that another assault on France was to follow. Other Allied leaders did the same. "The Germans appear to expect landings elsewhere," President Franklin Roosevelt said in an address to the nation. "Let them speculate. We are content to wait on events."

To perpetuate the idea that another huge strike was imminent, all the activity that preceded the invasion of Normandy was mimicked for the benefit of the enemy. Special forces and intelligence teams were parachuted to the Pas-de-Calais. Submarines and mine sweepers appeared off the French coast, while air and naval forces began to bombard potential landing areas. Messages to the French Resistance were relayed, just as they had been before D-Day. In England, FUSAG's dummy ships, along with a sprinkling of real ones, were brightly lit at night to make it appear from the air that they were being loaded with cargo and mobilized. Increased radio traffic between air and ground crews made it appear that a mammoth operation was underway. Double agents sent false messages to their controllers. One, code named Brutus, reported that he had seen "with my own eyes the Army Group Patton was preparing to embark at east coast and southeastern ports." Brutus also quoted Patton as saying, "Now that the diversion in Normandy is going so well, the time has come to commence operations around Calais." Another agent, called Garbo, sent a long, detailed report to his Nazi handler about gathering operations, and concluded, "I transmit this report with the conviction that the present assault [on Normandy] is a trap set with the purpose of making us move all our resources in a rushed strategic redisposition which we would later regret."

Meanwhile, Erwin Rommel and other German generals pleaded for reinforcements from the Pas-de-Calais to Normandy. Their forces were being slaughtered by the Allies, they said, while the army at Calais idled. Hitler, having been thoroughly hoodwinked by the Allied deception campaign, refused. He was adamant in his belief that another attack was in the works, and insisted the Pas-de-Calais remain strongly defended. So, while the Germans utilized their best troops to defend against a phantom force in Calais, the real one established itself at Normandy. The enemy, General Omar Bradley wrote in his memoirs, "played into our hands in the biggest single hoax of the war."

Bismarck itching for a fight with Napoleon III

# *Part IV*

~~

# STATE-SPONSORED
# DECEPTIONS

*"He who has known best how to employ the fox has succeed-
ed best. It is necessary . . . to be a great pretender and dissembler; and [citizens] are so simple, and so subject to present
necessities, that he who seeks to deceive will always find someone who will allow himself to be deceived."*
    —NICCOLÒ MACHIAVELLI, *The Prince*

Machiavelli understood how difficult the pursuit and mainte-
nance of power could be, and that it often required every
available means to keep it from collapsing. "A wise ruler cannot and should not keep his word when such an observance of
faith would be to his disadvantage," he counseled five centuries ago. It was a lesson many leaders throughout history
knew instinctively, or learned quickly. And that's why fraud has
flourished so abundantly in the great halls of state.

# *1*

~~

# A Bogus Bequest

Being pope in the eighth and ninth centuries was no picnic. His Holiness was often at the mercy of grasping Roman aristocrats or murderous mobs, such as the rabble who in 799 tried to blind Leo III and tear out his tongue. The Lombards loomed as a constant threat from the north. And as far as the Byzantine emperor and the Frankish king were concerned, the Vicar of Christ was just another bishop of a vassal state to be controlled and manipulated. These were Dark Ages indeed.

Out of this chaotic era emerged a remarkable forged document, known as the *Donation of Constantine,* designed to prop up the papacy and bestow upon it unprecedented power and supremacy. It was supposedly written in the fourth century by the first Christian Roman emperor, Constantine the Great, as a solemn legal bequest to Pope Sylvester I and his successors. The *Donation* was divided into two parts. In the first part, entitled "Confessio," Constantine— or rather the guy impersonating him on paper—recounted how he was instructed in the Christian faith by Pope Sylvester, and how he was miraculously cured of leprosy at his baptism (a legend widely believed when the forgery was produced sometime between 750 and 850). The "emperor" also made a full profession of faith in the "Confessio."

In the second part of the forgery, called "Donatio," Constantine supposedly made the pope all-powerful, setting him above all other bishops and churches throughout the world and giving Sylvester "all the prerogatives of our supreme imperial position and the glory of our authority." That included the right to wear the imperial crown, "which we have transferred from our own head." The pope turned down that particular honor, according to the *Donation*, but he did allow the emperor to hold the bridle of his horse and perform "the office of groom for him." Finally, "to correspond to our own empire and so that the supreme pontifical authority may not be dishonored" by a temporal ruler in Rome, "Constantine" supposedly gave the pope and his successors not only that city, "but all the provinces, districts, and cities of Italy and the Western regions." (In 330, Constantine had moved the imperial capital east from Rome to the city that bore his name, Constantinople, now Istanbul, thus giving the *Donation* a touch of historic credibility.)

Historians are uncertain who authored the fake document. Because of its obvious benefits to the papacy, many believe it originated in Rome. Others, however, think the *Donation* may have been produced by the Franks—an attempt to buttress the papacy, then under the protection of King Pépin and his successor Charlemagne, against the Byzantine emperor in Constantinople and his claims to the papal states. Whatever the case, Constantine's "donation" was for centuries believed to be genuine. And though the popes did not enjoy any immediate benefits from the forgery—they were still murdered, maimed, and deposed with alarming regularity—it did serve as part of the foundation upon which later medieval popes reigned with imperial power and grandeur.

The fraud was finally exposed in 1440 by Lorenzo Valla in his *Discourse on the Forgery of the Alleged Donation of Constantine*. Valla showed with devastating precision just how preposterous the *Donation* really was, citing its historical anachronisms and other glaring errors. Valla also noted that the temporal claims derived from the document had made the popes not leaders of the faithful, but oppressors of Christians—"so far from giving food and bread to the household of God . . . they devoured us as food . . . the Pope himself makes war on peaceable people, and sows discord among states and princes."

Valla's lesson was apparently lost on Pope Clement VII, who less than a century later had Raphael decorate his staterooms with frescos glorifying the *Donation of Constantine* and the supremacy of Rome. During that same reign, the city was sacked by Emperor Charles V. And no words put in a dead emperor's mouth could save it.

# 2

~~≈~~

# Three Kings with Aces
# Up Their Sleeves

The sack of Rome in 1527 was just one episode in a tangled series of plots and counterplots among three of Europe's most powerful monarchs: Francis I of France, Henry VIII of England, and the Holy Roman emperor Charles V (who was also Charles I of Spain). Theirs was an international game of trickery and betrayal, played beneath a veneer of courtly civility that sometimes bordered on farce.

The rivalry between Henry and Francis was perhaps the most intense, infused as it was with the longstanding enmity that existed between England and France. Centuries of intermittent warfare between the two kingdoms had left mutual antipathy and mistrust practically encoded in their genes. The fact that each king fancied himself the Renaissance ideal of a royal stud only added to the tension. They were like two strutting peacocks stuck on the same world stage. Close in age, both were handsome and athletic,[1] patrons of artists and scholars, at ease equally on the battlefield and the dance floor.

Charles V had none of Henry and Francis's more refined qualities. Sullen and remote, with a freakishly deformed lower jaw, he

---

1. This was before Henry VIII became the bloated tyrant of his later years; the Venetian ambassador described him early in his reign as "the handsomest sovereign" he had seen.

could hardly be described as Prince Charming. But what the emperor lacked in looks and style, he more than compensated for with power. From his four grandparents he inherited half of Europe, along with vast riches from the New World. His potential hegemony made him dangerous to Henry and Francis, and it was this threat that in 1520 brought the two together for an extravagant summit known as The Field of Cloth of Gold.

Ostentation was the theme, and both monarchs nearly went bankrupt in the effort to outshine one another. Their entire courts accompanied them to the encounter, held in a valley between the French towns of Guînes and Ardres. Fountains of wine flowed beside tents woven in gold and pavilions studded with precious gems. The ladies and gentlemen of the French and English courts all dressed sumptuously and ate lavishly, while Francis and Henry jousted and wrestled in outwardly friendly tournaments. Each king paid due homage to the other's queen and accorded to each other all the proper dignity and respect. "The Field of Cloth of Gold was the last and most gorgeous display of the departing spirit of chivalry," wrote historian A. F. Pollard; "it was also perhaps the most portentous deception of record."

Festering beneath all the glittering opulence and diplomatic niceties was toxic animosity. "These sovereigns are not at peace," wrote a Venetian observer. "They adapt themselves to circumstances, but they hate each other very cordially." Indeed, no sooner had the last empty formalities concluded than Henry was off to conspire with Charles V against Francis. Their meeting was a lot less flashy than The Field of Cloth of Gold, but it was far more productive.

King and emperor came to a secret accommodation against France and sealed it with the marital commitments so characteristic of royal diplomacy. Henry promised to break off the engagement of his daughter Mary to the French dauphin, and Charles agreed to pursue no further his commitment to marry Francis's daughter. There was even talk of the possibility that the emperor might take Princess Mary as his wife. (Charles was the nephew of Henry VIII's first wife Katherine of Aragon, which made Princess Mary Tudor his first cousin.)

The pact between Henry and Charles at the expense of Francis made little political sense for England, as it risked giving the emperor complete dominance over European affairs. It was in Henry's best interests to play Charles and Francis off each other, and thus maintain a balance of power. Pope Clement VII was among those bewildered by the secret alliance.

"The aim of the King of England is as incomprehensible as the causes by which he is moved are futile," observed the pope. "He may, perhaps, wish to revenge himself for the slights he has received from the King of France and from [France's allies] the Scots, or to punish the King of France for his disparaging language; or, seduced by the flattery of the Emperor, he may have nothing else in view than to help the Emperor; or he may, perhaps, really wish to preserve peace in Italy [where both Francis and Charles vied for dominance], and therefore declares himself an enemy of anyone who disturbs it. It is even not impossible that the King of England expects to be rewarded by the Emperor after the victory, and hopes, perhaps, to get Normandy."

Not long after Henry and Charles sealed their alliance, King Francis took advantage of a rebellion the emperor faced in his Spanish realm and invaded Navarre, a kingdom wedged between France and Spain. The conflict soon spread to other regions that both the French king and the emperor claimed. Each turned to England, which had guaranteed in an earlier treaty to fight against whichever monarch proved to be the aggressor against the other.

Henry sent his minister, Cardinal Wolsey, to mediate the dispute, but it was a trick. The English king had every intention of siding with the emperor against France, and Wolsey's role was to delay a resolution of the dispute while Henry and Charles prepared for war. "The cardinal might be profuse in his protestations of friendship with France, of devotion to peace, and of his determination to do justice to the parties before him," wrote Pollard. "But all his painted words could not long conceal the fact that behind the mask of the judge were hidden the features of a conspirator."

Wolsey served his master well. "Henry agrees with Wolsey's plan that he should be sent to Calais under color of hearing the grievances of both parties," wrote Charles V's ambassador, "and when he cannot arrange them, he should withdraw to the Emperor to treat of matters aforesaid"—specifically, the plot against France. Wolsey's excuse for suspending the hearing in Calais—prearranged with Charles—was that he had to meet with the emperor personally in Bruges because Charles's representatives claimed to have no authority to negotiate for their master. Wolsey further delayed the proceedings by feigning illness. Meanwhile, he finalized with Charles plans for an attack on France and secured the emperor's engagement to King Henry's daughter Mary. Charles also promised to use his influence in Rome to help Wolsey get elected as the next pope.

The invasion of France was set. The Duke of Bourbon, Constable of France and the most powerful peer in the kingdom, was to betray his king and stir up rebellion among Francis's disaffected subjects. Charles V was to attack from Spain, and the Duke of Suffolk was to lead English forces into the heart of France from Calais. But the plan fizzled. Bourbon's treason was discovered and he became a fugitive. Suffolk got within sixty miles of Paris but was forced to retreat. And Charles never bothered to invade at all. Furthermore, the emperor reneged on his promise to help Wolsey get elected to the papacy, and negotiated a marriage not with Princess Mary, as promised, but with Isabella of Portugal instead. Such were the fruits of the secret alliance between England and the emperor.

In a huff, Henry refused to assist Charles when the emperor finally did get around to storming France. He then sat back and watched his entire foreign policy backfire. Charles attacked Marseille, but was repelled by Francis's army. The French king would have done well to bask in the victory and leave it at that. Instead, he decided to chase Charles down through the Alps and into Italy, where he hoped to regain Milan. Francis was captured at the Battle of Pavia in 1525 and held as a prisoner of war. "The victory is complete," wrote the Abbot of Najera to Charles from the field of battle, "the King of France is made prisoner. . . . The whole French army is annihilated. . . . Today is the feast of the Apostle St. Mathias, on which, five and twenty years ago, your Majesty is said to have been born. Five and twenty times thanks and praise to God for his mercy! Your Majesty is, from this day, in a position to prescribe laws to Christians and Turks according to your pleasure." Just what Henry VIII had dreaded.

The emperor demanded some extremely harsh terms for the release of Francis, including the French territory of Burgundy and the king's renunciation of all claims in Flanders and Italy. "I am resolved to endure prison for as long as God wills rather than accept terms so injurious to my kingdom!" declared Francis. But in 1526 he signed the Treaty of Madrid, seeming to accept Charles's demands. To ensure the French king's compliance, the emperor demanded Francis's two sons as hostages. The pact was then sealed with Francis's betrothal to Charles's sister Eleanor. That part of the bargain the French king kept (and eventually gave his second wife a scorching case of the clap as a wedding present).

After Francis was released from his gloomy prison cell in Madrid, Charles rode with him part of the way to the border. When the emperor gave his hand in a farewell gesture, he asked, "Do you remember all that you have promised?"

"Set your mind at rest, brother," Francis replied. "My intention is to keep it all, else you may call me a wicked coward."

Francis, however, had no intention of keeping his word. He had signed the Treaty of Madrid under duress, he said, and repudiated it within a week of his release. He then organized the League of Cognac against the emperor, while Henry VIII and Cardinal Wolsey secretly urged him on from England. Charles was infuriated by the French king's duplicity and even challenged him to a duel. When the emperor heard the pope was in cahoots with Francis (hoping to check Charles's power) he reproached him: "Certain people are saying that Your Holiness has absolved the King of France from the oath by which he promised to keep to what was agreed; this we do not wish to believe, for it is not a thing that the Vicar of Christ would do." Yet that's just what the Vicar of Christ had done. He would pay a heavy price for siding with the king of France when the emperor's armies stormed Rome in 1527.

"All the churches and the monasteries, both of friars and nuns, were sacked," wrote a cardinal present at the scene. "Many friars were beheaded, even priests at the altar; many old nuns beaten with sticks; many young ones violated, robbed and made prisoners; all the vestments, chalices, silver, were taken from the churches. . . . Cardinals, bishops, friars, priests, old nuns, infants, pages, and servants—the very poorest—were tormented with unheard-of cruelties—the son in the presence of his father, the babe in the sight of its mother. All the registers and documents of the Camera Apostolica were sacked, torn in pieces, and partly burnt."

The sack of Rome proved to be a major headache for Henry VIII, as well as a turning point in the Reformation. The king looked to the pope for permission to shed his first wife, Katherine of Aragon, and marry his mistress Anne Boleyn. The request was a relatively routine one among monarchs of the era, but in this case the pope was in no position to cooperate. He was a prisoner of the emperor with whom Henry had foolishly allied himself. Now Charles controlled his destiny. And he wasn't about to let the king of England divorce his aunt Katherine. Thus Henry's eventual split with Rome.

Henry, Francis, and Charles continued to plot and scheme against one another in various combinations for the next two decades. The king of England and the king of France, rivals to the end, both died in 1547. Charles abdicated and went into a monastic retirement nine years later, pooped, it's said, from decades of duplicity.

# 3

## Cardinal Sin

In 1634, Cardinal Richelieu—the power behind the French throne, not to mention a prince of the Roman Catholic Church—leagued himself with the Prince of Darkness, aka the devil himself, to destroy a priest who had dared to defy him.

The town of Loudun was reeling from the apparent mass possession of a group of nuns who lived in a local monastery. People were understandably upset to see the good sisters suddenly behaving like Linda Blair in *The Exorcist,* spouting obscenities with contorted faces and lewdly thrusted hips. Even the mother superior appeared possessed. "My mind was often filled with blasphemies," related the Reverend Mother, Jeanne des Anges. "I felt a continual aversion against God. . . . My thought was often busy with seeking inventions to displease Him, and cause others to displease Him. Also, [the Devil] gave me a very great aversion against my religious profession, such that, sometimes when he occupied my head, I would tear up all my veils, and those of my sisters that I could get my hands on; I would trample them underfoot, I would eat them while cursing the hour that I entered into religion."

It is unclear whether Richelieu organized the charade, or whether the nuns really were in some kind of psychotic state. But the cardinal certainly seized upon the episode to accomplish a murderous scheme. A priest named Urban Grandier had offended Richelieu with a scathing tract he was accused of having written.[2] It attacked the cardinal's policies and urged his dismissal. Plus, Grandier was a bit of a libertine who spoke openly against the rule of celibacy for priests.

Grandier was the confessor to the local Ursuline nuns, and it was he, the disturbed women claimed, who conjured the demons that tormented them. The roster of the unholy was most imaginative. Seven of the beings, for example, were said to have resided in the mother superior, including Leviathan, lodged in the middle of her forehead; Balaam, who took up residence in the second rib of her right side; and Behemoth, who sat in her stomach. Grandier, the nuns cried, had welcomed them all. Worse, he had defiled the women when they were under Satan's spell.

"At that time," wrote Jeanne des Anges, "the priest I spoke of used demons to excite love in me for him. They would give me desires to see him and speak to him. Several of our sisters had these same feelings without communicating them to us. On the contrary, we would hide ourselves from one another as much as we could. . . . When I didn't see [Grandier], I burned with love for him . . ."

Richelieu was pleased when Grandier was arrested for sorcery, among other charges. He assigned the Baron de Laubardemont—"a faithful henchman of the central power," as historian Michel de Certeau described him—to take charge of the process against Grandier and ensure the priest would suffer the state's most hideous retribution for his unholy crimes. The trial was sure to end with the desired results. That's because the prosecution had the most powerful piece of evidence possible: the pact Grandier signed with the devil himself. The forged document, *extract ex inferis (extracts from hell),* still resides in France's Bibliothèque Nationale. It reads:

> I deny God, Father, Son, and Holy Ghost, Mary and all the Saints, particularly Saint John the Baptist, the Church both Triumphant and Militant, all the sacraments, all the prayers prayed therein. I promise never to do good, to do all the evil I can, and would wish

2. Whether he wrote it or not is uncertain.

not at all to be a man, but that my nature be changed into a devil
the better to serve thee, thou my lord and master Lucifer, and I
promise thee that even if I be forced to do some good work, I will
not do it in God's honor, but in scorning him and in thine honor
and that of all the devils, and that I ever give myself to thee and pray
thee always to keep well the bond that I gave thee.

—Urb. Grandier

The verdict was, of course, guilty. Grandier now faced a terrible
end. For the crimes of "magic, enchantments, irreligion, impiety,
sacrilege," and others, the official pronouncement read, the condemned priest was to humble himself in front of several local
churches. "Which being done," the sentence continued, "to be led
to the public courtyard of Sainte-Croix of that town, to be tied to a
stake on a pile of wood . . . and there his body to be burned alive
with the pacts and magic figures remaining with the clerk of the
court, together with the book written by his hand, composed
against the celibacy of priests, and his ashes cast to the winds." As he
was tied to the stake, Grandier begged to be strangled before the
flames started to consume him. That request was denied.

Having been liberated from the clutches of Grandier's demons,
Jeanne des Anges went on a triumphal tour of France. She was feted
by some of the most prominent people in the kingdom, including
Louis XIII himself, and in Paris stayed at the home of Laubardemont, the man "devoted to the state," as Richelieu said, who
presided over Grandier's demise. People marveled at the nun's hand,
said to have been "sculpted by the devil" as he departed with the
names of Jesus, Mary, and Joseph. When Cardinal Richelieu saw the
hand, he was most impressed, and exclaimed: "Now this is ad-
mirable!" Satan had rendered him a great service.

# 4

~~

# Tricking a Fight

Otto von Bismarck needed a war. The Prussian prime minister's dream of a united German empire—a Second Reich—was stalled, and he knew a good old-fashioned clash with France, the perennial enemy, was just the thing to give unification a jump. (Germany at the time was a loose confederation of independent states, the most powerful of which was Prussia.) A contest of "blood and iron," as Bismarck called it, was guaranteed to arouse the Teutonic spirit and rally those reluctant states, like Bavaria, that were wary of Prussian militarism and dominance.

But, alas, in 1869 the prospects for war were dim. Relations between France and Germany, while not exactly warm, were at least civil, and neither the French emperor, Napoleon III, nor Bismarck's boss, King Wilhelm I of Prussia, was prepared to disrupt the peace, at least for the time being. "German national feeling is gradually melting away," warned one of the prime minister's associates, "and without a new crisis I can see no means of checking the process." Bismarck hardly needed to be reminded. "I too think it probable that German unity would be advanced by violent events," he replied. "But it is quite another matter to assume responsibility for bringing about a violent catastrophe and choosing the right time to act. Arbitrary interference in the course of history, on purely subjective grounds, has always resulted in the shaking down of unripe fruit. In my opinion it is obvious that German unity is not a ripe fruit. . . . The gift of waiting while a situation develops is an essential requirement of practical politics."

Though Bismarck urged restraint, he was far too ambitious a politician to sit around and wait for fruit to ripen when he was hungry. Alert for anything that might precipitate a crisis with France, he found fertile opportunity in Spain. In 1868 a military junta had deposed Queen Isabella II and offered the throne to a member of the Prussian royal house of Hohenzollern, King Wilhelm's cousin Leopold. Bismarck knew the French would never stand for a Prussian monarch in Spain, which would leave them surrounded by Hohenzollern power. It looked like the perfect chance to provoke a clash, if only he could get his king to cooperate.

Wilhelm I was stubbornly opposed to the Spanish offer, and Leopold himself was disinclined to accept so unstable a throne. Bismarck, who regularly manipulated the royal master he was supposed to serve, badgered Wilhelm relentlessly until, "with a heavy, very heavy, heart," he agreed. Yet as soon as the French discovered what had happened, and indignantly demanded Prussia's rejection of the Spanish crown, Wilhelm backed off. Bismarck was furious. "My first thought was to leave the service," he later recounted. "I regarded this enforced yielding as a humiliation of Germany for which I would not be officially responsible." But the wily prime minister soon saw a new opportunity in a telegram sent to him by the king.

Wilhelm wired Bismarck with the news that the French foreign minister had met with him at Ems, where the king was on vacation, and presented another demand from Napoleon III. It was not enough that Leopold had renounced the Spanish throne. The emperor also wanted a guarantee from the king that no Hohenzollern would *ever* accept it. Wilhelm advised his prime minister in the wire that he had firmly but politely refused to make such a promise and declined the French minister's request for a second interview to discuss the matter further. The king's telegram, while reflecting his irritation at France, was essentially diplomatic in tone. Bismarck transformed it entirely with a little editing trick and released it to the press.

Not a word was added to the text of the telegram, but Bismarck excised just enough of it to make it read as if the king had been rudely accosted by the French minister while on vacation and had snubbed him in response. "This will have the effect of a red rag on the Gallic bull," the self-satisfied prime minister said to his associates as he prepared his version of the telegram for release. And indeed it did. "From a long and shapeless balloon," historian Emil Ludwig wrote of the edited telegram, "containing too little gas and therefore unable to rise in the air, an empty portion has been ligatured off; the remainder is now a round and well-filled bag which will rise quickly into the firmament and become visible to thousands of eyes."

Less than a week after the publication of the edited dispatch in France on July 14, 1870, Bismarck had his war. The French were defeated and Napoleon III was deposed. King Wilhelm became kaiser of the new German empire, and Bismarck its famed "Iron Chancellor."

# 5

~

# The Lies and Fraud of the
# Third Reich

*"The broad mass of a nation . . . will more easily fall victim to a big lie than to*
*a small lie."*

—ADOLF HITLER, *Mein Kampf*

The devil, it's said, wears many disguises. After he finished with the nuns of Loudun, for example, Satan slapped on a silly little moustache and called himself führer. He was most successful in his Hitler guise, helping an evil empire grow atop millions of corpses and a mountain of lies. They were often clumsy lies, unimaginative and easily disproved. Still, they were brazen and relentless enough to draw in masses of people, including a number of world leaders, and sufficient to spread terror and destruction across Europe and beyond.

A bold subterfuge and a failed Nazi coup known as the Beer Hall Putsch first propelled the future dictator to national prominence in 1923. Germany was a mess at the time, still staggering from its defeat in World War I and the humiliating peace terms it was forced to accept in the aftermath. The mark was virtually worthless; billions of them could barely buy a decent meal. France occupied the Ruhr, Germany's industrial heart, while other territorial losses and the hobbling of its once-proud military further sapped the national spirit. Many blamed the democratic government, called the

Weimar Republic, that had been established in Germany after the war, and by 1923 the atmosphere was ripe for revolt. Hitler sniffed opportunity.

His Nazi party—based in the conservative state of Bavaria, where hatred of the Weimar Republic ran high—was still in its larval stage in 1923, but Hitler had a daring plan to seize power. He read an announcement that Bavaria's three-man leadership was to hold a public meeting at a large beer hall outside Munich to discuss the sorry state of the nation. On the night of November 8, Hitler showed up with a gang of Nazi thugs and took over the meeting by threat of violence. He forced the Bavarian leaders at gunpoint into a back room, where he demanded they join his revolt against the Weimar government in Berlin and accept appointments in the new government he would form. The leaders declined, even with a gun pointed at their heads. Hitler was surprised, but not defeated. He raced back into the main hall and announced to the thousands gathered there that the leaders had agreed to join his cause. The throng believed him and roared their approval.

Hitler's first grab at power came to nothing. The Bavarian leadership slipped away from the beer hall and denounced the bold upstart. During a subsequent clash with government forces, a number of Nazis were killed. Their leader scurried away to safety as they fell around him. Hitler was later arrested and briefly imprisoned, and his nascent Nazi movement appeared to be finished. But the beer hall fiasco was rewritten in the Nazi annals as a glorious moment in the party's history. In fact, after he came to power in 1933, the führer commemorated the failed coup every year with extravagant rallies and celebrations. There was, of course, no mention of his cowardice under fire.

While in prison Hitler outlined his twisted political philosophy in his autobiography, *Mein Kampf (My Struggle)*. Though the book itself is a toxic collection of myth, distortion, and rabid anti-Semitism, it nevertheless documents one of the rare occasions when Hitler actually told the truth. For in the midst of all the blather about Aryan superiority, he articulated a vision of a new German empire restored to its ancient glory, expanding eastward (at the expense of Poland, Russia, and Czechoslovakia, among other nations), and rid of such subhuman elements as Jews and Slavs. Indeed, *Mein Kampf* was a blueprint for almost every action Hitler took when he came to power. Too bad few read the tedious tome carefully, because it stood as a clear rebuttal to every lie Hitler told as he struggled to build and maintain the Nazi state.

After the failed Beer Hall Putsch and his stint in prison, Hitler regrouped the Nazi party and reasserted an ultranationalistic political platform that started to draw wide support. He used the democratic process he aimed to destroy to get party members elected to the Reichstag (Germany's legislative body) and, eventually, himself appointed chancellor in 1933. Having reached this level of power, he immediately set about to do away with the democratic government and establish himself as dictator. The first step was to gain a majority in the Reichstag, at the expense of the Communist Party. Hitler arranged for the Reichstag to be dissolved and new elections held, an ostensibly legal way of seizing power. The Nazis were confident they would sweep the elections. "Now it will be easy to carry on the fight," gloated Joseph Goebbels, who was about to be appointed minister of propaganda, "for we can call on all the resources of the State. Radio and press are at our disposal. We shall stage a masterpiece of propaganda. And this time, naturally, there is no lack of money." Yet the propaganda extravaganza Goebbels envisioned, targeted against the Communists, failed miserably. No one seemed to believe a Bolshevik revolution in Germany was a looming threat. It then became clear to the Nazis that a crude deception was in order.

On the evening of February 27, 1933, just one month after Hitler was sworn in as chancellor, the Reichstag building in Berlin erupted in flames. It is almost certain that the Nazis started the fire, but they immediately blamed the Communists. "This is the beginning of a Communist revolution!" Hermann Göring, Hitler's second-in-command, shouted outside the burning building. "We must not wait a minute. We will show no mercy. Every Communist official must be shot, where he is found. Every Communist deputy must this very night be strung up." The next day, Hitler prevailed upon the German president, Paul von Hindenburg, the once mighty leader now weakened by old age and encroaching senility, to sign a decree "for the protection of the People and the State" that essentially abolished individual and civil liberties in Germany. With this flimsy legal sanction, a terror campaign against the Communists began. Mass arrests, torture, and murder were accompanied by the official suppression of Communist newspapers and political gatherings. The party was shattered, but still the Nazis failed to get the necessary majority in the elections that followed. No matter. Hitler had a simple solution. He would pave the way for his dictatorship by arranging for the Reichstag to legislate itself out of existence.

He proposed the Enabling Act, which gave all the Reichstag's legislative powers to him for a period of four years. The act required a constitutional amendment, but with the Communist Party suppressed, and members of others parties forcibly barred from voting, the amendment easily passed with the necessary majority. "The government," Hitler declared, "will make use of these powers only insofar as they are essential for carrying out vitally necessary measures." He declined to mention that those "necessary measures" included the destruction of democracy, the subjugation of the individual German states, and the establishment of a fascist dictatorship. With the passing of the Enabling Act, author William Shirer wrote in his history of the Third Reich, "parliamentary democracy [was] finally interred in Germany. . . . Parliament had turned over its constitutional authority to Hitler and thereby committed suicide." And, as Hitler loved to boast, it was all legal.

As he consolidated his dictatorship at home, Hitler sent tidings of goodwill to the rest of the world. On May 17, 1933, before the now impotent Reichstag, he delivered his "Peace Speech," for which he put on a mask of perfect benevolence. It was a soothing, reassuring message issued by a coiled snake poised to strike at its neighbors. War was "unlimited madness," declared the man who would soon plunge the world into the bloodiest conflict humanity has ever known. As if to distance himself from the territorial ambitions of Germany's past—and his own words in *Mein Kampf*—Hitler asserted that the Nazis had no wish to "Germanize" other peoples: "The mentality of the last century, which led people to think that they would make Germans out of Poles and Frenchmen, is alien to us. . . . Frenchmen, Poles, and others are our neighbors, and we know that no event that is historically conceivable can change this reality." Shirer called this speech one of the greatest of Hitler's career, "a masterpiece of deceptive propaganda that deeply moved the German people and unified them behind him and which made a profound and favorable impression on the outside world." Over the next four years, Hitler would make more false peace speeches as he rearmed Germany, in defiance of the Treaty of Versailles, and prepared to conquer his neighbors.

Austria was first. "Germany neither intends nor wishes to interfere in the internal affairs of Austria, to annex Austria, or to conclude an Anschluss [Union]," Hitler said of his native land in a 1935 speech. He even signed an agreement with the small nation in 1936 in which he promised to respect Austria's independence and not interfere with its internal affairs. Less than two years later, Austria was swallowed whole. It should have come as no surprise. "German-Austria must be restored to the great German Motherland," he wrote in the first chapter of *Mein Kampf*. "People of the same blood should be in the same REICH. The German people will have no right to engage in a colonial policy until they shall have brought all their children together in the one State."

Austria was absorbed under the flimsiest of pretexts. For years the Nazis had stirred up trouble there. They even went so far as to assassinate the Austrian chancellor Engelbert Dollfus in a 1934 putsch attempt. After that murder failed to achieve the desired results, Hitler bided his time while his goons continued to agitate. By 1938, he was ready to occupy his homeland. He insisted that his Austrian puppet, Arthur Seyss-Inquart, installed as chancellor after the forced resignation of his predecessor, send a telegram to the German government asking for help in quelling (Nazi-generated) unrest. This contrivance was Hitler's justification to the rest of the world for the bloodless invasion that followed, never mind that he had threatened immediate attack if the Austrian leadership did not cooperate fully and hand over power. The world simply shrugged as Austria ceased to exist. Czechoslovakia was next.

"It is my unshakable will that Czechoslovakia shall be wiped off the map!" Hitler shouted during a meeting with Nazi leaders in May 1938. The führer absolutely meant what he said, but he would never be so blunt in public. Such naked aggression might provoke Britain and France to come to Czechoslovakia's aid, and Germany at the time did not have the resources to fight them. An excuse was needed to invade, a feint to lull the Western European powers into complacency while he executed his designs. For this, Hitler fabricated intolerable abuses he claimed had been, and continued to be, inflicted on the German minority that lived in Czechoslovakia's Sudetenland.

"A petty segment of Europe is harassing the human race," Göring thundered at a Nazi rally at Nuremberg. "This pygmy race [the Czechs] is oppressing a cultured people [the Sudeten Germans] and behind it is Moscow and the eternal mask of the Jew devil." No one ever accused the Nazis of subtlety. Even so, the world seemed determined to believe that Hitler's interests in Czechoslovakia extended only to the welfare of the German populace living there, and that once satisfied on this issue, he would behave himself. Again, someone should have read *Mein Kampf*.

The last thing Hitler wanted was to be appeased on the "plight" of the Sudeten Germans. That would clear away the screen behind which he planned to crush Czechoslovakia. British prime minister Neville Chamberlain just didn't get it. A man of peace, yet astonishingly naïve, Chamberlain actually believed Hitler's concern for the German people in Czechoslovakia was real, and tried desperately to accommodate him. "In spite of the hardness and ruthlessness I thought I saw in his face," the prime minister remarked after one meeting, "I got the impression that here was a man who could be relied upon when he had given his word." It was a fatal misjudgment.

Chamberlain's timid acquiescence to every one of the führer's increasingly outrageous demands—which ultimately included the Sudetenland being handed over to Germany and Czechoslovakia's complete withdrawal from the territory—infuriated Hitler. He was being robbed of the crisis he wanted to create, and thus a reason to destroy Czechoslovakia. Aides reported seeing the führer fling himself to the floor in a fit of fury and chew on the carpet. "The Germans are being treated liked niggers," he screeched in frustration. "On October first [1938] I shall have Czechoslovakia where I want her. If France and England decide to strike, let them . . . I do not care a pfennig."

The Czechoslovakian government was also understandably distressed by Chamberlain's agreement to allow the dismemberment of its small country, among other concessions to keep Hitler happy. "If you have sacrificed my nation to preserve the peace of the world, I will be the first to applaud you," Czechoslovakian foreign minister Jan Masaryk told Britain's leaders. "But if not, gentlemen, God help your souls!" Chamberlain sincerely believed he had achieved "peace in our time" by his appeasement of Hitler. His eventual successor, Winston Churchill, then a lone voice of dissent, knew otherwise. "We have sustained a total, unmitigated defeat," he declared before being shouted down in the House of Commons. Churchill was right. Hitler soon gobbled up the rest of Czechoslovakia, as he had always planned to do. And having seen firsthand how weak a stomach Britain and France had for fighting, he turned his greedy glare to Poland. World war was on the horizon.

～

As Czechoslovakia gasped its last breaths in the fall of 1938, the Nazis orchestrated what Goebbels called "spontaneous demonstrations" against Germany's Jewish population. On the night of November 9–10, which would become known as *Kristallnacht,* or Night of Broken Glass, Jewish-owned shops and homes were destroyed, synagogues were burned, and thousands of Jews were arrested or murdered. This pogrom, the worst yet seen in Germany, was ordered in retaliation for the killing of a Nazi official by a Jewish refugee in Paris. The government issued specific instructions for how these "spontaneous demonstrations" were to be carried out. For example, synagogues were to be burned only when there was no danger to adjacent properties owned by gentiles. And, to compound the horror of the night, the government insisted Jews were to pay for all the damages to property that occurred. "German Jewry shall, as punishment for the abominable crimes, et cetera, have to make a contribution for one billion marks," Göring announced. "That will work. The swine won't commit another murder. Incidentally, I would not like to be a Jew in Germany."

Although anti-Semitism was nothing new in Germany, Hitler made it government policy. He started with laws intended to exclude Jews from every facet of the community, and steadily escalated the persecution to genocide. His hate-filled lies about the Jews would be almost laughable had they not been responsible for such massive suffering. An excerpt from *Mein Kampf:*

> The Jew offers the most powerful contrast to the Aryan. . . . Despite all their seemingly intellectual qualities the Jewish people are without true culture, and especially without a culture of their own. . . .
>
> He batters the national economies until ruined state enterprises are privatized and subject to his financial control.
>
> In politics he refuses to give the state the means for its self-preservation, destroys the basis of any national self-determination and defense, wipes out the faith in leadership, denigrates the historic past, and pulls everything truly great into the gutter. . . .
>
> In cultural affairs he pollutes art, literature, theater, befuddles national sentiment, subverts all concepts of beauty and grandeur, of nobleness and goodness, and reduces people to their lowest nature. . . .
>
> Religion is made ridiculous, customs and morals are declared outdated, until the last props of national character in the battle for survival have collapsed.

The führer's fierce anti-Semitism infected almost every element of German society through relentless propaganda. William Shirer, who lived in Germany during the Nazi era, wrote about the effect it had on him: "It was surprising and sometimes consternating to find that notwithstanding the opportunities I had to learn the facts and despite one's inherent distrust of what one learned from Nazi sources, a steady diet over the years of falsification and distortions made a certain impression on one's mind and often misled it. No one who has not lived for years in a totalitarian land can possibly conceive how difficult it is to escape the dread consequences of a regime's calculated and incessant propaganda."

Little children were a particular target of the terrible lies. "This new Reich will give its youth to no one," Hitler declared, "but will itself take youth and give to youth its own education and its own upbringing." Teachers were required to instruct their students in

Aryan superiority and the danger posed to the Reich by Jews. Even the smallest children were not immune. The government provided vicious storybooks to be read to wee Nazis at *nacht-nacht* time.

One of the most popular of these was a book produced by Julius Streicher called *The Poisonous Mushroom*. Save for the grotesque Jewish caricature on the front cover, it looked like any child's storybook, with colorful illustrations and simple stories. The message, however, was pure hate. In one story, a mother and her son are walking in the woods looking for mushrooms. The mother explains to the boy that some mushrooms are good to eat, but that others are very bad.

"Look, Franz," the mother says, "human beings in this world are like the mushrooms in the forest. There are good mushrooms and there are good people. There are poisonous, bad mushrooms and there are bad people. And we have to be on our guard against bad people just as we have to be on guard against poisonous mushrooms. Do you understand that?"

Franz tells his mother that he does understand. She then asks him if he knows who these bad people are, these poisonous mushrooms. "Of course I know, mother!" Franz says. "They are the Jews! Out teacher has often told us about them."

Franz's mother is very proud that her son understands. Then she tells him that he must help other children understand. "Our boys and girls must learn to know the Jew," the mother warns. "They must learn that the Jew is the most dangerous poison mushroom in existence. Just as poisonous mushrooms spring up everywhere, so the Jew is found in every country in the world. Just as poisonous mushrooms lead to the most dreadful calamity, so the Jew.is the cause of misery and distress, illness and death."

Lest it be lost in the subtle and nuanced tale of *The Poisonous Mushroom,* the author helpfully explains the moral: "German youth must learn to recognize the Jewish Poison-mushroom. They must learn what a danger the Jew is for the German Volk and for the whole world. They must learn that the Jewish problem involves the destiny of us all."

The Nazi response to the "Jewish problem" was, of course, another grotesque euphemism, the "Final Solution." The systematic murder of six million Jews began in Germany and spread to each nation the Nazis conquered. Poland would be the setting for some of the worst atrocities.

～

Poland had long been on Hitler's list of nations to be destroyed in his obsessive quest for *Lebensraum* (living space for the German people). But before he finally pounced in September 1939, the führer played the familiar role of friendly neighbor. In a pact with the Polish government, he agreed "to renounce all application of force in the relations with each other for the consolidation of European peace." He even invited Poland to take a slice of Czechoslovakia as a gesture of goodwill. The Poles eagerly snatched up their piece of the ruined nation, oblivious to the fact that they were the next target.

Before Hitler could safely invade Poland, however, he had to placate the Soviet Union, Germany's mortal enemy. Though he despised Soviet leader and fellow monster Joseph Stalin, and planned eventually to add Russia to the ever expanding Nazi empire, he had to keep his giant neighbor to the north neutral in the event Britain and France came to Poland's rescue. That meant he had to lure Stalin away from any alliance with the Western powers, and assure him of his own peaceful intentions. This he managed to do with false promises and empty concessions, including the guarantee of a chunk of Poland once it was defeated and a free hand in the Balkan states. Stalin bit, and a nonaggression pact was signed. The path to Poland was now clear.

The crisis Hitler concocted to justify the invasion of Poland to the world, and to his own people, was one of the lamest of all his lies. An attack on a German radio station near the Polish border was staged, carried out by SS men disguised in Polish uniforms. Condemned prisoners, also dressed in Polish uniforms, were drugged and then shot to make them appear to be casualties of the fake raid. A German who spoke Polish broadcast a speech from the "captured" radio station and announced it was time for Poland to rise up against Germany. Hitler, for his part, appeared unconcerned about the transparency of the provocation he had arranged. "I shall give a propagandist reason for starting this war," he had stated several weeks earlier, "never mind whether it is plausible or not. The victor will not be asked afterward whether he told the truth or not. In starting and waging a war it is not right that matters, but victory."

Thus, with the invasion of Poland, began World War II. Hitler knew a clash with the Western European powers was inevitable. In fact, he was itching for it. "Everyone must hold the view that we have been determined to fight the Western powers right from the start," he said. Germany needed this life or death struggle. "A long period of peace would not do us any good," he declared. The Third Reich had to be tempered by an epic clash of arms, just as Bismarck's Second Reich had been. Nevertheless, he continued to make bogus pronouncements of his benign intentions, and even called for a conference of European nations (those that he had not yet conquered) to promote peace. "It is impossible," he stated in a speech, "that such a conference, which is to determine the fate of this continent for many years to come, could carry on its deliberations while cannon are thundering or mobilized armies are bringing pressure to bear upon it. If, however, these problems must be solved sooner or later, then it would be more sensible to tackle the solution before millions of men are first uselessly sent to death and billions of riches destroyed." These shamelessly contrived sentiments were uttered just before Hitler sent his war machine to crush, in short order, Denmark, Norway, Holland, Belgium, France, Yugoslavia, and Greece. Then, after the Battle of Britain, it was Russia's turn.

"It is war," said Russia's stunned foreign minister, Vyacheslav Molotov, upon hearing what amounted to yet another of Hitler's fabricated excuses for invasion. "Do you believe that we deserved that?" Historians have long debated whether or not the Nazi invasion of the Soviet Union really took the wily and suspicious Stalin by surprise. Some have argued that he knew all along that the pact between Germany and Russia offered him no protection, and that he was buying time to build up defenses when he signed it. Others maintain that Stalin, though crafty, nevertheless was caught off guard, and that the USSR was nearly destroyed as a result.

Stalin certainly seemed smug and complacent as much of Europe fell to the Nazis. He dismissed Britain's repeated warnings of Hitler's intentions, and even mocked them in an official statement just a week before the invasion of Russia began. They were, he declared, an "obvious absurdity . . . a clumsy propaganda maneuver of the forces arrayed against the Soviet Union and Germany." If the Soviet dictator really was blind to the führer's intentions, he missed a number of obvious clues that should have at least nudged his suspicions. For starters, of course, there was *Mein Kampf*. "When we speak of new territory in Europe today we must think principally of Russia and her border vassal states," Hitler had written fifteen years earlier. "Destiny itself seems to wish to point out the way to us here. . . . This colossal empire in the East is ripe for dissolution, and the end of the Jewish domination in Russia also will be the end of Russia as a state."

As it turned out, Russia spelled the end for Hitler's Thousand Year Reich. And when it came to grasping the futility of the Nazi offense there, the führer only fooled himself. "The continual underestimation of enemy possibilities takes on grotesque forms and is becoming dangerous," lamented one of Hitler's generals in his diary. "Pathological reaction to momentary impressions and a complete lack of capacity to assess the situation and its possibilities give this so-called 'leadership' a most peculiar character."

With Soviet forces closing in on his Berlin bunker, Hitler dictated one last lie before he blew out his brains. He called it his "Political Testament," and asserted for the sake of posterity that he never wanted a world war, nor was he responsible for the suffering of tens of millions that his policies caused. Others bore the blame. And it's not hard to imagine who they were. "Centuries will go by," he declared, "but from the ruins of our towns and monuments the hatred of those ultimately responsible will always grow anew. They are the people whom we have to thank for all this: international Jewry and its helpers."

# 6

~

# Elena's Padded Résumé

She billed herself as a brilliant scientist—Romania's own Marie Curie—but Elena Ceausescu was really just a poorly educated peasant who gathered enough power to fabricate for herself an impressive list of scholarly credentials. It was one of the perks of being the wife and cohort of Romania's dictator Nicolae Ceausescu.

Elena managed to obtain her doctorate in chemistry despite some fairly significant educational gaps, like high school. Her thesis was on "the Stereospecific Polymerization of Isoprene on the Stabilization of Synthetic Rubbers and Copolymerization," though some snickered (privately, of course, for fear of arrest) that she couldn't even pronounce the title. No matter. Upon this wobbly academic foundation, Elena added a long list of other titles and honors to her résumé, like president of the National Council for Science and Technology and chairman of the Section for Chemistry in Romania's Supreme Council for Economic and Soviet Development. "Being an ignorant, uneducated, primitive kind of woman, she really thought that if she had some titles after her name, it would change her image," one Romanian official told author Edward Behr.

The accumulation of titles corresponded with Elena Ceausescu's ever increasing political power, which culminated in her position as her husband's second-in-command, a sort of vice despot whom no one dared defy. She slapped her name on reams of scientific books and papers she couldn't possibly have written, let alone understood, and demanded honorary degrees when she made official trips abroad. Sometimes she was obliged, like at the University of Tehran, but not always. On a state visit to the United States in 1978, Elena wanted a degree from a university in Washington, D.C., but was told President Carter couldn't guarantee that. Instead, she was offered an honorary membership in the Illinois State Academy of Science. According to Ion Mihai Pacepa, former chief of Romania's espionage service, Elena wasn't pleased. "Come off it!" she reportedly snorted. "You can't sell me the idea that Mr. Peanut can give me an Illiwhatsis diploma but not any from Washington. I will not go to Illiwhatever-it-is. I will not!"

Eleven years later, in 1989, Elena was on trial for her life after Ceausescu's regime was overthrown. The couple was charged with grave crimes against the Romanian people, which they haughtily dismissed by refusing to acknowledge the court or answer any questions. They waved away allegations of genocide and charges that they lived in gross extravagance while the people starved. These were apparently not sore spots for the couple. It was only when Elena was called an academic fraud that they actively engaged the court. The prosecutor referred to her as "the so-called academician Elena Ceausescu," to which she responded, "So-called! So-called! Now they have even taken away our titles!" Stung by the assault on his wife's credentials, Nicolae declared, "Her scientific papers were published abroad!"

"And who wrote the papers for you, Elena?" the prosecutor asked.

"Such impudence!" she snapped. "I am a member and chairwoman of the Academy of Sciences. You cannot talk to me in such a way!"

At the conclusion of the brief trial, Elena and her husband were taken outside and shot. Thus with her execution, Romania lost one of its great scientists—at least on paper.

# 7

⌁

# Gadhafi:

# Dead to Rights

Egyptian president Hosni Mubarak once cooked a terrorist's goose, with a little bit of ketchup.

In 1984, Libyan dictator Mu'ammar Gadhafi wanted to assassinate his enemy, former prime minister Abdul Hamid Bakkush. Bakkush was living in exile in Egypt. So Gadhafi ordered his ambassador to Malta to hire four intermediaries, who would then find four killers, who in turn would travel to Egypt and whack Bakkush.

President Mubarak got word of the plot, however, and immediately set out to foil it. He had Egyptian undercover police pose as assassins for hire, and when the offer was made, the four intermediaries were sent to prison. Bakkush was whisked away to a secret location, where an elaborate death scene was staged. Bakkush lay on the floor, his mouth agape like a flounder, ketchup oozing from ersatz bullet holes. Photos of the scene were sent to the Libyan ambassador, as requested, along with a letter requesting payment.

Within days, Libya's official radio was crowing triumphantly that the "stray dog" Bakkush had been executed by a death squad devoted to obliterating enemies of Gadhafi's revolution. Celebration, though, soon turned to humiliation when Mubarak announced that Bakkush was alive and well. He proved it several hours later at a news conference. A grinning Bakkush was flanked by two Egyptian officials holding up the staged photos.

# 8

~~

# Red, White, and
# Not Always True

L egend has it that George Washington never told a lie. Although
that's an impossible standard for any man to meet, at least the
first president had the goods to inspire such a myth. Few of his successors could claim similar virtue. Presidents are politicians, after all,
and thus not always willing to let the truth stand in the way of an
agenda. This has most often been the case when the commander in
chief wants war.

In 1846, James K. Polk stood before Congress and declared that
Mexico posed an immediate threat to the United States. Foreign
troops, he said, had crossed the border, "and shed American blood
upon the American soil." It wasn't true. Mexico had not invaded,
but had clashed with U.S. troops on disputed land occupied by
Mexican civilians. In fact, the only real threat Mexico represented
was that it stood in the way of American Manifest Destiny. Though
Polk got his war, his claims were disputed throughout the conflict
by a young congressman from Illinois named Abraham Lincoln,
who challenged the president to show him the spot on U.S. soil
where American blood had been shed. Though branded a traitor in
some circles, Lincoln was mostly ignored. The United States was
winning the war—and would ultimately gain an enormous swath
of new territory—and no one was overly eager to question why it
started.

⁓

A number of twentieth-century presidents were equally dishonest about their foreign entanglements. In 1960, during the cold war, an American U-2 spy plane was shot down over the Soviet Union. President Dwight D. Eisenhower assumed the plane was destroyed in the crash, and with it any evidence that it had been on an espionage mission. He felt secure enough, therefore, to order a cover-up of the spying operation, and approved this false statement about the crash issued by the National Aeronautics and Space Administration: "One of NASA's U-2 research airplanes, in use since 1956 in a continuing program to study meteorological conditions found at high altitude, has been missing since May 1, when its pilot reported he was having difficulty on the Lake Van, Turkey, area."

The next day, Soviet premier Nikita Khrushchev released a photograph of a wrecked airplane and described it as the U-2 that had been shot down. It wasn't the same plane, but Khrushchev wanted to trick the president into believing that the actual U-2 plane had been destroyed so that Eisenhower would stick to his story about it being a weather research plane. Ike stepped right into the trap. Khrushchev then appeared before the Supreme Soviet and gleefully declared, "We have parts of the plane and we also have the pilot, who is quite alive and kicking. The pilot is in Moscow and so are parts of the plane."

Though President Eisenhower had been humiliated by the truth, he compounded the crisis with more lies. He recognized that there was no point in continuing the charade that the U-2 had been a research plane, but he was not prepared to admit that he was personally involved in the spy operations. He authorized the State Department to issue a statement that denied the pilot had any authorization to fly over the Soviet Union. The press, however, immediately questioned who, if not the president, had authorized such a flight. This resulted in yet another false statement, which said in essence that the U-2 flights were carried out under a very broad directive from the president issued early in his administration. Eisenhower insisted that the statement make clear that he had no knowledge of this specific flight.

"This is a sad and perplexed capital tonight," reported James

Reston in *The New York Times* after the statement was released, "caught in a swirl of charges of clumsy administration, bad judgment, and bad faith. It was depressed by the United States having been caught spying over the Soviet Union and trying to cover up its activities in a series of misleading official announcements." As a result of the debacle, a planned arms summit between Eisenhower and Khrushchev was scuttled, and the cold war continued.

As the Eisenhower administration ended with a pack of lies, so began the John F. Kennedy administration that followed. The new president agreed to a secret plan, concocted during the previous administration, to back anti-Communist exiles in an invasion of Cuba with the aim of overthrowing its dictator, Fidel Castro. Yet while Kennedy had made up his mind to back the invasion at the Bay of Pigs, he told the world something entirely different. He pledged in a news conference on April 12, 1961, that U.S. armed forces would not "under any circumstances" intervene in Cuba. "The basic issue in Cuba is not one between the United States and Cuba," he said. "It is between the Cubans themselves. I intend to see that we adhere to that principle, and as I understand it, this administration's attitude is so understood by the anti-Castro exiles from Cuba in this country." Meanwhile, U.S.-backed rebel forces were gearing up.

On the morning of April 15, six B-26 bombers supplied by the United States, but disguised to hide their country of origin, attacked three Cuban air bases. The damage they inflicted was minimal, but the reaction was ferocious. Castro put his nation on full military alert, and announced that the United States was behind the attack. "Our country has been the victim of a criminal, imperialistic attack which violates all the norms of international law," he thundered. Though the White House denied any involvement in the air raids, the claim was compromised somewhat by the fact that two of the B-26s ended up in Florida. "If President Kennedy has one atom of decency, he will present the planes and pilots before the United Nations," Castro challenged. "If not, the world has a right to call him a liar."

Kennedy, now thoroughly shaken, was persuaded by Secretary of State Dean Rusk to cancel a second planned air strike, considered crucial to the coming invasion, for fear American involvement would be further exposed. It was a fateful decision, and the invasion that followed was a fiasco. The tiny fleet of invaders, escorted but unaided by seven disguised U.S. destroyers, was battered by coral reefs and fierce counterattack. Castro's forces, vastly superior in number, quickly captured or killed the invaders on the beach, and took a large cache of U.S.-supplied weapons. Yet as the disaster unfolded, the president refused any overt American assistance. "The present struggle in Cuba . . . is a struggle by Cubans for their own freedom," Dean Rusk said in a statement. "There is not and will not be any intervention there by United States forces."

Kennedy's successor, Lyndon Johnson, inherited a commitment to the protection of South Vietnam's independence, and with it an emerging mess. Americans in 1964 were queasy about any escalation in the ill-defined, undeclared war in Southeast Asia, as was President Johnson himself. But he was also afraid that any faltering on the part of the United States would send a dangerous signal of weakness to the aggressive Communists in North Vietnam. Plus, the president was to face Barry Goldwater, a committed hawk, in the upcoming November elections.

On August 4, 1964, Johnson received a report that two U.S. destroyers had been attacked in the Gulf of Tonkin off the coast of North Vietnam. The president immediately leapt to action. He and his advisors mapped out a military response that included an air strike against North Vietnamese torpedo-boat bases. He sought congressional support for military action, as well as a resolution that backed a firmer policy in Southeast Asia. That night the president went on television to tell the nation what had happened. "Aggression by terror against the peaceful villagers of South Vietnam has now been joined by open aggression on the high seas against the United States of America," he announced. The next day, in a speech at Syracuse University, he said: "The attacks were deliberate. The attacks were unprovoked. The attacks have been answered. . . . Aggression—deliberate, willful, and systematic aggression—has unmasked its face to the entire world."

What Johnson neglected to say was that there were serious doubts at the White House as to whether the attacks ever occurred. The commander of one of the destroyers reported that "a review of the action makes many reported contacts and torpedoes fired appear doubtful. Freak weather effects on radar, and overeager sonarmen may have accounted for many reports. No visual sightings have been reported." The commander suggested that "a complete evaluation be undertaken before any further action."

"Hell, those dumb, stupid sailors were just shooting at flying fish," Johnson was reported to have said in one conversation, and in another he told Secretary of Defense Robert McNamara, "We concluded maybe [the North Vietnamese] hadn't fired at all." Nevertheless, the Gulf of Tonkin resolution for escalated force passed in Congress. Nine years later, more than fifty-eight thousand Americans had died in Vietnam, and more than three hundred thousand were wounded.

~

The Constitution provides quite adequately for an incapacitated president. Theoretically, the government would barely miss a beat. But perception is an entirely different matter. People tend to equate a sick king with a sick kingdom. As a result, a number of chief executives, or those serving them, have gone to extreme lengths to conceal illness and disability.

Grover Cleveland risked his life in 1893 when he had a portion of his jaw, which showed signs of cancer, secretly removed aboard a pleasure yacht at sea rather than in the relative safety of a hospital. The nation was in a financial crisis at the time and Cleveland, who had recently been reelected after losing the White House to Benjamin Harrison four years earlier, didn't want a cancer scare to jeopardize his economic recovery program. What resulted was an elaborate ruse perpetuated by the president and his doctors.

To keep the press at bay, Cleveland called a cabinet meeting on June 30 and announced that he would reconvene Congress in August to address the serious economic depression. He instructed the cabinet members not to discuss the meeting with reporters, and the White House withheld the announcement until 6 P.M. that evening.

That allowed the president time to slip out of town on a train bound for New Jersey, from where he would ostensibly continue on to a vacation at his summer home at Buzzards Bay, Massachusetts.

After he arrived in New Jersey, the president boarded a yacht anchored several hundred yards offshore in the lower Hudson River. He was joined by a team of doctors and dentists who would secretly perform the operation while the yacht made its way up the Atlantic coast to Massachusetts.

The surgery was extremely dangerous for the overweight, fatigued president, and made more so by the makeshift facilities aboard the boat. There was the risk of his bleeding to death, or succumbing under the strong anesthesia. Worse, Cleveland had kept the surgery a secret from his cabinet, Congress, and even his vice president. Had anything gone wrong, there would have been a power vacuum. "If the president dies during surgery," one of the physicians on board reportedly said, "I hope the yacht sinks and we all drown!"

Fortunately, Cleveland made it through the procedure and was soon up and walking about the deck. To avoid suspicion, the doctors left the yacht one by one at various stops along the journey, and by the time the president arrived at Buzzards Bay, he looked perfectly fine—at least from a distance. The operation had been performed entirely inside his mouth, so there were no visible wounds or dressings. Had he tried to speak, though, people would have known immediately that something was wrong. Therefore, he stayed in seclusion.

Despite the elaborate scheme to fool the public, reports started to surface that the president was seriously ill. Cleveland's doctors denied it, but the stories persisted. The *Philadelphia Press,* in fact, correctly reported almost everything that had happened aboard the yacht. In response, President Cleveland launched a campaign to discredit the newspaper, and was largely successful. Eight weeks after the surgery, he was looking quite well. A prosthesis inserted into his jaw allowed him to speak normally, and he had regained weight. The *Philadelphia Press* stopped pursuing the story, and the true account of Grover Cleveland's secret surgery remained hidden for many years after his death in 1908.

Woodrow Wilson had just completed a tour of the western United States to advocate U.S. participation in the League of Nations when, on October 2, 1919, he suffered a massive stroke. "The President lay stretched out on the large Lincoln bed," recalled White House usher Ike Hoover. "He looked as if dead. There was not a sign of life. His face bore a long cut above the temple [sustained in a fall during the stroke] from which the signs of blood were still evident. . . . He was just gone as far as anyone could judge from appearances."

The president was indeed utterly incapacitated, and powerless to carry out his executive duties for a month after the stroke. His doctor and his secretary conspired with the first lady to conceal his wretched condition from the nation and the rest of the world, while Vice President Thomas Marshall, whom Wilson called "a small calibre man," was reluctant to take on any presidential powers or responsibilities. "During this period," wrote Wilson biographer August Heckscher, "no proclamations were issued, no pardons granted; bills became laws without a signature. The regular meetings of cabinet members gave the country the impression that some matters were being dealt with. They sat, these lieutenants who had once gathered around a formidable chief, discussing for the most part trivial matters, and even then were often unable to make decisions."

With the executive branch broken, the government effectively stopped running. And though Mrs. Wilson never assumed the power of the presidency, as is sometimes maintained, she wielded an enormous amount of influence by determining who would be granted access to her ailing husband, and who would not. Those who did get in found his behavior erratic and unsettling and saw that he was in no condition to steer the nation. Still, misleading reports of his recovery continued to emanate from the White House.

Though President Wilson did gradually improve, he was a broken man, both mentally and physically. The conclusion of his second term was a sad coda to a once brilliant career. His most dearly held policies were rebuked, and this shadow of a president left office with his administration in shambles. Perhaps fate would have been kinder after that horrible October day in 1919 if Wilson and his handlers had not tried to fool the nation, and simply let the Constitution do its job.

Unlike Wilson's, there was nothing about Franklin Roosevelt's disability that would have interfered with his ability to perform his duties as president. But people didn't always recognize that. Polio was a dreaded disease in the first half of the twentieth century, and those paralyzed by the effects of the virus, as Roosevelt was, were sometimes perceived to be lesser people. FDR was determined no one would ever think of him that way. His efforts to conceal the true extent of his condition, what author Hugh Gregory Gallagher called his "splendid deception," were extraordinary—as was the press's cooperation. There are only two known photographs of the president in his wheelchair, and news stories never mentioned that he used one.

In public appearances, Roosevelt seemed to stand on his own, an excruciating effort that involved leg braces, a strong upper body developed through years of vigorous exercise, and lots of practice to make his stance appear natural. He was usually drenched in sweat by the time he was finished. On one occasion in 1936, before an enormous crowd at Franklin Field in Philadelphia, Roosevelt took a terrible fall on the podium from where he was to accept the renomination of his party for president. Aides surrounded him and helped him up before anyone in the crowd noticed, and not a word of the incident was ever reported. (President Gerald R. Ford should have been so lucky thirty years later when he took so much grief after he slipped on some steps coming off an airplane.) Given his desire to hide his disability, it is ironic that in 2001, after much debate, a statue of President Roosevelt in his wheelchair was added to his memorial in Washington, D.C.

Few American myths have ever stampeded over reality more than those that still surround John Fitzgerald Kennedy—"the pride of

Western civilization," as he was called in one glowing tribute, "a bright racing star who lighted men's thoughts and their dreams." Thanks to a meticulously crafted public image, abetted by adoring biographers and an undeniable photogenic brilliance, the thirty-fifth president remains in the minds of many one of the most enlightened, heroic, and compassionate men ever to occupy the White House. The truth, however, stands in glaring contrast to the stubbornly entrenched Camelot legend. So many elements of the Kennedy legend don't stand up—from his military service to his stand on civil rights—that, for the sake of space, we'll simply focus, briefly, on sex.

"It doesn't matter who you are," Kennedy's father once admonished. "It's who people *think* you are." JFK and his handlers wanted the public to think he was a devoted family man, when in fact he was a shameless philanderer. Select photographers took pictures of the president as he romped with his children in the Oval Office, while behind the scenes he cheated on their mother with a staggering number of women—from secretaries to movie stars—with little regard for consequence. So reckless was he, in fact, that he even shared a mistress, Judith Campbell Exner, with mob boss Sam Giancana. "There's no question about the fact that Jack had the most active libido of any man I've ever known," said his friend Senator George Smathers. "He was really unbelievable in that regard, and he got more so the longer he was married." Kennedy himself once shed a little insight into his insatiable drive. "Dad told all the boys to get laid as often as possible," he once told Clare Boothe Luce. "I can't get to sleep unless I've had a lay."

Thanks to a remarkably compliant press, the American people never knew of their president's shenanigans. "They can't touch me while I'm alive," Kennedy once said, "and after I'm dead who cares."

~

The press's selective reporting during the Kennedy administration turned to intense scrutiny after Richard Nixon's abuses of office were exposed. "I am not a crook," Nixon declared, thus becoming perhaps the first president to actually lie about being a liar. Thanks to Tricky Dick, modern presidents rarely get away with anything. And when they do inevitably get trapped under the media microscope, the lies they tell tend to be doozies.

Take Ronald Reagan: "We did not—repeat, did not—trade weapons or anything else for hostages, nor will we," the president said vehemently in November 1986 during the Iran-Contra scandal. Just four months later, when it became clear that story simply wouldn't wash, Reagan had to reverse himself. His televised address to the nation was an inspired bit of obfuscation: "A few months ago, I told the American people I did not trade arms for hostages. My heart and my best intentions still tell me that's true, but the facts and the evidence tell me it is not."

Just over a decade later, President Bill Clinton pointed his finger in the face of the American public and indignantly declared, "I did not have sexual relations with that woman, Miss Lewinsky." He later made the same claim under oath, and then defended it by claiming that in his mind only intercourse constituted sexual relations, not the type of dress-staining activities he engaged in with the White House intern.

Clinton's slippery game of sex and semantics gave way to George W. Bush's pledge "to restore honor and dignity to the White House." Did he? Well, that all depends on what your definition of honor and dignity, and weapons of mass destruction, is.

# THE ILLUSTRATED LONDON NEWS

No. 3845.—VOL. CXLI.    SATURDAY, DECEMBER 28, 1912.    With Eight-Page Supplement in Photogravure.    SIXPENCE.

*Piltdown Man: The so-called "missing link"*

# Part V

~

# SCIENCE FICTIONS

Seekers of the truth follow the rigid requirements of the Scientific Method. Those less interested in genuine discovery skip such pesky steps and create scientific mayhem. And then there are those who simply lie. Through the ages, their deceptions have sometimes stalled human progress—or at least made a mockery of it.

# 1

~~

# Monkey Business

In 1913, amateur archeologist Charles Dawson uncovered what many scientists believed was the pivotal figure in man's evolution from ape. There wasn't much to Piltdown Man—popularly named for the site in southern England where he was found—just a few skull fragments and a portion of jaw that appeared remarkably simian. But he was a sensation, perhaps the most famous Englishman of his day. People made pilgrimages to the site where he was found, and scores of scholarly books and papers were devoted to what appeared to be the most important discovery in the relatively new field of human paleontology.

"In Eoanthropus Dawsoni [the scientific name given to Piltdown Man] we have in our hands, at last, the much-talked-of 'missing link,'" wrote scientist Ray Lankester in *Divisions of a Naturalist,* adding that the Piltdown jaw was "the most startling and significant fossil bone that has ever been brought to light." Another scientist, Arthur Keith, pronounced Piltdown Man "the earliest specimen of true humanity yet discovered." And Sir Arthur Smith Woodward, keeper of geology at London's Natural History Museum, was so excited about the find that he devoted the rest of his life to studying the fantastic fossils.

In the midst of all the excitement, however, there were a few scientists who noted the incongruity between the skull and apelike

jawbone. One of them, Gerrit S. Miller of the Smithsonian Institution in Washington, D.C., prepared a reasoned analysis of the Piltdown find and concluded that the jaw and cranium, if combined,
would create some kind of freakish specimen that would never be
found in nature. Miller's observations were utterly dismissed.
William Pycraft, a zoologist at London's Natural History Museum,
wrote a twenty-page screed in *Science Progress* that slammed the pre-
sumptuous Yankee. Miller, Pycraft wrote, had "woefully misread"
the data, demonstrated a disgraceful "lack of perspective," and had
obviously set out "to confirm a preconceived theory, a course of action which has unfortunately warped his judgment and sense of
proportion."

Pycraft's smug self-assurance seemed validated when Charles
Dawson produced some more bone fragments that matched Piltdown Man's. He claimed to have found them about two miles away
from the site where he had discovered the original. "If there's Providence hanging over the affairs of prehistoric man it certainly manifested itself in this case," wrote Henry Fairfield Osborn, president
of the American Museum of Natural History. A second Piltdown
Man appeared to prove there was indeed a first. As he looked at the
remains side by side, Osborn was forced to admit that "they agree
precisely; there is not a shadow of a difference." Thus, with most
traces of scientific skepticism effectively banished, Piltdown Man
was firmly established as the first true missing link. It would take
another four decades until he was exposed as one of the greatest of
all scientific frauds.

Joseph Weiner, a professor of physical anthropology at Oxford
University in the 1950s, was troubled by the fact that Charles Dawson had never revealed the precise spot where he had uncovered the
second Piltdown Man. His investigation into that significant omis-
sion in 1953 led to the complete unraveling of what he called "a
most elaborate and carefully prepared hoax," the perpetration of
which was "so entirely unscrupulous and inexplicable, as to find no
parallel in . . . paleontological history."

In short order, Weiner learned that Piltdown Man's teeth had
been chiseled down to resemble a humanlike chewing pattern and
had been stained with what appeared to be ordinary house paint to

give them the patina of age. Other fossils recovered from the discovery site, such as ancient elephant and hippopotamus teeth, were determined to have been planted, as were some Paleolithic tools. Testing on the skull and jaw fragments proved they were planted as well. The cranium, stained like the teeth, was judged to be about five hundred years old, and the jaw apparently belonged to an orangutan. Thus, wrote author John Evangelist Walsh, "Piltdown Man, the most famous creature ever to grace the prehistoric scene, had been ingeniously manufactured from a medieval Englishman and a Far Eastern ape."

This was no merry prank. One scientist called it "the most troubled chapter" in the study of man's origins. It set back for years the search for understanding, compromised reputations, and, in the process, really gave creationists something to crow about. The deception "was nothing short of despicable," opined Walsh, "an ugly trick played by a warped and unscrupulous mind on unsuspecting scholars." So who was the maniacal schemer behind it all?

A variety of suspects has been put forth over the years. One of the more compelling is Sir Arthur Conan Doyle, the man behind Sherlock Holmes (and later himself the victim of a fabulous hoax: see Part X, Chapter 1). Sir Arthur lived near the Piltdown discovery site and had plenty of access to fossils. Also, many of his works of fiction indicate a close familiarity with archeology and paleontology. *The Lost World,* for example, features curious apelike men. Most of all, Doyle had a motive. He deeply resented the scientists who mocked spiritualism, a realm that obsessed him in his later years. What better way to make fools of the "materialists," as Doyle contemptuously called scientists, than with the Piltdown concoction?

Doyle certainly makes an interesting suspect, but evidence points to a far more obvious culprit: Charles Dawson himself, the one who first discovered Piltdown Man. Beneath his affable surface, Walsh and others have noted, Dawson was fiercely ambitious and desperate to be inducted into the prestigious ranks of the scientific elite in the Royal Society. An amateur archeologist, he was responsible for a number of other frauds in that field, some of them quite successful.

His writings also show him to be a shameless plagiarist. If Dawson, who died in 1916, really was responsible for the hoax, it was by far his greatest success. It's ironic, then, that the man so eager for recognition has never been given official credit for the scheme. And that, it seems, is the most appropriate punishment.

# 2

## Bunny Tale

Imagine if some of the nation's top scientists responded to a *Weekly World News* report, like HOUSEWIFE GIVES BIRTH TO BUNNIES, and then actually endorsed it! Well it happened, almost three centuries ago in Britain, during what was supposed to be the Age of Enlightenment. In 1726 a woman named Mary Tofts was said to have delivered a litter after being ravished by a rabbit. (Could it possibly have been of the same breed that President Jimmy Carter said attacked him in 1977?)

A local doctor witnessed the woman's labor and was stunned to see the dead animals she produced. Soon news of the incredible bunny mum spread across Britain and generated so much controversy that King George I ordered an investigation. His court surgeon, Nathanael St. André, went to see Mary Tofts in the town of Godalming in Surrey and found her in labor with her twelfth rabbit. The king's doctor saw for himself the lop-eared delivery. It was, he declared, a "preternatural" phenomenon. The air in the dead animal's lungs and the contents of its colon, both of which St. André had taken careful note of, might have given him a clue that this bunny had already been hopping about before it went up the, er, rabbit hole. But they didn't. The royal doctor took the dead animal and its siblings back to London, where he performed further scientific examinations before an awed king and court.

Meanwhile, Mary Tofts's strange deliveries became a national obsession, even among the intellectual elite. The poet Alexander Pope wrote to a friend about "the miracle of Guildford," and asked him if he believed. "There is a thing that employs everybody's tongue at present," wrote noted political observer Lord Hervey, "which is a woman . . . of Surrey who has brought forth seventeen rabbits, and has been there these days in labor of the eighteenth. I know you laugh now, and this I joke; but the fact as reported and attested by St. André the surgeon (who swears he has delivered her of five) is something that really staggers one."

St. André wrote of the amazing births in a tract entitled *A Short Narrative of an Extraordinary Delivery of Rabbits,* which became a bestseller—just before it made its author a laughingstock. The story that riveted the kingdom started to unravel when Mary Tofts was taken to London and put under strict gynecological observation. "Every creature in town, both men and women, have been by to see and feel her," wrote Lord Hervey. "All the eminent physicians, surgeons, and man-midwives in London are there day and night to watch her next production." Not surprisingly, it never came.

A boy came forward and claimed Mary had bribed him to sneak her a rabbit. Under threat of a medical procedure that Mary apparently thought would be worse than having dead rabbits shoved up her birth canal, she was compelled to confess her hoax. She had done it, she said, "to get so good a living that I should never want as long as I lived." After a brief stint in prison for fraud, Mary Tofts was allowed to return to her home in Godalming, where soon after she reportedly gave birth to an actual human.

# 3

~

# Casting Stones

The rush a scientist gets when he thinks he's discovered something new hit Johann Beringer like crack; it short-circuited all
his reason. The dean of medicine at the University of Würzburg,
who was also an amateur archeologist, came across some strange
stones in 1725 that he concluded were fossil proof of God's hand in
creation. The rocks were said to have been recovered from a mountain near the university. They featured prominent shapes of plants
and animals, Greek and Hebrew letters, as well as other objects, like
shooting stars and planets carved in sharp, three-dimensional relief.
Most scientists would have at least suspected a human hand in the
creation of these mysterious stones, but where was the glory in that?
To Dr. Beringer, they *had* to be some sort of divine signature left
upon the earth.

"God, the Father of Nature, would fill our minds with His
praises and perfections radiating from these wondrous effects," he
gushed, "so that, when forgetful men grow silent, these mute stones
might speak with the eloquence of their figures."

The prospect of fame, sure to accompany such an amazing discovery, intoxicated Beringer to such an extent that he ignored
other, far more rational explanations for the rock carvings—like
fraud. "The figures expressed in these stones, especially those of in-
sects, are so exactly fitted to the dimensions of the stones, that one

would swear they are the work of a very meticulous sculptor," he wrote, never once considering that the "meticulous sculptor" could be anyone other than the Almighty. The "strokes of a knife gone awry," and the "superfluous gouges in several directions" that Beringer discerned in some of the carvings were, he decided, little slips of the Lord's hand as he practiced his art.

Now granted, paleontology was primitive in the early eighteenth century—a time when scientists still scratched their heads and wondered how those little critters ever crawled into the rocks that fossilized them. But even in such an age, Beringer was shockingly oblivious. He produced a book on the miracle rocks, which featured expensive plates the doctor paid for himself to showcase God's handiwork. The treatise, *Lithographiae Wirceburgensis,* was a masterpiece of deluded self-promotion, and gives some indication as to why Beringer's colleagues thought him such an insufferable windbag.

"Behold these tablets," he wrote in one illustrative passage, "which I was inspired to edit, not only by my tireless zeal for public service, and by your wishes and those of my many friends, and by my strong filial love for [the German state of] Franconia, to which, from these figured fruits [the stones] of this previously obscure mountain, no less glory will accrue than from the delicious wines of its vine-covered hills!"

It was precisely this kind of pomposity that made Beringer's associates at the university so eager to humiliate him. Two of them, geography professor J. Ignatz Roderick and librarian Georg von Eckhart, had planted the carved stones on the "vine-covered hills" where Dr. Beringer's assistants uncovered them. They relished watching their arrogant colleague make an utter ass out of himself as he held forth on the divine origins of the rocks. But Roderick and von Eckhart began to worry that things had gone too far when they learned Beringer was planning to publish his book. They tried to alert their victim to the hoax by spreading stories that the stones were fake, and even produced some carved stones of their own.

The warnings were to no avail. Beringer, in fact, devoted a section of his book to his colleagues' attempt to "bring down to the dust all my sacrifices and labors, my very reputation." And, he

gloated, "their clever efforts might have succeeded had not my vig-
ilance discovered the deceit and throttled it at birth." When the
poor doctor finally realized he had indeed been duped, he reportedly spent the rest of his fortune trying to recover all the copies of
the book he had published. He might as well have saved his money.
*Lithographiae Wirceburgensis* was republished after Beringer's death,
not for any scientific insight it provided, but just for laughs.

# 4

*~*

# A Hoax in Perpetuity

A fundamental and inflexible law of nature is that energy can neither be created nor destroyed, just converted from one form to another. That inviolable rule, however, has never discouraged people from believing in perpetual-motion machines, sham devices purported to run forever on almost nothing.

One of the most successful purveyors of impossible apparatus was a nineteenth-century inventor and con man named John Worrell Keely, who convinced wealthy investors that he could convert a quart of water into enough fuel to run a thirty-car train seventy-five miles in seventy-five minutes. The Keely Motor Co. was formed around his idea, and millions of dollars were invested.

Keely called his illusionary source of energy the "hydro-pneumatic-pulsating-vacu-engine," which he said would use the vibrations from a device he called a "liberator" to disintegrate a few drops of water, freeing nature's basic "etheric force." Through the years he held demonstrations of prototype miracle engines at his Philadelphia home. They appeared to confirm his claim that revolutionary success was on the horizon. One engine seemed powerful indeed, its pressure gauge registering fifty thousand pounds per square inch. The machinery it drove ripped apart cable, twisted metal bars, and fired bullets through several inches of wooden boards—all apparently with only a few drops of water as fuel.

Keely was able to keep up the facade of a glorious invention about to emerge until his death in 1898. Though scientists spoke against it, and frustrated investors pulled out, the persistent and affable scam artist was always able to rally with demonstrable modifications of his idea and new influxes of investors. One of them, a wealthy widow named Clara Bloomfield Moore, even wrote an adoring book called *Keely and His Discoveries*. Her skeptical son, though, rented Keely's house after he died, and with the help of experts from the University of Pennsylvania, exposed the hoax. Compressed air was the secret to Keely's mysterious force.

*Scientific American* described the details: under the kitchen floor of the home was "a steel sphere forty inches in diameter, weighing 6,625 pounds . . . an ideal storage reservoir for air . . . at great pressure." The compressed air traveled up to the second-floor workshop, where Keely held his demonstrations, through strong steel and brass tubes. Between the first-story ceiling and the floor of the workshop was a sixteen-inch space "well calculated to hide the running tubes for conveying the compressed air to the different motors with which Keely produced his results." In short, his miracle machines were primitive pneumatic devices, not much more complicated than a drinking straw.

# 5

~

# Diagnostic Deception

*"There are no greater liars in the world than quacks—except for their patients."*
—BENJAMIN FRANKLIN

During the Golden Age of Quackery, when snake-oil salesmen and other great hucksters like Keely proliferated, a guy had to be pretty special to be dubbed "the dean of twentieth-century charlatans." The American Medical Association gave that distinction to Dr. Albert Abrams in 1924 based on his groundbreaking work in the fake diagnosis and fake treatment of disease. The good doctor, a professor at Stanford University, developed two bogus devices he called the "dynamizer" and the "ocilloclast," which were nothing more than a jumble of wires and other useless components described by physicist Robert Millikan as the type "a ten-year-old would build to fool an eight-year-old." Abrams made a fortune from them.

At a time when radio technology was still in its infancy, people believed it had almost infinite possibilities. This served Dr. Abrams well. "The spirit of the age is radio," he declared, "and we can use radio in diagnosis." He came up with an absurd theory of disease he called "Electronic Reactions of Abrams," or ERA, and published it in 1917. According to Abrams, the human body possessed a characteristic rate of electronic vibration both in health and in disease. The amazing dynamizer measured altered vibratory rates, he claimed, and could determine what kind of disease afflicted an individual, as well as its severity and location in the body. All it took was a drop of blood or a bit of flesh from the ailing person. Even a handwriting sample or photograph was sufficient because the vibratory rate was always the same.

The sample was fed into the dynamizer, which was connected to the forehead of a healthy subject, and voilà, an accurate diagnosis. The system was supposedly so advanced that it could also determine a subject's sex, or even his or her religion. Once a diagnosis was made, Abrams's other machine, the oscilloclast, guaranteed a cure. This was accomplished simply by setting the oscilloclast to the frequency of the disease and blasting it away, the way sound vibrations shatter a wine glass.

The ERA system became hugely popular, and Abrams sold thousands of his machines. A judge even accepted his opinion in a paternity suit after a sample of the alleged father's blood was put through the dynamizer. Author Upton Sinclair was among the most enthusiastic advocates of the Abrams system. "His name carried a brilliant and convincing story to the masses," noted *Scientific American* in 1929, though the public "quite overlooked the fact that Sinclair's name meant no more in medical research than Jack Dempsey's would mean on a thesis dealing with the fourth dimension or Babe Ruth's on the mathematical theory of invariance." Such was (and is) the nature of celebrity endorsements.

The scientific establishment set out to debunk Abrams by sending him blood samples from animals, and even red ink. Invariably, a terrible diagnosis, like cancer, was returned, along with the soothing assurance that the oscilloclast would, for a fee, provide a cure. One sample of sheep's blood, accompanied by the history of a fifteen-year-old boy, revealed a diagnosis of congenital syphilis, metastatic carcinoma of the left lung and pancreas, Neisserian infection, and tuberculosis of the genitourinary tract. Alas, the dynamizer seemed unable to detect the pneumonia that suddenly carried Dr. Abrams away at the height of his fame in 1924.

# 6

~~

# A Naked Lie

It started as an anthropologist's dream. In 1972 the Philippine minister of culture, Manuel Elizalde Jr., announced to the world that a tribe of Stone Age people, never exposed to civilization, had been discovered in the jungle. The Tasaday, as they were called, did not hunt or farm. They had no method for keeping time, no woven cloth, no metal, no art, and no domesticated animals or weapons. Indeed, their language did not even have a word for war. Wearing only loincloths made of orchid leaves, the Tasaday were said to live in caves, subsisting only on grubs, small animals, and berries.

Elizalde's news excited scientists and journalists alike, and a special helipad was built in the rain forest to ferry them in and out. The cavemen, nearly naked and grunting in their primitive language, became media darlings. *National Geographic* devoted a cover story to the Tasaday and NBC television offered Elizalde $50,000 to produce a documentary on them. Then, almost as suddenly as they appeared to the outside world, the ancient people were gone. Philippine president Ferdinand Marcos declared martial law in 1974 and made the Tasaday's region a government preserve.

It was not until 1986, when the Marcos regime was ousted, that a Swiss journalist traveled back to the Philippines to revisit the mysterious people. He was stunned to find the erstwhile cave dwellers living in villages, dressed in colored T-shirts and shorts and sleeping on beds. They told him that they had been instructed by Elizalde to pretend to be savages, with an invented language and lifestyle. When people were coming to visit, members of the group were warned in advance to assume their primitive identities.

To this day some scientists can't believe it was a hoax. But it was. It was all a ploy to allow Marcos to declare the Tasaday region a government preserve, seize its natural resources, and rape them. And he did.

# 7

~~

# Duplicity

Dolly the cloned sheep? Bah! Try Eve the cloned human. In 2002, a company calling itself Clonaid announced to the world that it had created a child out of skin cells taken from its mother. After being implanted in her womb, the bouncing baby replicant, called Eve, was reportedly delivered by Caesarean-section on December 26 of that year. Mother and identical daughter were doing well, according to Clonaid, but wished to remain anonymous.

The media breathlessly reported the amazing scientific development, while the Vatican and the president of the United States, George W. Bush, were quick to condemn it. Of course there were some mainstream scientists and others who were skeptical, especially given the mixed results of animal cloning, but Clonaid's CEO, Brigitte Boisselier, promised DNA testing within a week or so to resolve all doubts. "You can still go back to your office and treat me as a fraud," she said at a press conference. "You have one week to do that." In the meantime, Boisselier implored people not to treat little Eve as a freak. "The baby is very healthy," she said. "The parents are happy. I hope that you remember them when you talk about this baby—not like a monster, like some results [sic] of something that is disgusting."

Weeks went by, however, and no testing was performed. Clonaid said it needed to protect the mother and her clone from harassment by the law. This prompted Michael Guillen, a former science editor at *ABC News* who was to arrange expert testing on the mother and baby, to walk away in disgust, his reputation battered. Instead of DNA proof, Clonaid offered more announcements of cloned births from around the world. And it promised even greater advances.

"In a not-too-distant future," the company Web site proclaimed, "advanced cloning technologies will allow us to even re-create a deceased person in an adult body, with all his past experiences and memories, allowing mankind to enter the age of immortality as it has been announced by his Holiness Rael, founder of Clonaid . . . after his contact with Elohim, mankind's extraterrestrial creators." Meanwhile, the company claimed, two thousand people had signed up for cloning at a cost of $200,000 each. According to the Web site, the list included "families of celebrities, business leaders, and political leaders—we are currently working on the case of a prime minister whose son has been killed."

Cloning, like human paleontology a century ago, is still in its infancy. Without independent DNA verification, a fraud as fresh as this one is almost impossible to prove. Seekers of the truth are left with only circumstantial evidence. But there's plenty of that. Start with Clonaid's founder and spiritual guru, "his Holiness Rael," a former French journalist and pop singer who heads a cult that claims life on earth was created scientifically twenty-five thousand years ago through genetic engineering by a human extraterrestrial race called the Elohim.

Rael, or Claude Vorilhon, as he was once known, says he was enlightened in 1973 by an alien being, just over a meter in height, with pale green skin, almond-shaped eyes, and long dark hair, who emerged from a flying saucer somewhere in France. A trip to the Elohim planet several years later revealed more truths to Rael, including the scoop that Jesus was actually resurrected by cloning. Tapped by the Elohim as a prophet, Rael spread the good news and now claims fifty-five thousand followers. Brigitte Boisselier, the CEO of Clonaid who once taught college chemistry, is one of them. "I do believe we've been created by scientists," she said at the press conference announcing the delivery of Eve. "And I'm grateful to them for my life."

"Dear Diary: because of the new pills I have violent flatulence, and—says Eva—bad breath."

# Part VI

~⌒~

# FANTASTIC FORGERIES
# AND LITERARY FRAUDS

Man's capacity to create has many expressions. Some use their talents to create fine art; others to create facsimiles of fine art . . . and literature . . . and cultural treasures of every sort. Call this a gallery of great fakes by the masters of deception.

# 1

~~

# Shrouding the Truth

What if all the medieval hucksters who claimed to have a piece of the true cross really did? Well, it would mean that Jesus had to carry a sequoia-sized cross up Calvary. Relics were big business in the Middle Ages; pilgrims paid dearly to be blessed in the presence of one. For con men, the opportunities for fraud were heaven sent, and fake relics abounded. One of the most famous, and profitable, was the Shroud of Turin.

With its full-sized image of an apparently crucified man, the shroud has been revered for centuries as the burial cloth of Jesus. However, evidence that it is a clever medieval hoax has been accumulating since the shroud first appeared in the 1350s after a knight presented it to a local church in Lirey, France. As rumors of its divine origin spread, the Roman Catholic Church launched an investigation into the shroud's authenticity. Bishop Pierre d'Arcis reported to Pope Clement VII that he had located the artist who had "cunningly painted . . . by a clever sleight of hand" the double image reported to be that of Christ. Although the pope ordered a disclaimer when the cloth was displayed, a relic of this magnitude was too valuable to allow any doubt. The shroud made numerous tours around Europe before it eventually landed in Turin. The pontiff's command was ignored.

The Church never did declare the shroud to be authentic, and in recent years the archbishop of Turin allowed it to be scrutinized in a variety of scientific tests. In 1988, three laboratories in the United States, Britain, and Switzerland each took a small piece of the cloth and independently performed radiocarbon dating tests. All three declared with 100 percent certainty that the cloth was made after AD 1200. Nevertheless, a powerful need to believe has obscured even scientific certainty. Many still argue that radiocarbon dating does not fully address some miraculous elements of the shroud, such as the negative image they say could not possibly have been produced by a medieval forger. Even some scientists are not ready to close the case. A team from the University of Texas, for example, recently declared that carbon dating of ancient textiles is not reliable.

For those whose faith is dependent on or deeply enhanced by the Shroud of Turin, it will remain a miracle. Others, however, may be interested to know how it was most probably created. Joe Nickell, in his book *Inquest on the Shroud of Turin,* convincingly demonstrated that medieval technology was capable of producing negative images. Wet cloth is molded to an image and allowed to dry. Powdered pigment (Nickell used a mixture of myrrh and aloe) is then rubbed on with a cloth-over-cotton dauber and, behold, a relic is born.

# 2

～

# To Be . . .
# Or Not to Be the Bard

In an era of giants like Blake, Coleridge, and Burns, literary hoaxers of the eighteenth century had to produce extraordinary poetry and prose if they expected to impress anyone. Some did. A Scottish schoolmaster named James MacPherson had the literati of the day convinced that the epic poetry he produced was the work of a third-century Gaelic bard he called Ossian, while young Thomas Chatterton—Wordsworth's "marvelous boy"—became the darling of the Romantic movement after he wrote a body of work he attributed to an imaginary priest of the fifteenth century named Thomas Rowley. William Ireland, on the other hand, wasn't nearly as successful as his contemporaries, perhaps because of hubris. Rather than conjure works from the murky medieval past, Ireland tackled a true heavyweight, Shakespeare, and was pummeled in the process.

Ireland's attempt to foist onto the public a "lost" play by the Bard was inspired by his success as a forger of other Shakespearean relics. His father worshipped the famed playwright and often said he would give anything—including his treasured book collection—for just one scrap of the great one's handwriting. Young William, then seventeen, obliged his dad with a sixteenth-century land deed supposedly written by Shakespeare. He told his father that the document had come from a collection of old papers that belonged to an acquaintance who wished to remain anonymous. Ecstatic, the elder Ireland asked if there might be more treasures to be discovered in the cache—completely unaware that it was merely a matter of his son making more.

William purchased some blank sheets of antique paper from a bookseller and produced another gem that sent his poor unsuspecting father reeling with joy. It was a document entitled *Profession of Faith,* and it seemed to settle once and for all the controversy over whether Shakespeare was a Catholic or Protestant. In what appeared to be his own words, the playwright openly espoused the Protestant faith. The elder Ireland was so excited by the find that he immediately shared it with friends in the literary community, many of whom were equally impressed and clamored for more. As a result, William Ireland became a one-man factory of fake Shakespeareana. He produced an original manuscript of *King Lear,* complete with playhouse receipts and other documents tied up in a bundle with string taken from an old tapestry. He followed it with portions of the original manuscript for *Hamlet.*

Enough experts were taken in by the fakes to inspire Ireland to create a "lost" play, based on an obscure English legend, called *Vortigen and Rowena.* It was truly bad, riddled with leaden lines and strained verse that surely would have made the real bard barf. Even so, it was enough to fool William Sheridan, a prominent figure in the theater world, who decided to stage *Vortigen and Rowena* at London's famed Drury Lane Theatre. It wasn't that Sheridan failed to notice the poor quality of the work; he just came to the wrong conclusion about it, noting that "one would be led to think that Shakespeare must have been very young when he wrote the play." Audience reaction on opening (and, as it turned out, closing) night was devastating. They groaned at the poorly constructed speeches and howled for a full ten minutes when an actor uttered the line, "I would this solemn mockery were over." It was, soon enough.

Ireland had planned to give the world another "lost" play, *Henry II,* but the charade he had perpetuated was losing momentum. People blamed William's father for the fraud because of his stubborn belief in his son and the authenticity of his discoveries. With the senior Ireland's good name at stake, William was finally forced to admit he was to blame for everything. In the end, all he proved was that a clever forger does not necessarily make a compelling playwright.

# 3

~≈~

# They Just Can't Be Etruscted

Millions of visitors to New York's Metropolitan Museum of Art were awed for half a century by two large warrior statues (and a huge warrior's head) said to have come from the ancient Etruscan culture that preceded Roman rule in central Italy. The artifacts, discovered in pieces and carefully restored, were thought to be about twenty-five hundred years old. No one seemed to notice that they looked like props from a B-movie set, and so the "Etruscan" treasures remained on view until 1961.

It was then that a massive fraud was exposed. An art expert and cultural sleuth named Harold Woodbury Parsons tracked down an old man who was said to have forged Etruscan art earlier in the century. His name was Alfredo Fioravanti, and he shared with Parsons stories from his career in the bogus art trade. He and two brothers named Riccardi worked together for a firm that specialized in the repair of antique pottery. Soon enough, Fioravanti and the Riccardi brothers parlayed their skills into the manufacture of Etruscan vases and small statues. This proved so profitable that the three men got more ambitious and commenced work on their giant figures.

They fashioned the clumsy looking figures in clay and mixed in manganese dioxide (unknown in the sixth century BC) to simulate a type of old glaze called Greek black. There was one problem, however. Their kiln was too small to accommodate the large statues. The solution was to break the hardened clay and fire the pieces separately. The fragments were then sold to an acquiring agent for the Metropolitan Museum of Art, complete with a fictitious provenance.

Armed with this information, Parson wrote a letter to *The New York Times* stating that the museum been displaying fake Etruscan statuary since early in the century. He offered simple proof if anyone doubted it. One of the statues was missing a thumb. When the museum's curator of Greek and Roman art went to Italy with a cast of the hand, he was dismayed to find that the thumb Fioravanti had snapped off decades before fit perfectly. Not only that, it was also revealed that the fake statues had been modeled on an Etruscan figure from the British Museum that the forgers had seen in a photograph. It too was a fake.

"So on Valentine's Day of 1961," wrote Thomas Hoving, former director of the Metropolitan Museum of Art, "the world learned that the three Etruscans, so admired for so long, published hundreds of times, taught in schools as exemplars of the spirited and bellicose Etruscan civilization, were really prime examples of modern Italian sculpture of the 1910s and 1920s."

# 4

*~*

# French Fraud

Vrain-Denis Lucas was among the most audacious forgers of historic documents during the nineteenth century. With a client as spectacularly gullible as the illustrious mathematician Michel Chasles, he could afford to be. Chasles was a member of France's prestigious Academy of Sciences, so he couldn't have been completely stupid. Nevertheless, he snatched up virtually every fake Lucas presented him, twenty-seven thousand in all, many of them patently absurd, and all very expensive.

The first batch of forgeries Lucas sold to Chasles was letters from French literary heroes like Molière and Racine, part of a collection the seller claimed to have inherited from his prominent forebears. Lucas produced the fakes on paper ripped out of antique books, using ink appropriate for the period. Chasles was so thoroughly duped that Lucas got a little bolder. He produced some rarer items, like a letter said to have been written by Charlemagne some one thousand years earlier. Chasles happily paid the price for such a valuable piece of French history.

The forger, apparently convinced by now that he was dealing with a complete dolt, started to produce thousands of items too outrageous to believe. There were letters from Alexander the Great to Aristotle, and Cleopatra to her "dearly beloved" Julius Caesar— all written in *French!* One letter, again in French, was supposedly written by Judas just before he hanged himself, and another from Pontius Pilate to the Roman emperor Tiberius expressed regret for the crucifixion of Jesus. Chasles was delighted with them all. Here's an excerpt from a letter penned by Mary Magdalene, while on vacation in France, to her brother Lazarus (wrong Mary, by the way; Mary of Bethany was Lazarus's sister):

> *My dearly beloved brother, that which you have sent me regarding Peter the apostle of our gentle Jesus gives me hope that soon he will appear here and I am prepared to receive him well, our sister Martha rejoices at the prospect also. Her health is failing badly and I fear her death, that is why I recommend her to your good prayers. . . . It is as you say my dearly beloved brother that we are very fond of our sojourn in these provinces of Gaul, that we have no desire to leave it, just as some of our friends suggest to us. Do you not find that these Gauls, who we were told are barbarous peoples, are not at all that way. . . . I will say nothing more except that I have a great desire to see you and pray our Lord to hold you in grace this tenth day of June 46.*
>
> *Magdalene*

Lucas knew Chasles believed that it had been a Frenchman, Blaise Pascal, who had first formulated the laws of gravity, not Sir Isaac Newton. Therefore, he presented his favorite customer with a batch of fake letters between Pascal and Newton that seemed to validate his point of view. Chasles excitedly announced the discovery to the French Academy of Sciences in 1867; his enthusiasm was unhampered by the fact that Newton was still a teenager when Pascal died.

The relationship between Lucas and Chasles ended not with the humiliating episode at the Academy, but with the forger's failure to produce more documents, paid for in advance. Chasles sued. At the trial that followed, Lucas's fraud was finally exposed—as was Chasles's astonishing credulity.

# 5

~

# A Thin Vermeer

The great Dutch artist Jan Vermeer of Delft was not known for his religious themed paintings, but his forger was. Beginning in 1936, Hans van Meegeren, another Dutchman, painted six Biblical scenes in the style of the master and passed them off as original. The art world trembled with excitement. Museums snatched up the newly discovered "Vermeers," and van Meegeren got rich. It all backfired, though, when a Nazi art aficionado obtained his own "lost" work.

Van Meegeren was an ornery sort of fellow, a drug-addled artist with a point to prove and little to lose. Frustrated by years of dismissive reviews, he set out to humiliate his critics in the most spectacular way possible. What resulted was a meticulously produced forgery he called *Christ and the Disciples at Emmaus*. Van Meegeren took an original seventeenth-century painting and stripped it to the canvas. He recreated Vermeer's colors with materials the master used, like white lead, lapis lazuli, and crushed insect shells. Then, with a special mix of chemicals added, he baked the work to give it the appearance of age. Finally he concocted a fake provenance for the painting and foisted it onto the unsuspecting art world.

The critics were awed. "It is a wonderful moment in the life of a lover of art," enthused renowned expert Abraham Bredius, whom van Meegeren particularly despised, "when he finds himself suddenly confronted with a hitherto unknown painting by a great master, untouched, on the original canvas, and without any restoration, just as it left the painter's studio! And what a picture!"

The forger no doubt relished Bredius and other critics blathering on breathlessly about the Italian influence on the picture and other empty analyses. But the temptation he must have felt to reveal the hoax, and thus embarrass his enemies, was tempered somewhat by an unexpected windfall. Bredius and a group of investors actually raised money to buy the fake Vermeer, for a fortune. *Christ and the Disciples at Emmaus* went on display at the Boymans Museum in the Netherlands and stayed there for seven years. Van Meegeren quickly graduated from proving a point to the far more lucrative business of minting other imitation Vermeers. Works like *The Last Supper,* with the figure of John copied rather amateurishly from the original *Girl with the Pearl Earring,* made lots of money for van Meegeren. But when Nazi field marshal Hermann Göring got his hands on another fake, *Christ and the Adulteress,* the deception turned dangerous.

At the end of World War II, the painting was discovered among the thousands of art works Göring had looted from German-occupied territories across Europe, and traced back to van Meegeren. He was arrested and charged by the Dutch government with the capital crime of collaboration with the enemy. To save himself, van Meegeren admitted he had forged Göring's "Vermeer," and the others as well—spurred, he said, "by the disappointment of receiving no acknowledgments from artists and critics. . . . I determined to prove my worth as a painter by making a perfect seventeenth-century canvas." Furthermore, he argued that he had actually done his nation a great service by trading the fake with Göring for more than two hundred genuine Dutch paintings that had been stolen by the Nazis.

The presiding judge was skeptical, but allowed the prisoner the opportunity to prove himself. With the court closely watching, van Meegeren created *The Young Christ Teaching in the Temple* using the same techniques he had applied to his other forgeries. The result was incontrovertible, and the charges of collaboration were dropped. Van Meegeren was instead convicted of forgery and sentenced to a year in prison. He died soon after, while the experts still reeled. "It is unbelievable that it fooled me," remarked one. "A psychologist could explain it better than I can."

# 6

~~

# Not Quite the Surreal Deal

Van Meegeren's fakes had all the right ingredients, but they still lacked something essential, like Vermeer's talent. A truly great forgery requires the soul of a master. Or, in the case of Spanish surrealist Salvador Dalí, the *sold* soul of a master.

The production of fakes by great artists was nothing new. Michelangelo, for example, churned out a few phony ancient sculptures in his day. But Dalí was different. He copied himself, and he did it with crappy, mass-produced prints that made millions. "Dalí sleep best after receiving tremendous quantity of checks," he used to say. In his later years, a sad coda to a once brilliant career, the eccentric artist found it was easier, and a lot more lucrative, to sign thousands of blank sheets. A machine would do the rest. The result was a glut of worthless Dalí "lithographs" and "original prints" that circulated around the world.

The artist was unapologetic for his participation in the gigantic fraud. "If people want to produce poor representations of my work and other people want to buy them," he said shortly before his death in 1989, "they deserve each other."

# 7

≈

# "Con Man of the Year"

Clifford Irving may have been a bit of a hack when it came to his own prose, but as a literary hoaxer he bordered on brilliant. He managed to convince two publishing powerhouses, McGraw-Hill and Time-Life, to hand over a small fortune in 1971 for what would have been a major literary coup, had it been real: *The Autobiography of Howard Hughes.*

The reclusive billionaire had not been photographed or interviewed for more than a decade, and rumors about him were rampant. In the minds of many, the aviation pioneer and onetime Hollywood mogul had devolved into an insane old man with wild hair and six-inch fingernails. Some even said he was dead. Intense public interest made Hughes irresistible to journalists, but he was unapproachable, hidden away in an impenetrable cocoon. Even his closest associates never saw him. "It is easier for a camel to go through the eye of a needle than for a poor reporter to enter into the kingdom of Howard," quipped one *New York Times* writer. And anyone who even thought about writing a book on Hughes was subject to lawsuits and other forms of intimidation. So, the opportunity to have him on the record for a sanctioned book was enough to prompt a publishing feeding frenzy. Clifford Irving set out the chum.

A second-rate writer with less than stellar sales on a number of previous books—including one, ironically enough, on the great art forger Elmyr de Hory called *Fake!*—Irving had little to recommend him. He did, however, seem to have the cooperation of Howard Hughes himself. He told Beverly Loo, executive editor at McGraw-Hill, which had published a number of his other books, that he had sent the latest, *Fake!*, to Hughes and had received an enthusiastic reply. A correspondence between the two had ensued, Irving said, during which he broached the idea of writing Hughes's biography. And, surprisingly enough, the publicity-averse hermit appeared intrigued by the idea. Irving showed McGraw-Hill executives letters that he said were from Hughes, but that he had actually forged himself.

"I am not entirely insensitive to what journalists have written about me," Hughes supposedly wrote in one letter, "and for that reason I have the deepest respect for your treatment of de Hory, however much I may disapprove of his morals. I do not question your integrity and I would not expect you to question mine." The next few paragraphs indicated the very real possibility of a book, which the gathered executives knew could bring their company enormous profits: "It would not suit me to die without having certain misconceptions cleared up and without having stated the truth about my life. . . . I believe in obligations. I regret many things in my past, but I have little feelings of shame about them. I would be grateful if you would let me know when and how you would wish to undertake the writing of the biography you proposed."

Irving made a show of involving the McGraw-Hill people in secret and sensitive negotiations with Hughes. He took Beverly Loo with him to the American Express office where he said Hughes had left him a plane ticket to Mexico to discuss the proposed book. She had no idea that Irving had purchased the ticket himself and would use it for a Mexican romp with his mistress, not to meet Howard Hughes, who was actually holed up in the Bahamas at the time. After the trip, Irving returned to New York with a copious diary of his supposed meetings with Hughes, as well as the authoritative pronouncement that the famed capitalist expected to be well compensated for his cooperation. McGraw-Hill obliged with a fantastic offer of $500,000. Irving then went to Puerto Rico, ostensibly to present the offer to Hughes. He came back with his forged signature on a bogus contract.

The conditions set forth in the contract were most unusual. For example, McGraw-Hill was required to keep the agreement secret until after the complete manuscript had been accepted. This, of course, gave Irving plenty of room to maneuver without any interference. The contract also stipulated that all checks were to be made out to H. R. Hughes. When it was later discovered that a blonde woman named Helga R. Hughes had been depositing and cashing the checks in a Swiss bank, a media frenzy over her identity ensued. The London *Daily Express* dubbed Helga "the most wanted woman in the world," and Henry Kissinger joked to the press about his keen desire to meet her. As it turned out, Helga was actually Irving's wife, Edith, who used a forged passport.

Long before the Helga episode erupted, though, Irving's scam was still unfolding. The folks at McGraw-Hill were overjoyed with the prize they believed they had won. Beverly Loo set up a secret meeting with *Life* magazine's managing editor Ralph Graves, who agreed to buy world magazine and newspaper serialization rights to the Hughes book for $250,000. That covered half the money McGraw-Hill had committed, and the sale of book club and paperback rights later added hundreds of thousands more. It looked like a bonanza for the publisher, until Irving threw them an unexpected curve.

Hughes, he said, demanded more money, never mind that a contract had already been signed. To emphasize the point, Irving presented the executives with a note he said was from Hughes that authorized him to renegotiate with another publisher if McGraw-Hill failed to meet his new demands. He also showed them a bogus check from H. R. Hughes made out to them for the $100,000 the company had already paid in advance. It was a bold move on Irving's part, but he sold the executives with his assurance that the interviews with Hughes were going so well that the book was evolving from an ordinary biography to an astonishing autobiography. Plus, he said he was able to talk Hughes down from his new demand of one million dollars to $850,000. In what they thought was hard-nosed bargaining, McGraw-Hill got the price down to $750,000, which was still a good price for the prize property they believed they were to receive. Furthermore, they had been treated to an early version of the manuscript and were delighted with what they read.

"It was outspoken," Ralph Graves later wrote in *Life,* "full of rich and outrageous anecdotes, as well as detailed accounts of Hughes's youth, his moviemaking, his career in aviation, his business affairs, his private life, his opinions and crotchets." It was also lifted almost entirely from an unpublished manuscript by veteran journalist Jim Phelan based on interviews he had conducted with Noah Dietrich, a member of Howard Hughes's inner circle.[1] Irving peppered the manuscript he gave the publishers with marginal notes he said were from Hughes, which gave it an added sense of authenticity. For some executives at McGraw-Hill, the quality of the work alone was enough to convince them that Clifford Irving hadn't fabricated anything. "He's not a good enough writer to have made it up," pronounced one.

Still, a few doubts lingered. *Life*'s Ralph Graves sought to reassure himself with a professional handwriting analysis of one of the notes Hughes had purportedly sent to Irving. The expert he retained, Alfred Kanfer, compared the note to writing known to be Hughes's. "It can be stated that the two handwriting specimens were written by the same person," Kanfer declared in his report. "The chances that another person could copy this handwriting even in a similar way are less than one in a million." Irving, perhaps inspired by his onetime biographical subject Elmyr de Hory, had proved himself. (De Hory later dismissed the idea that Irving could be behind the Hughes hoax. "He would have to be a genius," the great forger sniffed, "and Cliff, dear boy, is no genius at anything.")

On December 7, 1971, Pearl Harbor Day, McGraw-Hill announced that one of the world's most enigmatic characters, a man once described as "a dozen personalities rolled into one," was finally going to tell his story in a book to be published the following

---

1. In a complicated chain of events, Irving obtained Phelan's manuscript from a fringe Hollywood "referral agent" named Stanley Meyer, who was supposed to be helping Noah Dietrich pitch the Phelan-penned book to literary agents and publishers. Irving was approached by Meyer after Phelan was dismissed from the project.

March. The news release quoted what was said to be an extract from Hughes's preface to the book:

"I believe that more lies have been printed and told about me than about any living man—therefore it was my purpose to write a book which would set the record straight and restore the balance. . . . I have lived a full and, perhaps, what may seem like a strange life—even to myself. I refuse to apologize, although I am willing now to explain as best I can. Call this autobiography. Call it my memoirs. Call it what you please. It is the story of my life in my own words." And lest Clifford Irving be overlooked in this great enterprise, he concocted a glowing acknowledgment from Hughes that was included in the press release: Irving had been chosen for the project "because of his sympathy, discernment, discretion and, as I learned, his integrity as a human being." Indeed.

McGraw-Hill and *Life* were so convinced of Irving's integrity that a subsequent disavowal of the forthcoming book by the Hughes organization barely rattled them. "Well," said Ralph Graves, "what did you expect?" From the publisher's point of view, it was entirely consistent with Hughes's bizarre behavior to deny his cooperation in his own autobiography. Plus, it wasn't Hughes himself who denounced the book, just one of his companies. "We have gone to considerable efforts to ascertain that this is indeed the Hughes biography," Albert Leventhal, head of the books division at McGraw-Hill, told *The New York Times*. "And we believe what we say is correct." Donald M. Wilson, an executive at *Life*, was downright cocky. "Oh, we're absolutely positive," he said. "Look, we're dealing with people like McGraw-Hill, and, you know, we're not exactly a movie magazine! This is Time, Inc., and McGraw-Hill talking. We've checked this out. We have proof."

Even an angry phone call from Howard Hughes himself failed to raise red flags. *Time*'s Frank McCullough, who had once interviewed Hughes in 1958, took the call. There was no mistaking the voice, or the message. The book was a fraud, and so was Clifford Irving. Having read the manuscript, though, McCullough was convinced otherwise. The tone, language, and style were all vintage Hughes. The executives at McGraw-Hill simply concluded that

Hughes was either having second thoughts, or that for some mysterious reason of his own he wanted his autobiography to come out under a cloud of suspicion. Yet despite their confidence, the executives decided another handwriting analysis would banish all doubt. The firm of Osborn, Osborn and Osborn was retained, and their report was more than reassuring. "We were jubilant at the totality of the report," Ralph Graves later admitted—jubilant enough to utterly ignore a warning from Howard Hughes's personal attorney, Chester Davis.

"There is no doubt that you have been deceived into thinking you have acquired material which you could publish and that someone is responsible for most serious representations to you and through you to the public," Davis wrote Harold McGraw. McGraw dismissed him by questioning his credentials: "If you represent Mr. Hughes as legal counsel, we must insist upon the receipt by us of a copy of your specific written authorization from Mr. Hughes relating to the autobiography."

Clifford Irving meanwhile kept busy perpetuating his fraud by writing a bogus letter to Hughes and sending a copy to the president of McGraw-Hill, Shelton Fisher. The letter advised Hughes of the efforts his lawyer Chester Davis and others had made to undermine the book, and requested that he "call off the dogs." Almost as a direct response to the letter he never received (because, of course, it was never sent), Hughes did something Clifford Irving never imagined possible. The famous hermit called a press conference and broke his silence for the first time in fourteen years. "I don't know him," Hughes said of Irving in a telephone call with seven journalists. "I have never even heard of him until a matter of a few days ago when this first came to my attention." The checks that had been cashed in his name—a fact that had reassured the people at McGraw-Hill—infuriated Hughes. "Chester Davis will tell you that I have been very, very critical of him for not being able to uncover the path of these funds." ("Helga" had not yet been exposed.)

That Howard Hughes would break years of silence to expose Clifford Irving should have been enough to end the elaborate fraud.

But the conference call actually had the opposite effect. The publishers believed that Hughes had denounced the book on the advice of his lawyers. There was too much authenticating evidence for them to think otherwise. For his own part, Irving was characteristically bold with his take on the Hughes press conference. "In my opinion it was a damn good imitation of his voice as it may have been three or four years ago," he told reporters. "My obligation, of course, is to Howard Hughes and not to the voice on the telephone." Irving even faced the Grand Inquisitor himself, Mike Wallace, with calm self-assurance on *60 Minutes.* "I don't know why [Hughes] hasn't surfaced," he lied to Wallace in reference to his "attempts" to reach Hughes and have him vindicate the book. "It puzzles me. It upsets me. It distresses me. And I don't mean on my own account because I can handle this. And we have the proof and that's no problem. It just distresses me that he seems unable to respond."

On January 12, 1972, Hughes's attorney Chester Davis sought an injunction in the Supreme Court of the State of New York to prevent McGraw-Hill and *Life* from publishing what he called a fraudulent autobiography. The publishers responded with affidavits that would soon come to haunt them. "I believe the book Clifford Irving has produced is precisely what it is represented to be," declared Harold McGraw, "the story of Howard Hughes in the words of Howard Hughes himself." *Time*'s Frank McCullough said in his affidavit, "I am convinced beyond a reasonable doubt as to the authenticity of the Howard Hughes autobiography. This conviction is based upon my long-standing personal familiarity with Howard Hughes, my readings of the manuscript, and my interviews with Clifford Irving. My belief in that authenticity is not shaken by denials of that story, nor is my belief in the autobiography shaken by the denials which I have heard from a man I believe to be Howard Hughes. Such actions are perfectly consistent with the Hughes I know." The affidavits were submitted just before the publishers discovered that it wasn't Howard R. Hughes who cashed their checks, but the woman known as "Helga R. Hughes," Clifford Irving's wife, Edith.

It wasn't long before Irving's epic lie was exposed. Trapped, he admitted his misdeeds, was convicted of fraud, and served fourteen months in federal prison. He also had the dubious distinction of being featured on the cover of *Time* in 1972, dubbed "Con Man of the Year."

# 8

~~~

# Führer over a Fraud

The Russian archives contain a bullet-pierced skull fragment said to be Adolf Hitler's. If genuine, it's a rare relic indeed—all that remains (other than a few teeth) of one of history's most notorious monsters. Yet while morbidly fascinating, the skull remnant reveals nothing of the demented mind it once contained. An artifact that did that—a diary, say—would not only be a historical bonanza, but extremely lucrative as well.

Konrad Kujau, a German dealer in Nazi memorabilia, had that sense when he embarked on a major forgery that briefly captured the world's attention in 1983. He produced sixty-two volumes of nonsense that he passed off as Hitler's diaries. His efforts were well rewarded when the West German magazine *Stern* purchased the rights for more than $3 million.

"After assessment of the diaries," *Stern* triumphantly announced, "the biography of the dictator and the history of the National Socialist Nazi state will have to be rewritten." As it turned out, all that was ever rewritten were the careers of the weekly's top editors. They had been duped by one of their own staffers. Reporter Gerd Heidemann, in cahoots with Kujau, told his bosses that he had tracked down the diaries after an exhaustive search over several continents. They had been retrieved, he said, from a Luftwaffe plane that had been shot down in the final days of the war. Heidemann insisted that his source—supposedly a German army officer who had found and hidden the diaries—would have to remain anonymous for reasons of safety in what was then East Germany.

"I can't tell you where the diaries came from because I don't even know," *Stern*'s editor in chief Peter Koch said in an interview at the time. "We asked Heidemann many times but he refused to tell us. We respect his desire to keep it secret because we never had any reason to distrust him. He has worked here for thirty years."

Koch's faith in Heidemann was buttressed by the fact that a plane believed to have been carrying Hitler's personal papers had crashed en route from the dictator's bunker in Berlin to his Alpine retreat at Berchtesgaden. Also, experts in handwriting had confirmed the diary script was indeed the führer's. "There can be no doubt that these samples were written personally by Hitler," the London *Sunday Times* quoted Max Frey-Zuker, described by the newspaper as "one of Europe's best-known graphologists." (Apparently no lessons had been learned from the Hughes debacle a decade before, when several handwriting "experts" proved to be less than reliable.) Finally, there was the glowing endorsement of British historian and Hitler scholar Hugh Trevor-Roper, who declared the discovery of the diaries to be "the most significant historical event of the last decade."

Amid all the hoopla, however, was a chorus of skeptical scholars. "I don't believe a word of Heidemann's story," Hitler biographer Joachim Fest told *The Washington Post*. He dismissed the *Stern* reporter's account of his search for the diaries as "a lot of bally hoo, nothing more." Even Hugh Trevor-Roper's initial enthusiasm cooled considerably. At a press conference *Stern* believed would settle all doubts about the authenticity of the diaries, Trevor-Roper stated that a "final judgment cannot be given until the whole text has been examined." (He had only been allowed a brief look at the diaries in a bank vault.) "As a historian I regret that this process has been sacrificed to the requirements of the journalistic scoop."

Faced with a storm of doubt and criticism, the editors at *Stern* remained defiant. "All I can say is that we paid a lot of money for the diaries and we will be paid back with our good reputation," declared Peter Koch. "All our critics will have to eat their words."

Alas, it was Koch who had to eat crow. Just two weeks after *Stern* announced its coup, Hans Booms, president of the Federal Archives Office of West Germany, officially debunked the diaries. He told a press conference that close scrutiny by history and crime experts indicated that "with regard to contents, the alleged Hitler diaries are a grotesque, superficial forgery."

Indeed they were, replete with glaring errors, anachronisms, and scientific impossibilities. Tests proved, for example, that the diaries contained paper and glue manufactured only after 1955, when Hitler had long been dead. Passages allegedly written in 1934, 1935, and 1937 were lifted directly from a 1962 book of the führer's speeches, which was itself full of errors. In addition, there were expressions used in the diaries that didn't exist when Hitler was alive. Even the initials in gothic print on the *imitation* leather diary covers were wrong. Some read "FH," not "AH." And then there were the inane entries, like "Must not forget to get tickets for the Olympic Games for Eva [Braun]" and "Because of the new pills I have violent flatulence, and—says Eva—bad breath."

Confronted with the overwhelming evidence of fraud, *Stern* publisher Henri Nannen said, "We have reason to be ashamed that something like this could happen to us." Editors Peter Koch and Felix Schmidt tendered their resignations, and Gerd Heidemann, needless to say, was fired. He and Konrad Kujau served prison sentences. As a result of the debacle, the publishing world became far more wary of such brazen tricks—until a decade later when publishers in Canada, Australia, Germany, France, Britain, Holland, Spain, Italy, Japan, and the United States eagerly snatched up the rights to *The Diary of Jack the Ripper,* which was, of course, yet another hoax.

# 9

~

# Murder, Ink

Deception turned deadly in 1985, when Mark Hofmann, a fallen Mormon and forger of historic documents, murdered two people with pipe bombs in a desperate effort to keep his fraudulent schemes concealed. Rarely had Salt Lake City been racked so hard by a crime, especially when the killer was revealed.

People in the city's tightly knit Mormon community believed Hofmann to be a gentle family man, a dutiful son of the church, and a respectable dealer of historic documents. There was, however, another side to this soft-spoken man that few in the City of Saints would have recognized. "Mark looks like all of us, he talks like us, he was raised here," said county attorney David Biggs. "But after 11:30 at night, he would forge documents and build bombs."

By most accounts, Hofmann was quite adept at creating history. He managed to fool the FBI, the Library of Congress, and the Mormon Church with his meticulously crafted fakes. Charles Hamilton, a renowned expert in historic documents, dubbed him "the World's Greatest Forger" (although, as Hofmann himself suggested, Hamilton's approbation may have had something to do with the fact that he too had been deceived, and being tricked by the best may have been a bit more palatable). Hofmann forged documents from American history, like letters written by George Washington, Betsy Ross, Miles Standish, and Daniel Boone, as well as "the Oath of a

Freeman," said to be the first document printed in the colonies, and for which the Library of Congress was prepared to pay a million bucks. Hofmann also traded in Mormon history, although in this sphere, profit was not his only motive.

The forger was outwardly faithful, but he had long been alienated from the Church of Jesus Christ of Latter-day Saints. He viewed the church's founder, Joseph Smith, as a charismatic fraud. And while most Mormons idolized the man, "Hofmann seemed to admire him as a deceiver, the ultimate con artist," wrote authors Linda Sillitoe and Allen Roberts. He made it his mission to rewrite the church's history to better reflect his deeply cynical view of it.

At first Hofmann forged letters and papers that tended to validate the faith and fill in some of its historical gaps. Gradually, though, he produced more disturbing documents that undermined the church's very foundation. Perhaps the most notorious of these was the so-called "Salamander letter," which offered a far different account of how Joseph Smith came to discover the sacred gold plates that he translated into the *Book of Mormon*. Church doctrine holds that Smith had been led to the plates by the angel Moroni. The "Salamander letter," however, hinted at something darker and more sinister. It was supposedly written in 1830 by Martin Harris, an associate of Joseph Smith.

"I hear Joseph found a gold bible," the letter opens, "& he says it is true I found it 4 years ago with my stone but only just got it because of the enchantment." The text continues with a description of how Smith was led to the plates by a white salamander, a creature associated with the occult in folklore. "The story of Joseph Smith finding the gold plates was present [in the letter]," wrote Sillitoe and Roberts, "but embedded in a context that suggested ceremonial magic and ghoulism, a strange contrast to the traditional story of the Angel Moroni." Hofmann sold the letter to his friend Steven F. Christensen, an idealistic Mormon bishop who later donated it to the church. The following year, Christensen would become the forger's first murder victim.

He was blown up by a pipe bomb at his office on the morning of October 15, 1985. Three hours later, Kathleen Sheets, the wife of Christensen's former business partner, was killed the same way when she picked up a package left at her home and addressed to her husband. Both bombs had been planted by Hofmann early that morning as his wife and children slept. "Why would this meek-looking, scholarly, respectable, almost a wimp of a man commit this horrible crime?" Salt Lake County prosecutor Robert L. Stott asked rhetorically as he reconstructed the crime at a symposium held at Brigham Young University almost two years after the murders.

Simply put, Hofmann had gotten himself into a jam. He had promised the church another amazing find known as the McLellin Collection, a series of letters from a former Mormon who had fallen out with Joseph Smith. It was expected to be very critical of the church, which paid Hofmann $165,000 to acquire it. The problem was, he had also received a $150,000 advance from an antiquities dealer for the very same papers—which did not actually exist. Deeply in debt, and in danger of being exposed as a fraud by his friend Christensen, the broker on the nonexistent McLellin Collection, Hofmann turned to murder. One bomb would silence Christensen, and the other, intended for Christensen's former partner Gary Sheets, was supposed to cast suspicion on disgruntled investors in Sheets and Christensen's failed business venture.

A third bomb, which investigators believe was intended for another Mormon bishop, blew up in Hofmann's van the day after the murders. The killer was grievously wounded, and the explosion produced evidence that led to his arrest. Hofmann pleaded guilty to two counts of murder and two counts of document fraud. The Utah Board of Pardons, which was ultimately responsible for determining a sentence after a complicated plea bargain, found that the killer showed no remorse for his crimes and recommended that he serve the rest of his life in prison. There Hofmann reportedly offered fellow inmates cash from a secret stash to have members of the board of pardons killed—preferably with pipe bombs.

Anti-Semitic cartoon featuring the Jewish
monster devouring the world

# Part VII

~≈~

# THE DEADLIEST LIES
# EVER TOLD

*"Not a word from their mouth can be trusted; their heart is
filled with destruction. Their throat is an open grave, with their
tongues they speak deceit."*

—PSALMS 5:9

Evil thrives on lies, the most malignant of which have metas-
tasized throughout nations—even the world—with devastating consequences. What follows is a mere glimpse of the
misery wrought by the obliteration of truth. A fuller account
would, sadly, occupy volumes.

# 1

~

# The Blood Libel

On the day before Easter, 1144, the body of a twelve-year-old boy named William was found in a forest just outside Norwich, England. Though there were signs of violence on the young apprentice, his death would have been unremarkable in an age when a child's life was often short and brutal. But a zealous monk named Thomas of Monmouth made William a martyr when he claimed the boy was murdered by Jews in a gruesome ritual that mocked the crucifixion of Jesus.

Most historians agree that Thomas's tale—detailed in his epic *The Life and Passion of Saint William the Martyr of Norwich*—was the seed from which grew what professor Alan Dundes called "one of the most bizarre and dangerous legends ever created by the human imagination." The widespread belief that Jews routinely killed Christian children in secret rituals, commonly called the Blood Libel, has endured for nearly nine centuries, influenced anti-Semites from Martin Luther to Adolf Hitler, and caused untold misery to millions of innocent people over the ages. And to think it all flowed from one stupid little story.

A contemporary chronicler summarized the tale of William around 1155: "In [King Stephen's] time, the Jews of Norwich brought a Christian child before Easter and tortured him with all the torture that our Lord was tortured with; and on Good Friday hanged him on a cross on account of our Lord, and then buried him. They expected it would be concealed, but our Lord made it plain that he was a holy martyr, and the monks took him and buried him with ceremony in the monastery, and through our Lord he works wonderful and varied miracles, and he is called St. William."

No one in Norwich seems to have given William a second thought after he died, except for a few distraught family members, one of whom eventually accused the local Jews of killing the boy (not by crucifixion) based on another relative's dream. The bishop who heard the charge was rightfully skeptical, and the story faded into a bit of provincial folklore—that is, until Thomas of Monmouth arrived in town about five or six years later. The monk became obsessed with William's murder and soon launched a campaign to create a saint. A product of the twelfth century, Thomas, wrote historian Gavin I. Langmuir, was "concerned with his status on earth and in heaven, and convinced that loyal service to William would benefit him in both realms." Plus, saintly relics and shrines often meant big money in the Middle Ages. (See Part VI, Chapter 1.)

The "evidence" Thomas gathered for his hagiography of William was, to be generous, a joke. It was based on rumor, speculation, and, perhaps, a little of the monk's imagination. One of his most incendiary sources was a converted Jew named Theobold, who supposedly told him that "in the ancient writings of his Fathers it was written that the Jews, without the shedding of human blood, could neither obtain their freedom, nor could they ever return to their fatherland. Hence it was laid down by them in ancient times that every year they must sacrifice a Christian in some part of the world." Norwich apparently had that honor in 1144.

Despite the obvious absurdities of Thomas's story of St. William, it quickly gained currency throughout England. Soon other accusations of Jewish ritual murder popped up across the kingdom. The charge was heard in Gloucester in 1168, in Bury St. Edmunds in 1181, in Bristol in 1183, and in Winchester in 1192, 1225, and 1235. Then, in 1255, came one of the most famous cases of all—that of little St. Hugh of Lincoln. Nineteen Jews were hanged for the alleged crimes against this child, one of them dragged to the gallows tied to the tail of a horse. And nearly one hundred more blameless people were imprisoned in the Tower of London.

According to one chronicler, the Jews had been summoned "to be present at a sacrifice to take place at Lincoln, in contumely and insult of Jesus Christ." Like St. William of Norwich, St. Hugh was said to have been crucified. "They scourged him till the blood flowed," the chronicle continued, "they crowned him with thorns, mocked him, and spat upon him, each of them also pierced him with a knife, and they made him drink gall, and scoffed at him with blasphemous insults, and kept gnashing their teeth and calling him Jesus, the false prophet."

Predictably, all sorts of miracles were attributed to this allegedly martyred boy. One of the more colorful held that Hugh actually spoke, prayed, and sang—despite being dead. The story of St. Hugh eventually became embedded in the English psyche through popular ballads and the immortal literature of Geoffrey Chaucer. His *Prioress's Tale*—which tells the story of another Christian child slaughtered by Jews "in Asie in the gret citee"—ends with a tribute to St. Hugh (reproduced here in a modern translation):

> *Hugh of Lincoln, likewise murdered so*
> *By cursed Jews, as is notorious*
> *(For it was but a little time ago),*
> *Pray mercy on our faltering steps, that thus*
> *Merciful God may multiply on us*
> *His mercy, though we be unstable and vary,*
> *In love and reverence of His mother Mary.*
> > *Amen.*

The Blood Libel meshed well with other medieval superstitions about Jews—devils in disguise, it was said, who poisoned wells, corrupted children, and, of course, killed Christ. After incubating in England, the slur gradually infected the rest of Europe, where horrific images of ritual murder may still be seen in the paintings and stained-glass windows of some churches across the continent. Persecution inevitably followed the story wherever it spread. In 1492, for example, King Ferdinand and Queen Isabella of Spain ordered the expulsion of all the Jews residing in their kingdom. (Edward I of England had done the same thing two centuries earlier.) Some historians say the religiously motivated act was prompted in part by reports of an infant sacrificed by Jews in the town of LaGuardia several years before. Tomás de Torquemada, Spain's infamous inquisitor general, took a special interest in that case, which resulted in eight people burned at the stake before wildly cheering crowds.

Throughout the rest of the Renaissance, the Reformation, the Enlightenment, and the Industrial Revolution, the Blood Libel clung to the popular consciousness like a poisonous leech. And it wasn't just ignorant peasants who spread the tales of human sacrifice, but priests, professors, and politicians who kept the spirit of St. William of Norwich alive around the world. Eastern Europe at the turn of the last century was particularly receptive.

It was the Easter season, 1899. A nineteen-year-old Christian girl was found murdered outside the little Czech town of Polna, her corpse, it was said, suspiciously drained of blood. The Jews had done it, people surmised, just as they had in Tisza-Eszlar, Hungary, seven years before. The trial of a local Jew named Leopold Hilsner was a sensation that filled newspapers and dominated conversation. "All pretexts are to no avail," declared Dr. Karel Baxa, future mayor of Prague, as he appealed to the most primitive anti-Semitism with the assertion that a blood sacrifice had occurred. "This motive for murder really existed. The world has been made aware of the fact that there are people who try to kill their neighbors in order to get hold of their blood. That is ghastly and terrible." Hilsner was convicted and sentenced to hang. It fell to Tomáš G. Masaryk, founder and first president of Czechoslovakia, to plead for justice and reason. "People [like Dr. Baxa] who pretend to save the Czech nation actually poison it with base, incongruent lies and ignorance," Masaryk wrote. "Shame!"

# 2

### ~

# *The Protocols of the Elders of Zion*

As Masaryk struggled for the soul of the emerging Czech nation, the Blood Libel was supplemented by an especially goofy (though no less evil) conspiracy theory that has resonated across the globe: *The Protocols of the Elders of Zion*. For a century now, this silly forgery has been trotted out by fanatics everywhere as proof positive that Jews are out to rule the world.

The *Protocols* contain the master plan of an alleged Jewish conspiracy to take over the globe. "Soon we will start organizing great monopolies," reads one passage, "reservoirs of colossal wealth, in which even the large fortunes of the Gentiles will be involved to such an extent that they will sink together with the credit of their government the day after a political crisis takes place." The document, an amateurish (and extensively plagiarized) rehash of long-established anti-Semitic literature and mythology, is believed to have been fabricated in Paris under the auspices of the tsarist secret police. It was published in Russia around the turn of the last century—perfect fodder for the anti-Jewish pogroms that were then being carried out there. Tsar Nicholas II was among the *Protocols'* most ardent enthusiasts. "What depth of thought!" the gullible monarch jotted in the margins of his copy. "What foresight—What precision in the realization of the program!—Our year of 1905 has gone as though managed by the Elders—There can be no doubt as to their authenticity—Everywhere one sees the directing and destroying hand of Judaism." All this from the guy who believed Rasputin was a holy prophet.

The execution of Nicholas and the rest of the imperial family in 1918 was for many further evidence of the evil elders at work—especially paranoid fascists in Germany. The *Protocols* informed much of the Nazi philosophy Hitler spun in *Mein Kampf* and later put into practice. "The extent to which the whole existence of [the Jewish] people is based on a continual lie is shown in an incomparable manner in the *Protocols of the Elders of Zion,* which the Jews hate so tremendously," the future dictator wrote in his tedious screed. "*The Frankfurter Zeitung* [a leading liberal newspaper] is forever moaning to the public that they are supposed to be based on a forgery; which is the surest proof that they are genuine. What many Jews do perhaps unconsciously is here consciously exposed. But that is what matters. It's a matter of indifference which Jewish brain produced these revelations. What matters is that they uncover, with really horrifying reliability, the nature and activity of the Jewish people, and expose them in their inner logic and their final aims."

Hitler got a resounding *Amen!* from his pal in America, auto magnate Henry Ford. Both men were students of the *Protocols* and both hated Jews, shared passions which seem to have bonded them. Hitler kept a portrait of the industrialist in his office, and Ford proudly accepted from the führer the Grand Service Cross of the Supreme Order of the German Eagle, the highest honor for foreigners the Nazis bestowed. By helping to spread the word about the *Protocols* and the Jewish threat, Ford rendered Hitler a great service. He did it in a series of eighty articles that ran in his newspaper, the Dearborn *Independent.*

"Not only does the Jewish Question touch those matters that are common knowledge," the paper warned, "such as finance and commercial control, usurpation of political power, monopoly of necessities, and the autocratic direction of the very news that the American people read; but it reaches into cultural regions and so touches the very heart of American life."

The articles were assembled into a book, *The International Jew: The World's Foremost Problem,* which was translated into more than a dozen languages and became an international bestseller. At one point it was second only to the Bible in sales. Hate, like automobiles, was being mass-produced. "All in all," writes historian Norman Cohn, "*The International Jew* did more than any other work to make the *Protocols* world famous."

Ford was unfazed by evidence that proved the *Protocols* were a crude forgery. "The only statement I care to make about the *Protocols* is that they fit in with what is going on," he said in 1921. "They are sixteen years old, and they have fitted the world situation up to this time. They fit it now."

Hitler stood by his friend, and enthusiastically endorsed his presidential aspirations. "I wish that I could send some of my shock troopers to Chicago and other big American cities to help in the elections," he said. "We look to Heinrich Ford as the leader of the growing Fascist movement in America. . . . We have just had his anti-Jewish articles translated and published. The book is being circulated in millions throughout Germany." And throughout the rest of the world as well.

Today the *Protocols* are everywhere, from neo-Nazi Web sites to extremist newspapers in the Middle East. Many of the September 11 terrorists were reported to have studied the *Protocols,* as did Oklahoma City bomber Timothy McVeigh. Even a visionary like Henry Ford could never have imagined such a legacy.

# 3

~≈~

# Witchcraze

*"Thou shalt not suffer a witch to live."*
—EXODUS 22:18

James VI of Scotland (later James I of England) felt under siege in 1590. There were plots against his throne, and he knew exactly who was responsible: witches. That "these detestable slaves of the Devil" existed, the king had no doubt. In fact, he wrote a widely read treatise on their wicked ways called *Daemonologie,* intended, he said, "to resolve the doubting hearts of many; both that such assaults of Satan are most certainly practiced, and that the instruments thereof [witches] merits most severely to be punished." Accordingly, King James, patron of the Bible that would later bear his name, presided over the first major witch hunt in Scotland, during which nearly one hundred people were tortured and executed for allegedly engaging in diabolical acts against him.

It was just one episode in a savage era of European history, when an estimated two hundred thousand people, mostly women, were accused of being in league with the devil. Many were hideously tortured to elicit unfounded confessions, and about half were hanged, beheaded, or burned at the stake. One scholar called these witch persecutions "the greatest [European] mass killing of people by people not caused by war," and historians have long grappled with the reasons why the witchcraze ever occurred. Some attribute it to the religious upheavals of the era, while others cite economic and cultural shifts. What seems certain, though, given the vast numbers of women maimed and killed, is that this terrible lie thrived in an environment of toxic misogyny.

"All witchcraft comes from carnal lust, which in women is insatiable," declared the authors of the *Malleus Maleficarum (Witches' Hammer),* a fifteenth-century text by two German priests that became the bible of witch hunters for the next three centuries. With their high sex drive and low character, it was reasoned, women were far more susceptible to seduction by the devil. "For as that sex is frailer than man is," King James wrote in *Daemonologie,* "so is it easier to be entrapped in these gross snares of the Devil, as was over well proved to be true, by the serpent's deceiving of Eve at the beginning. . . ."

The very essence of womanhood was transformed into something evil during the witchcraze. As a mother suckles her child, for example, so it was said that witches nursed hellish spawn off a mark on their bodies called "the devil's teat." And the older, more outspoken or impoverished a woman was, so much greater the likelihood was that she would be named as a witch. Reginald Scot, a contemporary English observer who was actually skeptical about witchcraft, described witches this way: "Women which be commonly old, lame, bleare-eied, pale, fowle, and full of wrinkles." In other words, grandmothers. It was these women, writes historian Barbara Walker, who "could be called witches and destroyed, like domestic animals past their usefulness. . . . The old woman was an ideal scapegoat: too expendable to be missed, too weak to fight back, too poor to matter." But it wasn't just poor, older women who fell victim to the madness. Men, women of the establishment, children, and even entire families were persecuted. Mothers were often executed with their daughters and sons because witchcraft was believed to be hereditary and nurtured in the home.

By far the most vicious witch hunts occurred in Germany, where more than half of all the executions in Europe took place. The statistics are horrifying. Six hundred people were put to death by the bishop of Bamberg, for example, and 390 were burned at Ellwangen between 1611 and 1618. In Würzburg, forty-one young children were executed, while the hunt at Trier was so extensive that two local villages were left with only one woman each. The fate of the

Pappenheimer family in Bavaria graphically illustrates just how cruel the witchcraze in Germany could be.

The family lived on the fringes of society as beggars and privy cleaners, and in 1660 was accused of witchcraft by a condemned criminal. Under intense torture, Anna Pappenheimer confessed to all kinds of diabolical activities, like making a murderous powder out of the hands of dead children, and flying on a piece of wood to rendezvous with the devil. After a long, well-publicized trial, meant to reinforce the power of the local duke, the Pappenheimers were convicted and sentenced to death. The executions that followed were a ghastly public spectacle that drew thousands. Anna's breasts were cut off and, in a gross mockery of motherhood, forced into the mouths of her two grown sons. Chunks of flesh were gouged out of her husband and sons with red-hot pincers. The abused and bleeding family was then put on a cart and taken to the execution site in a long procession of clergymen, municipal officials, and other dignitaries as the crowd sang hymns and the church bells tolled. Upon reaching the appointed place, Paulus Pappenheimer's arms were broken by a heavy iron wheel, and he was impaled by a sharpened stick. Finally, the family was tied to stakes and set on fire. Eleven-year-old Hansel Pappenheimer was forced to watch the agonies of his parents and two older brothers before he was himself executed three months later.

Although the "orgy of hatred against women," as historian Anne Llewellyn Barstow called the witchcraze, subsided by the end of the eighteenth century, its spirit has been revived many times in subsequent centuries. Remember the Taliban?

# 4

~

# A Big Red Lie

*"People always have been and they always will be stupid victims of deceit and self-deception in politics."*

—NIKOLAI LENIN

Some political philosophies seem swell on paper, like Plato's *Republic* or More's *Utopia*. They're enlightened, but ultimately they are impractical. That's why they remain *ideas,* concepts to be bandied about in coffeehouses and college classrooms. Too bad the theories of Marx and Engels weren't left in the libraries as well. The workers' paradise they envisioned in the nineteenth century was a fantasy co-opted in the twentieth by a succession of monsters and tyrants who called themselves socialists. In the name of the people, these agents of misery unleashed corrupt, unworkable systems that consumed more than one hundred million lives, and spewed forth almost as many lies. Soviet leader Joseph Stalin told a good many of them. It was his brutal, totalitarian regime that inspired many of the world's Communist despots—from Mao to Pol Pot, Ceausescu to Castro.

One of the most obscene myths Stalin ever created around himself was the idea that he was the wise, benevolent father of the Russian Motherland, devoted to the welfare of his people, even as he massacred millions of them. "Of all the treasures a state can possess," he declared, "the human lives of its citizens are for us most precious." An estimated 14.5 million of his "precious" citizens died of disease and starvation when they were forced off their land and onto state collective farms. Many more were murdered for refusing to cooperate. "Liquidate the kulaks [prosperous farmers] as a class," Papa Joe ordered in 1929.

To bolster the fiction of paternal care and concern, thousands of sculptures and paintings of Stalin with children were commissioned. One image of him with an apple-cheeked little girl became an icon of the era, reproduced countless times and distributed across the Soviet Union. Stalin later had the child's father shot.[1] The iconography was all part of a vast propaganda effort in art, architecture, and literature to make Stalin the omnipotent god of the officially atheistic society. He loomed everywhere and was indeed adored.

"The worship and boundless cult with which the population surrounds Stalin is the first thing that strikes the foreigner visiting the Soviet Union," a German observer wrote. "On every corner, at every crossroads, in appropriate and inappropriate places alike, one sees gigantic busts and portraits of Stalin. The speeches one hears, not only the political ones, but even on any scientific or artistic subject, are peppered with glorification of Stalin, and at times this deification takes on tasteless forms."

Stalin was a jealous god. "He loved nothing more than he loved power," wrote author Dmitri Volkogonov, "full, unlimited power, consecrated by the 'love' of the multitudes. In this he was successful. No other man in the world has ever accomplished so fantastic a success as he: to exterminate millions of his own countrymen and receive in exchange the whole country's blind adulation."

History, of course, had to reflect Stalin's greatness—even if it had to be rewritten. During the Bolshevik rise to power, he had been a mere party functionary, albeit an efficient one. But in his version of history, the *required* version, he and Lenin had led the Russian Revolution together, side by side as equals. That's what the textbooks said, and the propaganda films, and every other tool used to "educate" the Soviet citizen. Lenin, however, had grave misgiv-

1. Perhaps a better representation of Stalin's fatherly treatment of the Russian people can be found in his own family portrait. He bullied his second wife Nadezhda into suicide; lovingly called his mother "the old whore"; and mocked his son's failed suicide attempt, snorting, "Ha! You missed!" And he ordered half his in-laws executed. No wonder he admired Ivan the Terrible so much.

ings about the man who became his surprise successor. "Having become General Secretary [of the Communist Party], Comrade Stalin has concentrated unlimited power in his hands," the revolutionary leader warned shortly before his death in 1924, "and I am not sure that he will always use that power with sufficient care."

Lenin was frighteningly prescient on this point. As Stalin consolidated his power in the 1930s, he went on a murderous rampage against so-called "enemies of the people." Millions were arrested in a vast terror campaign, from party leaders to ordinary citizens. "I have known Stalin for thirty years," wrote Budu Mdivani, former premier of Soviet Georgia, before he was shot on Stalin's orders. "[He] won't rest until he has butchered all of us, beginning with the unweaned baby and ending with the blind great-grandmother."

Justice became a sick joke as people were forced through torture to confess crimes against the state that they didn't commit. Hordes of unfortunates were summarily tried and executed, or sent away to gulags to die of disease and starvation. The engineer of one of the greatest holocausts in history oversaw it all with cold efficiency. He spent long hours poring over endless lists of those to be condemned and approving their death sentences, after which he often relaxed by watching a movie.

All the problems of the state, which Stalin's disastrous policies wrought, were blamed on "wreckers" and counterrevolutionaries. "The remnants of the dying classes," he declared in 1933,

> . . . they have all wormed their way into our factories, our institutions and trading bodies, our railway and river transport enterprises, and for the most part into our collective and state farms. They have wormed their way in and hidden themselves there, disguised as "workers" and "peasants," and some of them have even managed to worm their way into the party. What have they brought with them? Of course, they have brought their hatred of the Soviet regime, their feelings of ferocious hostility to the new forms of the economy, way of life, culture. . . . The only thing left for them to do is to play dirty tricks and do harm to the workers and collective farmers. And they do this any way they can, on the

quiet. They set fire to warehouses and break machinery. They organize sabotage. They organize wrecking in the collective and state farms, and some of them, including a number of professors, go so far in their wrecking activities as to inject the livestock in collective and state farms with plague and anthrax, and encourage the spread of meningitis among horses, and so on.

The Russian populace was so thoroughly indoctrinated by the official lies and slander that they clamored for the blood of the "traitors." And they were sated. "Stalin felt he had achieved much," wrote Volkogonov "in removing the truth from the people, he had turned them into a crowd for which he would take responsibility himself. Among all his other crimes, this was perhaps his worst."

The great purges of the 1930s had a devastating effect on the Red Army. An estimated forty thousand officers were executed in 1937 and 1938, more officers than were killed in all of World War II. And as that great calamity approached, the army that was to defend the Soviet Union from Hitler's onslaught was virtually decapitated. The führer was thrilled with the news. "It makes a worse impression than it did in 1933," he gloated over the Soviet military's dangerously weakened state. "Russia needs years to recover its previous level." Six months later, on June 22, 1941, he invaded Russia on a thousand-mile front in what was history's largest land attack. Stalin was not to be seen for weeks after the invasion, hidden away and reportedly paralyzed by fear.

The Soviet Union barely survived the war. More than twenty million men, women, and children were killed. But Stalin emerged stronger than ever. As the self-proclaimed father of the country, he was entirely identified with its victory over fascism, and its new place of power on the world stage. His deification was complete, his lies gospel, and his will absolute. The system over which he presided, however, was as unworkable as ever. Consequently, another massive purge was planned before his death in 1953.

With the collapse of communism in the Soviet Union and the Eastern Bloc, not to mention China's decisive turn toward capitalism, history has rendered its verdict on the great lie that once threatened to take over the globe. Nevertheless, the spirit of Stalin still lingers, perhaps most abundantly in the pudgy little person of North Korea's "Dear Leader" Kim Jong-il. In one of the world's most oppressive regimes, Kim reigns supreme by holding out the empty promise of paradise for his starving people.

His is a land of illusion, particularly the capital of Pyongyang. Many of the city's gleaming office towers and hotels sit empty—a facade of prosperity in a malnourished nation. Murals depict abundant harvests and cheerful peasants, though as many as two million people died of starvation during the 1990s. Policemen direct nonexistent traffic on empty boulevards, while stores display luxury goods that few can afford in a hopelessly failed economy. Citizens, mostly students, are used as props for massive, precisely choreographed demonstrations of devotion to the state and its leader. But their sunny faces belie the true condition of the Hermit Kingdom. "If you went a little outside the center of Pyongyang," wrote Hwang Jang Yop, a party leader who defected to South Korea, "the roads were filled with people who were reduced to mere skeletons."

Kim reserves some of the most grotesque distortions for himself and his late father Kim Il Sung, whom Stalin installed as a puppet in North Korea after World War II, and from whom Kim inherited the totalitarian regime in 1994. Father and son are worshipped as demigods by a people brainwashed from birth. Their portraits hang side by side in every building, and citizens are required to wear a picture of the father pinned to their clothes, right over their hearts. "It's a cult of personality like nothing in history," Korea scholar Kongdan Oh told *The Washington Post* in 2003. "In North Korea [Kim] and his father are like God and Jesus Christ."

The mythology built around both men makes even Stalin look modest. According to official doctrine, Kim's birth on Korea's sacred Mount Paekdu was heralded by a bright star, a double rainbow, and a swallow that descended from heaven to announce the blessed arrival of "a general who will rule all the world." (The true story is somewhat less glamorous. Kim was actually born in a Siberian army camp, where his father and a small band of communist guerillas had fled from the Japanese.) His presence is said to make trees bloom and snow melt, and he is supposedly so gifted that he wrote fifteen hundred books while in college. No wonder his proud pop called him "a genius of 10,000 talents." Of course it won't do to have a deity that stands only five-foot-three, so Kim compensates as best he can with platform shoes and a puffy pompadour.

The "Dear Leader's" quasi-divine status in North Korea is still relatively low-key next to that of his dad, the "Great Leader," who had erected more than thirty-four thousand monuments to himself by the late 1980s, and whose mummified corpse rests in a $900 million palace-*cum*-mausoleum. When he died in 1994, there was deep and genuine grief among the people whose minds he had manipulated for more than half a century. The propagandists had a field day. "When the Most Beloved Leader Kim Il Sung passed away," relates one widely believed official myth, "thousands of cranes descended from heaven to fetch Him. The birds couldn't take Him away because they saw that North Koreans cried and screamed, pummeled their chests, beat the ground and pulled out their hair. After ten days the heavenly birds decided to put Him to rest in a heavenly palace built on earth." He still reigns as "President for Eternity," and almost anything he ever touched has become a sacred relic.

Like his father before him, Kim depends on the faith and hope of the people for survival. Truth, therefore, is his greatest enemy. If his oppressed subjects ever learned that communism has proven to be an abysmal failure in the rest of the world, that their fellow Koreans in the South enjoy such relative prosperity, or that their woes aren't caused by the evil, decadent West, Kim would be booted from power. That's why he keeps his people in such an extreme state of isolation. If anyone did manage to gather news from the outside, he would instantly join hundreds of thousands of his countrymen in a prison camp, or worse. So, the people who know no better continue to eat bark and clay to fill their bellies, offer their paeans to the "Dear Leader," and wait expectantly for a better day. Meanwhile, the rest of the world waits anxiously to see what Kim's going to do with his nukes.

# 5

~~

# What in the Name of God!

God wills it!" Pope Urban II declared in 1095 as he launched the First Crusade. Rich rewards in heaven were promised for those who sacrificed themselves in the holy war against Islam. Almost a millennium later, Osama bin Laden guaranteed the very same thing, only he tossed in some heavenly virgins to sweeten the deal for those martyrs who died fighting the infidel.

Poor God has been misrepresented so many times throughout history, even *He* must find it difficult to keep track of all those false prophets who have hijacked His holy name. What follows are sound bites of some of the most obscene and ridiculous lies ever disguised as divine will.

*"By the grace of Auramazda [God] I am king; Auramazda gave me the kingdom."*
—Darius the Great of Persia (reigned 522–486 BC)

*"Are you the god-haters who do not believe me to be a god, a god acknowledged by all the other nations but not to be named by you?"*
—Caligula (reigned AD 37–41), the mad Roman emperor with divine pretensions, to an embassy of Alexandrian Jews

*"The sentence of God on this sex of yours lives on even in our times and so it is necessary that the guilt should live on, also. You are the one who opened the door to the Devil, you are the one who first plucked the fruit of the forbidden tree, you are the first who deserted the divine law; you are the one who persuaded him whom the Devil was not strong enough to attack. All too easily you destroyed the image of God, man. Because of your desert, that is, death, even the Son of God had to die."*

—Tertullian, ecclesiastical writer in the second and third centuries, *On the Apparel of Women*

*"The Roman Church has never erred, nor can it err until the end of time."*

—Pope Gregory VII (reigned 1073–1085), claiming infallibility ceded to the church by God

*"Piles of heads, hands, and feet were to be seen in the streets. . . . Men rode in blood up to their knees and bridle reins. Indeed, it was a just and splendid judgment of God that this place should be filled with the blood of unbelievers, since it had suffered so long from their blasphemies."*

—Report from the French cleric Raymond d'Aguilers on the slaughter of Muslims and Jews in Jerusalem during the First Crusade in 1099

*"Kill them all; God will recognize his own."*

—Papal commander Arnaud Amalric in 1208 when asked by his forces what should be done about the Catholic citizens of Béziers, who were indistinguishable from the "heretical" Cathars of the same town

*"In this way the battle of the Lord was triumphantly won, by God alone and through God alone. To God be the honor and the glory, who granted the victory of His Cross through Jesus Christ, our Lord."*

—Report to the pope from King Alfonso VIII of Castile after the defeat of the Muslims at the Battle of Las Navas de Tolosa in 1212

*"Alfonso—God curse him!—pulled out of this place after he and his men had taken their fill of the chattels and possessions of the Muslims. . . ."*

—Muslim account of the same battle

"It is the duty of every Catholic to persecute heretics."

—Pope Gregory IX (reigned 1227–1241), launching the Inquisition in 1232

"Infidels should all be dispatched to hell with the proselytizing sword."

—Tamerlane, the fierce Mongol warrior of the fourteenth century who built great towers in the shape of minarets out of human heads

"We come to conquer this land by [the King of Spain's] command, that all may come to a knowledge of God and of His Holy Catholic Faith; and by reason of our good mission, God, the Creator of heaven and earth and of all things in them, permits this, in order that you may know Him and come out from the bestial and diabolical life that you lead. . . . Our Lord permitted that your pride should be brought low and that no Indian should be able to offend a Christian."

—Spanish conquistador Francisco Pizarro to the Inca emperor Atahuallpa at Peru in 1532

"Alas, it cannot be anything but the terrible wrath of God which permits anyone to sink into such abysmal, devilish, hellish, insane baseness, envy, and arrogance. If I were to avenge myself on the devil himself I should be unable to wish him such evil and misfortune as God's wrath inflicts on the Jews, compelling them to lie and to blaspheme so monstrously, in violation of their own conscience. Anyway, they have their reward for constantly giving God the lie."

—Protestant reformer Martin Luther, On the Jews and Their Lies, 1543

"Who will venture to place the authority of Copernicus above that of the Holy Spirit?"

—Protestant reformer John Calvin (1509–1564) on the Copernican theory that the earth revolves around the sun

"The state of monarchy is the supremest thing upon earth; for kings are not only God's lieutenants upon earth, and sit upon God's throne, but even by God himself they are called gods."

—James I of England (reigned 1603–1625), firm believer in the Divine Right of Kings

*"We recognize the negro as God and God's Book and God's Laws, in nature, tell us to recognize him—our inferior, fitted expressly for servitude."*
—Jefferson Davis, president of the Confederate States of America, 1861

*"We, the Order of the Knights of the Ku Klux Klan, reverentially acknowledge the majesty and supremacy of Almighty God and recognize His goodness and providence through Jesus Christ our Lord."*
—From the Constitution and Laws of the Knights of the Ku Klux Klan, 1867

*"The natural and proper timidity and delicacy which belongs to the female sex evidently unfits it for many of the occupations of civil life. . . . The paramount destiny and mission of women are to fulfill the noble and benign office of wife and mother. This is the law of the Creator."*
—U.S. Supreme Court, 1873, upholding the Illinois Supreme Court's refusal of Myra Bradwell's application for admission to the bar because of her sex

*"The Catholic and Protestant religions are insolent to the gods, extinguishing sanctity, rendering no obedience to Buddha, and enraging Heaven and Earth. . . . But 8 million Spirit Soldiers will descend from Heaven and sweep the Empire of all foreigners."*
—The Chinese Society of Harmonious Fists, or Boxers, a nativistic terrorist group that tortured and killed foreigners and Chinese Christians during the Boxer Rebellion of 1900

*"[The royal crown is] granted by God's Grace alone and not by parliaments, popular assemblies, and popular decision. . . . Considering myself an instrument of the Lord, I go my way."*
—Kaiser Wilhelm II (reigned 1888–1918), militaristic emperor of Germany who helped instigate World War I, one of the most savage conflicts in human history

*"God is with us."*
—Motto on the belt buckles of Kaiser Wilhem's soldiers during the Great War

"*Hence today I believe that I am acting in accordance with the will of the Almighty Creator: by defending myself against the Jew, I am fighting for the work of the Lord.*"

—Adolf Hitler, *Mein Kampf*, 1925

"*I believe that it was God's will to send a youth from here into the Reich, to let him grow up, to raise him to be the leader of the nation so as to enable him to lead back his homeland into the Reich.*"

—Hitler, speaking in his Austrian homeland, after it was absorbed by Nazi Germany in 1938

"*Every deity and the spirits of your dead comrades are watching you intently.*"

—Excerpt from the suicide manual carried by Japanese kamikaze (Divine Wind) pilots during World War II

"*I am God.*"

—Jim Jones, leader of the Peoples Temple cult who called for the suicide of more than nine hundred of his followers in Jonestown, Guyana, in 1978

"*Those who are not Christians go to a place of suffering and torment called hell.*"

—Televangelist Pat Robertson, *Answers to 200 of Life's Most Probing Questions*, 1984

"*God has revealed to me that those doing battle for Allah and our country and meet death will immediately go to Heaven.*"

—The Ayatollah Khomeini in 1984, during Iran's bloody war with Iraq

"*I knew my God was bigger than his. I knew that my God was a real god and his was an idol.*"

—Lieutenant General William "Jerry" Boykin on his 1993 response to a Muslim warlord in Somalia who boasted Allah would protect him

"This is America, God has sent one of the attacks by God and has attacked one of its best buildings. And this is America filled with fear from the north, south, east, and west, thank God."
—Osama bin Laden, 2001

JERRY FALWELL: "What we have seen on Tuesday [September 11], as terrible as it is, could be minuscule if, in fact, God continues to lift the curtain and allow the enemies of America to give us probably what we deserve."
PAT ROBERTSON: "Well, Jerry, that's my feeling. . . ."
JERRY FALWELL: "I really believe that the pagans, and the abortionists, and the feminists, and the gays and the lesbians who are actively trying to make that an alternative lifestyle, the ACLU, People for the American Way—all of them who have tried to secularize America—I point the finger in their face and say 'you helped this happen.' "
—Christian evangelists Jerry Falwell and Pat Robertson during a 2001 broadcast on the Christian Broadcasting Network

"God is on our side, and Satan is on the side of the United States."
—Saddam Hussein, 2003

"Thou shalt not suffer a witch to live."
—Biblical justification (Exodus 22:18) for the torture and murder of hundreds of thousands of women and men accused of being in league with Satan

"If a man lies with a male as with a woman, both of them have committed an abomination; they shall be put to death, their blood is upon them."
—Biblical justification (Leviticus 20:13) for the hatred of homosexuals

"Everything in the water that has not fins and scales is an abomination to you."
—Biblical justification (Leviticus 11:12) for the hatred of shellfish

Perkin Warbeck, aka "Richard IV"

# Part VIII

~~

# THE GREAT
# PRETENDERS

"It's good to be the king!" the saying goes. And so it seemed—at least to the scores of ordinary folk over the centuries who tried, with varying degrees of success, to pass themselves off as royalty. Sure beat scrubbing floors for a living. Since antiquity, these imposters have made regular appearances around the world, especially in times of chaos and uncertainty. After the Roman emperor Nero was hounded into suicide in AD 68, for example, no fewer than ten fake Neros reportedly popped up and claimed to have escaped death by fleeing Rome. Plenty of people believed them too (although few of these frauds could have ever hoped to match the depravity of the original). The following is a look at some of history's more interesting royal impersonators.

# 1

~~

# The Paupers Who Would
# Be Prince

In medieval England, after the bloody struggle known as The Wars of the Roses,[1] two successive imposters posed grave threats to the throne of Henry VII, the first Tudor king. Though Henry had defeated and killed Richard III at the Battle of Bosworth Field in 1485, which ended the epic clash between the royal houses of York and Lancaster, his claim to the throne was rather remote. King Richard had left a number of Yorkist relatives with far better blood connections to the crown. One of them was his nephew Edward, Earl of Warwick, whose father was immortalized in Shakespeare's *Richard III* when he was drowned in a malmsey butt. Henry VII kept the young earl closely confined in the Tower of London, but that didn't stop an obscure lad named Lambert Simnel, the son of an Oxford tradesman, from claiming that he was the true earl and the rightful king of England.

Lambert Simnel was described by contemporaries as a "comely youth" with a strong resemblance to members of the royal house of York. (And in an age without mass media, few knew what they

---

1. Shameless Plug #2: For a more detailed account of the Wars of the Roses, see the author's highly acclaimed *A Treasury of Royal Scandals: The Shocking True Stories of History's Wickedest, Weirdest, Most Wanton Kings, Queens, Tsars, Popes, and Emperors.* (There's more on Nero in there as well.)

looked like anyway.) Lambert's teacher, an Oxford priest named Richard Symonds, seized on the similarities in appearance and embarked on a bold plan to pass his pupil off as the imprisoned Earl of Warwick. He nearly got away with it. As historian G. R. Elton wrote, "The very fact that such a wildcat scheme could spring from an obscure priest's brain—and that it came within a measurable distance of success—indicates the state of the country and the size of [King] Henry's problem."

One of Simnel's first supporters was Margaret, Duchess of Burgundy, sister of the late King Richard and center of Yorkist plots against the Tudor regime. Whether Margaret came to Simnel's side out of political expediency, as a way of undermining Henry VII, or because she really believed he was her nephew remains a mystery. But she was a powerful ally. Soon Simnel gained support in Ireland as well. Any opportunity to throw off the English yoke was welcomed there, and in May 1487, Lionel Simnel was proclaimed "King Edward VI" by the Irish. Henry VII recognized the danger he faced in Ireland and tried to quell the enthusiasm for the false Warwick by parading the real one around London. It didn't work. A force from Ireland, aided by two thousand mercenaries provided by Margaret of Burgundy, invaded England that June and began a march to London. Henry defeated them at the Battle of Stoke, during which many Yorkist leaders were killed.

Lambert Simnel was convicted of treason, but the English king demonstrated a trait not often associated with the Tudors when it came to rebels: a sense of humor. Rather than have Simnel hideously tortured and executed, the usual fate of traitors, Henry took him into his household and put him to work in the royal kitchens. When a group of Irish lords came to dinner one night, Henry made sure they saw the young man they had proclaimed king reduced to kitchen help. He thought it was a hoot.

But that flash of levity escaped the king entirely when another nobody named Perkin Warbeck emerged from obscurity and tried to claim Henry's kingdom. With many of Europe's monarchs behind him, Warbeck proved far more menacing than Lambert Simnel ever was. Consequently, he would meet a less savory fate.

As the imposter himself later recounted, the story began in 1491 when Warbeck, then a seventeen-year-old servant to a wealthy Breton merchant, was walking along the streets of Cork, Ireland, dressed in the silk finery of which his master traded. Unaccustomed to such a display of wealth, especially on someone so young, certain locals became convinced that he was the Earl of Warwick, whom Lionel Simnel had previously impersonated. When Perkin denied this, people then said he was a bastard son of Richard III. Warbeck again denied any royal connections, but the townspeople were insistent. He was, they declared at last, Richard, Duke of York, the younger of the two famed princes in the Tower who had been imprisoned and presumably murdered by their uncle Richard III after he stole the older boy's throne in 1483.[2] Worn down by their vehemence, or so he later claimed, Warbeck finally affirmed that he was indeed the long missing prince.

The great nobles of Ireland, perhaps still feeling burned after the Lambert Simnel fiasco, were less enthusiastic than the people of Cork over the discovery. On the other hand, Charles VIII of France, then at war with Henry VII, warmly welcomed Warbeck to his court with the idea that he might be a useful pawn in the ongoing negotiations with the English king. Charles could threaten to support the imposter if things didn't go his way, or repudiate him if conditions warranted. As it turned out, the French and English did sign a peace treaty. Warbeck was expelled from France—right into the arms of Margaret of Burgundy.

Once again the question arises as to whether Margaret was incredibly gullible or just very crafty when she accepted Warbeck as her nephew, just as she had Lambert Simnel. (It is worth noting that Margaret had been sent off to the Netherlands and married five years before her real nephew Richard, Duke of York, was born, and had never met him. Still, this was the second "nephew" of hers to turn up at her doorstep out of nowhere, which should have at least

---

2. After the death of his brother Edward IV, Richard III obtained the throne by falsely claiming that his late brother's sons, the princes in the Tower, were bastards, and thus ineligible to rule. The elder boy was King Edward V, but he was never crowned. Young Edward and his brother Richard disappeared during Richard III's reign, and were never seen again.

given her pause.) In any event, Margaret worked successfully to have Warbeck recognized by Pope Alexander VI and Emperor Maximilian of Austria as "Richard IV," the rightful king of England.

The official embrace Warbeck received was not appreciated by Henry VII, who ordered a trade embargo against the Netherlands in 1493. This was reciprocated the following year, but the situation was an economic disaster for both sides. The Dutch, eager to rid themselves of Warbeck, backed his invasion of England to claim the crown in 1495. The venture was a flop, but at least the Dutch had disposed of the troublesome pretender. Warbeck eventually made his way to Scotland, where King James IV gave him an allowance and official recognition as "Richard IV." He even gave him one of his royal relatives as a bride—not bad for the son of a Flemish farmer. The Scottish king's support did nothing to further Warbeck's cause, however. Discouraged, the imposter left Scotland in 1497 and attempted another invasion of England through Cornwall, then in rebellion against Henry VII over his taxation policies. It was yet another failure, and Warbeck was forced to surrender.

King Henry was lenient with his would-be usurper at first, but then Warbeck foolishly tried to escape. His subsequent confinement in the Tower of London was a lot less cushy and reportedly included torture. Still, he continued to enjoy the support of some European monarchs, and that's what ultimately doomed him. With a little help from the king, as some historians believe, Warbeck made a final escape attempt in 1498. That gave Henry the perfect excuse to kill him and do away with the real Earl of Warwick as well. Henry declared that the earl, still languishing in the Tower, had conspired with Warbeck and deserved death. The hapless young man, who had never done anything wrong other than be born into the wrong branch of the royal family, was fortunate enough to be dispatched quickly. Warbeck, by contrast, suffered a ghastly demise. He was hanged until almost dead, then castrated and disemboweled while still breathing. Finally he was chopped into four quarters. The remains were put on public display as a grisly warning to anyone else who might harbor kingly pretensions.

# 2

## Tsar Struck

Ruling Russia was often a dangerous business. Tsars were bumped off with alarming regularity, which, though unfortunate for the royals, opened fertile opportunities for the frauds. Russian history is rife with imposters who grasped for the imperial crown. In 1605, one actually got it.

After Ivan the Terrible's savage reign came to a close with his death in 1584, he was succeeded by his second son Fyodor. (Ivan had murdered his first son in a fit of rage.) Fyodor was a nice, pious fellow, if something of a dolt. He was completely controlled by the powerful boyar (noble) Boris Godunov, who effectively ruled Russia in Fyodor's name. After the dim tsar died in 1598, without a successor, Godunov took the crown. It was openly whispered, however, that Godunov had earlier ensured Fyodor would leave no heirs by ordering the murder of the tsar's younger half brother Dmitry in 1591.

Dmitry had been sent to live with his mother Maria Nagaia, one of the last of Ivan's seven or so wives, in the Russian town of Uglich after Fyodor's accession. One day in 1591, Dmitry's mother reportedly heard a terrible scream that came from the courtyard of her home. When she ran outside to see what had happened, she found Dmitry on the ground, bleeding to death from a knife wound to the throat. The townspeople immediately concluded that one of

Boris Godunov's local henchmen had killed the boy, and in a frenzy they killed the suspect and his family. Godunov sent a commission to Uglich to investigate Dmitry's death. The examiners came to the preposterous conclusion that the heir to the throne had fallen while playing and had accidentally slit his own throat. To bolster the commission's findings, Godunov ordered the townspeople who had killed his agent severely punished. Many were executed, the rest sent to Siberia. Dmitry's mother was forced into a convent, and her family scattered to remote corners of Russia. Although suspicions about Godunov's role in the murder of Dmitry lingered, his critics had been effectively silenced.

And so it happened that, seven years later, Boris Godunov came to the throne as Russia's first elected tsar. But he did not sit comfortably. Two years of crop failures, followed by terrible famine, made the people wonder whether this might be divine punishment for the murder of Dmitry. Besides, their tsar, on whom they were utterly dependent, had not been selected by God, but by them. Could this be the cause of their troubles? Agitation mounted. Then, in the summer of 1604, Godunov faced one of his greatest challenges. A young man, backed by an army of Cossacks, emerged from Poland and claimed to be Dmitry, the rightful tsar. It was the beginning of a dark period in Russian history known as the Time of Troubles.

The young man who came to be known as the False Dmitry began his career as a monk named Gregory Otrepyev. After traveling from monastery to monastery, Otrepyev eventually arrived in Moscow and became secretary to the patriarch of the Russian Orthodox Church. There, in the very heart of imperial power, Otrepyev absorbed useful information for his future ambitions. "Do you know," he remarked to some of his fellow monks, "one day I shall be tsar of Moscow." When Boris Godunov heard of the monk's impertinence, Otrepyev was banished to a monastery far away on the White Sea. He wasn't there long before he escaped to another monastery near the southern city of Chernigov. When he eventually departed this refuge, Otrepyev left a note in his cell: "I am the Tsarevich Dmitry, son of Ivan IV. I shall not forget your kindness when I am on my father's throne."

Otrepyev next went to Poland, where he entered the service of a

Polish prince and learned to fight from the fierce Cossacks. At one point, he pretended to be gravely ill and asked for a priest. When the priest arrived, Otrepyev handed him a piece of paper, a confession of sorts, which read, "I am the Tsarevich Dmitry, son of Ivan IV. I was saved from my murderers and hidden. A priest's son died in my place." (In another account, Otrepyev revealed his "true" identity when the Polish prince he served slapped him in anger. "If you knew who serves you," Otrepyev reportedly responded, "you would not treat me like this.") Otrepyev was duly presented before the king of Poland, who recognized his claim and granted him an annual pension. The False Dmitry was on his way.

He raised an army in Poland, and at the same time launched a propaganda campaign in Russia, through which he staked his claim to the throne and vowed to return and take it. The Russian people, disaffected by Godunov's rule, were eager to believe that the son of Ivan IV had survived and would soon come and save them. Though Godunov tried to counter Otrepyev's propaganda campaign with one of his own, the pretender's cause quickly gained momentum, even among the most powerful aristocrats.

When the False Dmitry finally marched into Russia, he was greeted as a savior with widespread support. His forces defeated Godunov's army in an initial clash. Although the tsar's troops crushed Otrepyev's in a second encounter, fate intervened when Boris Godunov died suddenly on April 13, 1605 (some said by poison). His son was immediately placed on the throne as Fyodor II but enjoyed little support. The citizens of Moscow stormed the Kremlin, seized the new tsar and his mother, and later killed them. "The time of the Godunovs is past!" the people shouted. "The sun of Russia is rising. Long live the Tsar Dmitry."

The False Dmitry marched into Moscow on June 20, greeted by cheering crowds. He went straight to the tomb of Ivan IV. "Oh, beloved father!" he cried. "You left me in this world an orphan, but your saintly prayers helped me through all the persecution and has led me to the throne." Witnesses to the scene were much moved, and Otrepyev's support was solidified. The following month he was crowned in the Kremlin's Cathedral of the Assumption. An imposter now sat on Russia's throne, but he would not rule for long.

It is unclear exactly why "Tsar" Dmitry became so unpopular so quickly. Some historians believe the Russians resented his Polish friends and associates, including his bride Marina Mniszech, a Polish princess. Ten days after their wedding, a group of boyars stormed the tsar's palace. The False Dmitry leapt out of a window to save himself, but broke his leg in the fall. He pleaded for his life in vain, and was quickly dispatched. His body was then put on public display before it was cut into pieces and burned. The ashes were mixed with cannon shot and fired westward back to Poland, from where he had come. "Dmitry" had reigned for less than a year.

The Time of Troubles did not end with the death of the False Dmitry, however. Chaos continued as a succession of tsars were enthroned and deposed. It was during this period that a second False Dmitry appeared, supported as the first had been by Poles and Cossacks. His army came within ten miles of Moscow and besieged the city for a year. To complicate matters, the second False Dmitry married the widow of the first, and was even acknowledged by the mother of the real Dmitry! But in the end his efforts failed. In 1613, Russia came under the rule of Michael Romanov, founder of the dynasty that would occupy the throne for the next three centuries.

# 3

~

# Queen-*Wanna*-Be

The allure of royalty must have been pretty potent for those close enough to witness firsthand the pampered luxury and fawning deference accorded monarchs and their families. Such was the case with Sarah Wilson, a young maid in the service of Britain's Queen Charlotte, consort of George III. The aura of majesty was apparently so intoxicating to the ambitious girl raised in rural England that she wanted a piece of it for herself. Her quest would eventually lead her to the American colonies, where she reinvented herself as a member of the royal family who in fact never existed. But that's getting ahead of the story.

At first all Sarah wanted was something that belonged to the queen. So one night she crept into Charlotte's closet and took a ring, along with a miniature portrait of the queen and one of her finest gowns. Greedy for more, Sarah slipped in again the following night but was caught. Stealing from the queen was a capital offense, and Sarah was duly sentenced to death. Fortunately, she was saved from the gallows through the intercession of Caroline Vernon, a lady-in-waiting to Queen Charlotte who had brought Sarah into the royal service. The death sentence was commuted to exile in the colonies.

The redeemed maid arrived in the New World in the fall of 1771, and was sold as an indentured servant to William Devall of

Bush Creek, Maryland. Life as a slave in all but name did not suit Sarah, though, and after several months she escaped to Virginia. There she commenced her imposture. Somehow she had managed to keep possession of the items she had stolen from Charlotte, and she used them to create her new identity: Princess Susanna Carolina Matilda, the queen's younger sister.

Sarah told people she had been banished after quarreling with her sister the queen. No one seemed to notice, or care, that the supposedly German-born princess could not speak a word of the language. And the fact that Charlotte had only one, *older* sister was apparently a nonissue as well. The onetime maid was feted in the American south by people eager to rub shoulders with royalty. The governors of Virginia and North Carolina warmly received her, and in both colonies, wrote historian Francis Xavier Martin in 1829, "she made astonishing impressions in many places, affecting the manners of royalty so inimitably that many had the honor of kissing her hand."

The presumed princess kept people interested with promises of rank or property when she eventually reconciled with her sister and returned home. "To some she promised governments," wrote Martin, "to others regiments or promotions of different kinds in the treasury, army, and navy. In short, she acted so adroitly as to levy heavy contributions upon some persons of the highest rank."

Yet while Sarah made her royal progress through the south, her master William Devall had not been idle. He advertised her as missing property and sent his lawyer to track her down. She was eventually captured in 1773, but escaped again two years later. By now the colonies were in revolt against Britain, and in the turmoil Sarah was able to avoid detection. She eventually married a young officer named William Talbot and settled with him in New York, where they raised a large family. In the midst of this simple domesticity, however, Sarah never forgot her stint as a princess. On the wall of her home she kept a portrait of her "sister," the queen.

# 4

~

# A School of Dauphins

Had Twain's fictional "Looy" actually existed, he would have been just one of a herd claiming to be the lost king of France. There were more than a hundred. Some of the fake dauphins caused quite a stir; others—like a half Native American in the Great Lakes region—never got very far with their frauds. All, however, traded on a tragedy and, in doing so, tormented the real dauphin's sister to her grave.

After the executions of Louis XVI and Marie-Antoinette in 1793, their two orphaned children were kept separated from one another in the fortress prison known as the Temple, where the deposed royal family had been imprisoned. Louis-Charles, the eight-year-old dauphin, was consigned to a hideous fate. His enchanted childhood at Versailles had ended abruptly when a murderous mob stormed the palace. He watched in terror as his mother and father were threatened and humiliated before they were finally dragged to the guillotine. Now the little boy was all alone and at the mercy of revolutionary fanatics. The "son of a tyrant," as they called him, was subjected to a brutal reeducation program designed, in the words of one, to make "the little whelp . . . lose the recollection of his royalty." Then, when physical, emotional, and sexual abuse had all but broken the boy, he was abandoned entirely—left to rot in his own filth in a dark cell.

"He lay in bed," wrote his older sister Marie-Thérèse, "which had not been made for more than six months, and he now had no strength to make it. Fleas and bugs covered him, his linen and person were full of them. His shirt and stockings had not been changed for more than a year. His excrements remained in the room; no one had removed them in all that time. His window, the bars of which were secured by a padlock, was never opened. It was impossible to stay in his chamber on account of the foul odor. . . . He might have taken rather more care of his person. . . . But the unhappy child was half dead from fear, so much had they terrorized him. He spent the day in doing nothing. They gave him no light; this condition did as much to harm him morally as it did physically. It is not surprising that he lapsed into a fearful marasmus."

When a doctor was finally allowed to attend the boy, now ten, he found him consumed by diseases, covered with tumors and sores, his joints grotesquely swollen and discolored. Louis-Charles was "a victim of the most abject misery and of the greatest abandonment," the doctor reported, "a being who has been brutalized by the cruelest treatments and who it is impossible for me to bring back to life. . . . What a crime!" On June 8, 1795, he died. An autopsy was performed, during which the boy's heart was secretly removed—a postmortem tradition for French kings that on this occasion seemed hollow, but would in time have enormous significance. The rest of the body was buried in an unmarked grave without ceremony or mourners. The child who would have been Louis XVII was no more, but his legend was launched.

Many believed the boy-king had not died, but had escaped the Temple and that a substitute child had been buried in his place. "Some contend that this death means nothing," reported Le Courrier Universel; "that the young child is in fact full of life and that it is a very long time since he was at the Temple." Sure enough, the first of a long parade of imposters soon made his appearance. A tailor's son who claimed to be Louis XVII had a noble bearing that convinced many people that he was indeed the young king. Royalists showered him with gifts and paid homage, while tales of his escape from the Temple and subsequent adventures excited imaginations across France. Nevertheless, Marie-Thérèse, by then living in exile in Vienna, believed the story of the young man who claimed to be her brother was "an idle fancy," as she wrote her uncle in 1798, which "according to everything I know thereon, is in no way probable." The imposter was eventually arrested by Napoleon's secret police and imprisoned. In his place, however, sprouted many more false claimants, and some of these Marie-Thérèse could not so easily dismiss from her mind.

One of the most successful, and most agonizing to Marie-Thérèse, was a Prussian clockmaker named Karl Wilhelm Naundorff, who made his claim official in 1834. Ironically, it was during the trial of another imposter. Naundorff's representative interrupted the proceedings to read a letter from his client, the *real* claimant: "Gentlemen of the jury and all you Frenchmen in whose hearts reign sentiments of honor and justice, learn that the son of your unfortunate king, Louis XVI, is still living. . . . Yes, Frenchmen, Louis XVII still lives and is relying upon the lively interest which the nation has never ceased to feel for the innocent son of the most unhappy of her kings . . ."

Like many of his fellow imposters, Naundorff told a compelling story of rescue from the Temple prison, and of harrowing adventures that followed. What set him apart, however, were the number of intimates of the deposed royal family who believed him and rallied to his cause. "Madame," the dauphin's childhood nurse, now an old woman, wrote Marie-Thérèse, "I am impelled by my conscience to take the liberty of writing respectfully to you to assure you of the existence of your illustrious brother. I have seen him and recognized him with my own eyes. . . . His long suffering, his resignation and submission to the will of Providence, as also his kindness, are beyond belief." Other former courtiers of Louis XVI and Marie-Antoinette were equally enthusiastic in their endorsements. Startled, Marie-Thérèse sent her trusted friend, Vicomte de La Rochefoucauld, a former French minister, to meet Naundorff.

"I found myself in the presence of a man who undoubtedly bears a certain resemblance—taking his age into account—to the more careful portraits of Louis XVII," the vicomte reported, "and who possesses the general features of the Bourbon family." More important, he continued, "There was nothing in his behavior, in his tone, his manner of speech which suggested impudence or fraud, let alone roguery and still less blackmail. . . . He is so calm, so convincing, that one is almost convinced oneself."

Marie-Thérèse had been harassed by a relentless horde of "brothers" for years, and was naturally wary of Naundorff. Still, the possibility that he might be telling the truth compelled her to at least receive letters from him through his agent. "I am ready to give *my sister alone, by word of mouth, indisputable proofs* which will remove all your remaining doubts," Naundorff wrote. In the end, though, Marie-Thérèse could not bring herself to meet the imposter, which made him furious. "It is sufficiently painful to me to find Frenchmen propagating by *command* lies and calumnies against me," he wrote, "but how bitter must be my feelings when I see my own sister at the head of my oppressors! My own sister, not content with protecting my enemies, assists them to crush my just cause. . . . I find myself utterly at a loss, Madame."

The imposter continued to stalk his "sister," and even filed suit against her. His efforts eventually got him arrested, after which a shady past that included allegations of forgery and insurance fraud was exposed. He was deported to England. "Thank God, I will not hear of the Prussian again," wrote Marie-Thérèse. "But I know it is not entirely over. . . . His threats do not frighten me a great deal. He is a cunning imposter who is being manipulated by political adventurers." Indeed, Naundorff would continue to haunt her.

He died in Holland in 1845, maintaining his royal pretensions to the end. Inexplicably, Dutch officials recorded on his death certificate that he was "Louis XVII, who has been known as Karl Wilhelm Naundorff, born at the Chateau of Versailles, in France, March 27, 1785 . . . the son of his late Majesty, Louis XVI, king of France, and her Imperial and Royal Highness, Marie-Antoinette . . ." And on his tombstone was engraved, "Here lies Louis XVII . . . King of France and Navarre." Naundorff's wife and children were determined to validate the epitaph. They pursued a claim in the French courts to have the death certificate of the real dauphin invalidated and the fake one recognized. In addition, as the (self-proclaimed) widow of Louis XVII and the rightful "princes" and "princesses," they demanded "rights and privileges" to which they claimed entitlement. Marie-Thérèse was summoned to appear before the court, but she refused. The case was eventually dismissed, and a month later Marie-Thérèse was dead at age seventy-two. Her epitaph was infinitely more appropriate than Naundorff's: "Oh, all those that pass by, come and see whether any sorrow is like unto my sorrow!"

Marie-Thérèse was at last free of the mysteries and torment that surrounded her brother's life and death, but for historians there was no such relief. For nearly two more centuries, scholars and amateurs alike tried to find the elusive proof that the little boy who died so miserably at the Temple was indeed the dauphin. It finally came in 2000, thanks to the now dry and hardened heart taken from the boy during his autopsy in 1795, and the miracle of DNA.

The shriveled organ, passed from hand to hand over the years, had survived wars and revolutions before it finally came to rest among the remains of other French royalty in the abbey of Saint-Denis. A sliver of the relic was analyzed and compared to hair samples taken from the dauphin's maternal aunts, which had survived in a rosary that belonged to their mother. "This is the end of two hundred years of uncertainty," declared Philippe Delorme, a historian who worked with the scientists on the case. "It puts to an end a mystery that has absorbed so many of us. The DNA analysis shows the child's heart is from a member of the Habsburg family [Marie-Antoinette's royal line]. The historical research shows that this heart came from the orphan of the Temple. Since, apart from Marie-Thérèse who survived, the only other relative of Marie-Antoinette in the Temple in 1795 was Louis-Charles, now we have an answer. It was Louis XVII, the little king of France without a crown, who died in the Temple prison. It is definitive."

# 5

~~

# The Last Tsarevna?

There was one royal imposter who reigned above all others in the world's imagination. From the time she was pulled sputtering out of a Berlin canal after an apparent suicide attempt in 1920 until just recently, a Polish peasant named Franziska Schanzkowska had a legion of believers convinced she was the Grand Duchess Anastasia, the only surviving child of Russia's last tsar, Nicholas II. The resemblance was indeed startling, as was her apparent intimate knowledge of the imperial court. And Franziska was certainly ornery enough to pass as royal. She barked orders and threw fits like any true spoiled princess. But what really captured the imagination of historians and Hollywood alike was the romantic notion that the tsar's youngest daughter, against all odds, had miraculously escaped her family's bloody fate.

At first Franziska was maddeningly evasive after being rescued from the canal and brought to a Berlin asylum. She refused to identify herself, or, for that matter, to say anything at all. Instead, she cowered under her bedcovers in apparent terror. They called her "Fräulein Unbekannt," or "Miss Unknown." Gradually, however, Franziska started to offer little hints to the hospital staff about who she might be. She muttered Russian in her sleep, but refused to speak it while awake, as if the language was somehow cursed. She also subtly encouraged comparisons between her appearance and photos of the real Anastasia, but pretended to be horrified if anyone made a connection. Her fear, she suggested, was that the Bolsheviks would come and kill her if they ever discovered who she was. Then, after nearly two years biding her time in the asylum, Franziska finally "admitted" that she was indeed the Grand Duchess Anastasia.

Some thought she was just another pathetic creature who thought she was royal. After all, Romanov claimants appeared all over the place after the massacre of the tsar and his family in 1918. Others, however, were thoroughly convinced she was the genuine princess. Her story, as it emerged in fragments, was fantastic. She said a Russian soldier named Alexander Tschaikovsky had somehow rescued her after the rest of her family was slaughtered in the basement of the prison home in the Siberian town of Ekaterinburg. How he managed this she claimed not to know, only what Tschaikovsky told her: "It was a dreadful mix up, then he saw that I was still alive [after the family had been lined up against a wall and shot]. He did not want to bury a live body and he escaped with me under the greatest dangers. It was very dangerous."

Grievously wounded in the assault, she was hidden in a farm cart and driven out of Russia with Tschaikovsky and his family. "Do you know what a Russian farm wagon is?" Franziska asked her rapt audience. "No, you do not know. You only know when you lie in one with a smashed head and body. . . . How long was it? My God! A long time. Many weeks. Tschaikovsky was really crazy to rescue me." Speaking of crazy, the tale continued. They ended up in Bucharest, Romania, Franziska said, where they were sheltered by a gardener and survived by selling off pieces of jewelry "Anastasia" had sewn in her clothing while in captivity. During this time she had a son with Tschaikovsky, whom she then married. Soon after he was killed, perhaps, she hinted, by the Bolsheviks. With her husband dead, she said, there was nothing to keep her in Bucharest. It was time to go to Berlin and find her surviving royal kinsmen there. Having left her son with Tschaikovsky's family, she set off with his brother. "It was always in my mind to go to my mother's relatives," she said. "It seemed so natural to me that they would recognize me; I did not think of any difficulties." But difficulties there were, she claimed, from the arduous trek to Berlin to her abandonment by her brother-in-law to the desperate realization that her royal relatives might not recognize her. It was in this confused and distressed state that she jumped into the canal from which she was rescued.

Farfetched as the story was, the faithful swallowed it. Nor were they deterred by the sharp denials of Franziska's claims by various royal relatives and intimates who agreed to meet the increasingly prominent imposter. "I saw immediately that she could not be one of my nieces," declared Princess Irene of Prussia, sister of Anastasia's mother, Empress Alexandra. "Even though I had not seen them for nine years, the fundamental facial characteristics could not have altered to that degree, in particular the position of the eyes, the ears, etc."

That should have settled it, but for every apparent exposure of the fraud, there was some tantalizing bit of evidence that kept it alive. The most compelling of these was the declaration of a few people who had known Anastasia in Russia that the frail, sickly woman now before them was the Grand Duchess herself—or very well could be. Anastasia's paternal aunt Olga, Tsar Nicholas's sister, was so open to the possibility that Franziska was her niece that she sent her sweet notes and little gifts. "I am sending you all my love," Olga wrote in one missive, "am thinking of you all the time. It is so sad to go away knowing that you are ill and suffering and lonely. Don't be afraid. You are not alone now and we shall not abandon you." That Olga eventually repudiated the imposter was of little consequence to her supporters. The tsar's sister, they concluded, had simply bowed to family pressure.

Meanwhile, Franziska played the part of Anastasia to near perfection. She often peppered her conversation with little anecdotes about life with the imperial family back in Russia. "Yes," she pretended to reminisce at one point, "we had kokoshniki [Russian headdresses] and red costumes, I and [sister] Maria danced, we did many performances for us children, Maria and I, we always danced together." In another conversation, while looking at a formal portrait of the Romanovs, Franziska feigned intimacy: "We were so bad, did not want to sit still. I and my brother. I still remember, Papa was so angry. Look, you can see here, he was really angry." She was also quite adept at avoiding specific questions. There were huge gaps in her memory, she suggested, as if the horrible events she had endured had somehow shut down a part of her psyche. She made a show of agonizing while trying to remember, clenching her fists and breaking out in a sweat. They were boffo performances that left few doubting her sincerity.

One thing was certain, the imposter did not try to win support by ingratiating herself to people. Quite the opposite, actually. Imperious and rude, she often exasperated those trying to help her. In 1926 one of her most ardent supporters, an artist named Harriet von Rathlef, discovered just how nasty "Anastasia" could be while on vacation with her in Switzerland. "I can't tell you all she's doing to make my life miserable," Frau von Rathlef exclaimed. "The other day she threw her stockings in my face and said 'You are supposed to darn them! What have I got a serving girl for!?'" Franziska also demanded that her companion be moved out of her room and down the hall because she could hardly be expected to share a room with "her service." This was the thanks Frau von Rathlef received for nursing the woman she thought was Anastasia and working tirelessly to advance her cause. "She's either crazy or truly wicked," the flabbergasted woman declared after a week of enduring "Anastasia's" nonsense. Indeed, Franziska alienated so many people who tried to help her that it raises the question: was the imposter herself unbalanced, or just perfecting her petulant princess act? Whatever the case, her behavior only grew more erratic as time went on.

And the controversy surrounding her increased as well, especially after Harriet von Rathlef wrote a book in 1927 designed to bolster "Anastasia's" claims and draw attention to her plight. The book was serialized in the *Berliner Nachtausgabe* and caused a furor. "The 'Anastasia' publications became the theme of all Berlin," wrote the editor in chief of the *Nachtausgabe*. "And it was no different in the rest of the land. In Breslau and in Stuttgart, in Düsseldorf and in Bremen—everywhere people were asking, 'Is Anastasia alive?'" Frau von Rathlef's account was soon followed by a detailed report in the same newspaper that exposed Franziska as a fraud. But the matter was hardly settled. For those in the Russian monarchist circles already convinced Franziska was an imposter, the *Nachtausgabe* account was simply more evidence of that conviction. For believers, though, the

newspaper exposé meant nothing. "We have often mutually observed with what fanaticism certain people have campaigned against
[her]," Grand Duke Andrew, Anastasia's uncle and one of the imposter's few supporters within the extended Russian royal family,
wrote to another true believer, Gleb Botkin, son of the physician
who had been murdered with the tsar's family.

The Anastasia mania that swept Germany was exported to the
United States when Franziska arrived in 1928 to live with the real
Anastasia's second cousin Xenia, who was married to a wealthy
American industrialist. The *Herald Tribune* called the presumed
grand duchess "the reigning enigma of Europe," and noted that the
true identity of the claimant mattered little to the American public.
"The mystery is too appealing," the paper editorialized, "the hope is
too dramatic. . . . The records of every social upheaval are studded
with these strange, half-furtive figures, who may have been somebody or who may only have been somebody else. Were they really?
Historians and enthusiasts produce their mountains of proof; but
one never really knows, and one is never quite sure that one would
want to."

"Anastasia," or Anna Anderson, as she became known,[3] was the
star of New York society, although she seemed to shy away from all
the attention. She often retreated to her room and, as usual, made
life extremely difficult for her sponsors. She was so taxing, in fact,
that "cousin" Xenia finally had to dump her. "You know," the
princess confided to friends, "she isn't normal." That became even
more evident during Franziska's subsequent stay with a wealthy society lady named Annie Jennings. The imposter was so abusive and
paranoid that she eventually had to be committed.

"Mrs. Anderson . . . has been the guest of, and supported by my
sister for 18 months," Walter Jennings wrote in the formal application for commitment to the Supreme Court of New York. "She believes attempts are being made to poison her, refuses medical
assistance, spends most of her time confined to her bedroom talking

3. The imposter used the name Mrs. Anderson as a pseudonym when she came to
the United States. She later added the first name Anna, a shortened version of
Anastasia, and Anna Anderson eventually became her legal identity.

to two birds. She believes my sister has stolen her property." This was no act. It seems the imposter really was seriously disturbed, which may help explain why she was so successful. Only a crazy lady could commit to a role with such intensity for so long. And all for so little obvious benefit. Perhaps a part of Franziska Schanzkowska actually believed she was the Grand Duchess Anastasia, or wanted to be so desperately that it consumed her. "One of the most convincing elements of her personality was a completely unconscious acceptance of her identity [as Anastasia]," Princess Xenia noted. "She never gave the slightest impression of acting a part."

Money did not appear to be the motivation for Franziska's charade, although for some of those around her she represented a potential bonanza. Tsar Nicholas II had reportedly stashed a fortune in the Bank of England for the benefit of his daughters. If it could be proved that Anastasia was alive, she stood to inherit millions—or so it was believed. Gleb Botkin went on a mission and, in 1928, hired an American lawyer named Edward Fallows to follow the money trail. For twelve years Fallows toiled. He formed a Delaware corporation under the acronym GRANDANOR (for Grand Duchess Anastasia Nikolayevna of Russia) to help fund his quest, and invited Miss Jennings's wealthy friends to invest. He also poured his own money into the venture. He sold his home, cashed in his insurance policy, and emptied his portfolio of stocks and bonds. The effort eventually killed Fallows, his daughter claimed, and in the end not a ruble was recovered.

While poor Fallows pursued his fruitless quest, Franziska sailed back to Europe in 1931. There she lived a nomadic existence for years, until 1949 when Prince Frederick of Saxe-Altenburg settled her in a small former army barracks in the German village of Unterlengenhardt. There she lived for the next two decades, imperious and controversial as ever. During this time, two more people who had been intimately acquainted with the real Anastasia saw the imposter and offered conflicting conclusions. "I have recognized her, physically and intuitively, through signs which do not deceive," said Lili Dehn, a friend of Anastasia's mother. Sidney Gibbes, a tutor for the Romanov children, had a decidedly different opinion. "If she is the Grand Duchess Anastasia," he declared, "I am a Chinaman."

Then there were those, with only Hollywood as a reference, who saw pictures of Franziska and complained that she looked nothing like Ingrid Bergman, who starred in the 1956 film *Anastasia.*

A legal action brought by Franziska in 1938 to contest the distribution of a small estate to Empress Alexandra's German relatives came very close to vindicating the claimant. (It was the longest legal action in the German courts during the twentieth century, proceeding on and off until 1970.) Two expert scientists appointed by the court testified in Franziska's favor. One of them, Dr. Otto Roche, an internationally renowned anthropologist and criminologist, compared more than one hundred photographs of Anastasia to ones of Franziska taken at the same angles and under similar lighting conditions. After a millimeter by millimeter analysis, Roche concluded that "such coincidence between two human faces is not possible unless they are the same person or identical twins. Mrs. Anderson is no one else than Grand Duchess Anastasia." Similarly, Dr. Minna Becker, a graphologist who assisted in the authentication of Anne Frank's diary, compared samples of Anastasia's handwriting with Franziska's. "I have never before seen two sets of handwriting bearing all these concordant signs which belonged to two different people," Becker concluded. "There can be no mistake. After thirty-four years as a sworn expert for the German courts, I am ready to state on my oath and on my honor that Mrs. Anderson and Grand Duchess Anastasia are identical." Compelling as the evidence was, the court ultimately determined that case *non liquet,* neither established nor rejected. Franziska seemed unphased by the outcome. "I know perfectly well who I am," she snapped. "I don't need to prove it in any court of law."

Meanwhile, as her case crawled through the German courts, Franziska's mental health was deteriorating. She lived alone with sixty cats and banned even close friends from entering her home. When the Unterlengenhardt Board of Health objected to the conditions at her home, especially the terrible odor of animals buried in graves too shallow to mask the stench of decay, an insulted Franziska decided to take up an invitation from her old friend Gleb Botkin and come to Charlottesville, Virginia. There Botkin introduced her to a wealthy genealogist friend of his, Dr. John Manahan. The two apparently hit it off and were married in December 1968. "Well, what would Tsar Nicholas think if he could see his new son-in-law?" Manahan, eighteen years "Anastasia's" junior, joked to Botkin.

The odd couple lived together for fifteen years in a Charlottesville home that came to resemble the dump Franziska had left behind in Germany. The yard was a jungle, while inside a large population of cats made quite a mess. Whenever one of them died, Franziska would cremate it in the fireplace. Manahan seemed happy to indulge his spouse's eccentricities. "That's the way Anastasia likes to live," he explained. Perhaps his tolerance had something to do with the fact that he was growing every bit as weird as his wife. In one nine-thousand-word tract sent out as a Christmas card, Manahan accused President Franklin Roosevelt of aiding in a Marxist conspiracy to take over the world. The CIA, KGB, and the British Secret Service, he said, were all monitoring him and his wife. Delusional as he appeared to be, it was Franziska who was eventually institutionalized in 1983. During her confinement, Manahan kidnapped her and drove around Virginia's back roads with her for three days. Police arrested them and returned Franziska to the psychiatric ward. Three months later, on February 12, 1984, she died of pneumonia and was cremated the same day.

The mystery of Franziska's identity outlived her, however. Like the lost king of France, it would take a scientific analysis of her DNA to finally close the case. Although Franziska's body had been cremated, a Charlottesville hospital held samples of her intestine from an operation performed in 1979. After a great deal of legal wrangling to obtain a sample of the tissue, DNA extracted from it was compared to samples provided by members of the true Anastasia's extended family, including Prince Philip, husband of Britain's Queen Elizabeth II. A series of tests finally proved that Franziska Schanzkowska was a fraud. Still it was hard for the true believers to accept.

"I knew her for twelve years," Peter Kurth, author of *Anastasia: The Riddle of Anna Anderson,* told historian Robert K. Massie. "I was involved in her story for nearly thirty years. For me—just because of some tests—I cannot one day say, 'Oh, well, I was wrong.' It isn't that simple. I think it's a shame that a great legend, a wonderful adventure, an astonishing story that inspired so many people, including myself, should suddenly be reduced to a little glass dish."

The Tower of London: escape-proof?

# Part IX

~

# ESCAPES HATCHED

The human spirit's resistance to confinement has been manifested over time by the remarkable ingenuity and determination people have used to overcome it. Deception was a key element in many of history's greatest escapes, some of which are recounted here.

# 1

A Bloody Good Ruse

The ancient rhetorician Polyaenus recorded a number of brilliant escapes in his *Stratagems of War*, a book he dedicated to the joint Roman emperors of the second century, Marcus Aurelius and Lucius Verus. One of the more imaginative concerned Amphiretus the Acanthian, who had been captured by pirates and held for ransom on the island of Lemnos. While in captivity, Amphiretus ate little food, but secretly drank a mixture of saltwater and vermilion. This potion, reported Polyaenus, "gave a [red] tinge to his stools that made his captors believe he was seized with the bloody flux." Concerned that they would be robbed of their expected ransom money if Amphiretus died, the pirates released him from close confinement and allowed him to exercise outside in the hope that this might restore his health. The relaxed security allowed Amphiretus to slip away under cover of night, board a fishing boat, and sail back to Acanthum a free man.

In another episode, Polyaenus wrote of the tyrant Lachares, who sought to escape from Athens after Demetrius Poliorcetes captured it in 295 BC. He blackened his face to resemble a slave and slipped out of the city with a basket of coins. When a group of soldiers saw through his disguise and gave chase, Lachares was ready. He reached into his basket and tossed the coins behind him. As his greedy pursuers stopped to collect the treasure, Lachares galloped away.

# 2

~~

# Cross-Dressed for Success

The Tower of London has served many purposes throughout its nearly one-thousand-year history—from royal palace to zoo—but it was as a prison for enemies of the state that the famous structure acquired its fearsome reputation. Behind the Tower's stone walls, where Jesuits were tortured on the rack and three queens beheaded on the Green, few could hope to ever find freedom again. Nevertheless, some did.

William Maxwell, the fifth Earl of Nithsdale, had his wife, Winifred, to thank for his cleverly engineered escape from the Tower in 1716. He and several other Scottish lords had been condemned to death for their role in the plot to overthrow King George I and replace him with the late Queen Anne's half brother James. Lady Nithsdale, at home in Scotland when she received the news of her husband's capture, immediately buried the deeds to the family property and other important documents in her garden, then set off to London in a heavy snow to plead for his life.

According to her own account, she found King George in an unforgiving mood when she met him at St. James's Palace. Dressed in mourning, she waited in a corridor through which she had been told the monarch would pass. When he did, she threw herself at his feet and begged him to show mercy, but the king impatiently brushed her aside. Desperate, she grabbed the skirt of his coat and was dragged along the floor as he strode away. All hope now seemed lost, but still Lady Nithsdale was resolved to save her husband from a traitor's death. And so she concocted a daring plan.

Prisoners at the Tower weren't always consigned to dark, bone-chilling cells as they awaited their fate. Some, especially persons of rank, were given relatively comfortable rooms, where their servants could attend them and family members could visit. So it was with Lord Nithsdale. He was confined in the Lieutenant's Lodgings (now called the Queen's House), one of many buildings within the Tower complex where Anne Boleyn and other prominent prisoners stayed before their executions. Lady Nithsdale's escape plan incorporated the access she had to her husband, and the relative inattention Tower guards gave to the comings and goings of women.

She enlisted four accomplices: her faithful maid Evans, her land-lords Mr. and Mrs. Mills, and a woman named Miss Hilton. On the evening before Lord Nithsdale's scheduled execution, his wife and her companions arrived at the Tower. Lady Nithsdale left the three women outside the Lieutenant's Lodgings while she went in and brightly announced to those gathered that her husband's death sentence was to be reconsidered. This was meant to diffuse the high-alert atmosphere that always preceded an execution. She then entered her husband's room on the second floor, shut the door, and immediately set about disguising him to look like Mrs. Mills, the landlady waiting outside. To achieve the effect, she gave him a red wig she had smuggled in, painted down his thick eyebrows with a chalky paste, and rouged his cheeks.

When the transformation was complete, Miss Hilton entered the room wearing two coats. She removed one and, after a few mo-ments, she left, still wearing the other. Lady Nithsdale accompanied her to the stairs, then, for the benefit of the guards, called after her to send her maid Evans to help her get ready for the presentation of the mercy petition. As Miss Hilton departed, Mrs. Mills arrived, her face buried in a handkerchief, shoulders heaving, as she pretended to sob uncontrollably for the condemned man. When she entered Lord Nithsdale's room, she took off her long hooded cloak, gave it to him, then put on the extra coat Miss Hilton had left. Her de-meanor was entirely different when she departed—dry-eyed and composed. The crushed and weeping persona Mrs. Mills had earlier affected would now be adopted by Lord Nithsdale, along with her appearance.

Everything was set; all that was needed now was an incredible amount of good luck. The couple opened the door and stepped out into the adjacent Council Room. It was filled with people gathered in anticipation of the execution the next day. Those who noticed saw that poor "Mrs. Mills" was still a mess, sobbing into her handkerchief and supported by the soon to be widowed Lady Nithsdale. The two walked through a short passage and down the stairs, at which point Lady Nithsdale loudly reminded "Mrs. Mills" to fetch her maid. She then turned around to go back to the room where her doomed husband supposedly waited, while he walked out of the Lieutenant's Lodgings. The maid Evans met him outside, and together they headed for the Tower's Bulwark Gate—the passage to freedom—where Mr. Mills waited with a carriage.

Meanwhile, Lady Nithsdale maintained the pretense that her husband was still in the building. "When I was in the room," she later wrote, "I talked to him as if he had really been present, and answered my own questions in my Lord's voice as nearly as I could imitate it. I walked up and down, as if we were conversing together, till I thought they had time enough to thoroughly clear themselves of the guards." As she left the room, she told the guard outside she was going to fetch her maid herself because Evans had still not arrived, and asked that he please leave his Lordship to his prayers. She then walked out of the Tower, and joined her husband in hiding at the home of a friend. They eventually fled to Rome, but not before Lady Nithsdale sneaked back up to Scotland to recover the vital documents she had buried there.

"For a man in my Lord's situation it was the very best thing he could have done," King George reportedly—and grudgingly—said of Nithsdale's bold escape. As for his wife, though, he swore that she had given him "more mischief than any woman in the whole of Christendom."

# 3

---

# Special Delivery from Bondage

I entered the world a slave," Henry Box Brown wrote in his autobiography, "in the midst of a country whose most honored writings declare that all men have a right to liberty." It was from the dehumanizing system of bondage, where his wife and children were sold away from him by men who called themselves Christians, that Henry Brown was determined to escape. "I now began to get weary of my bonds," he wrote of that terrible time when his family was taken away, "and earnestly panted after liberty." To achieve it, he came up with a simple, yet daring plan: he would have himself mailed to freedom in Philadelphia.

A carpenter built the shipping crate, barely large enough to contain him, while a sympathetic shopkeeper in Richmond agreed to arrange for a friend of his to take possession of the human cargo when it arrived in the North. Brown then had to contrive an excuse to be absent from work at his master's tobacco plant so he wouldn't be missed while the plan was executed. He had an injured finger, but it wasn't enough to satisfy the overseer. So Brown's friend Dr. Smith procured for him some corrosive oil of vitriol. It burned his finger to the bone when he applied it, and the damage convinced the overseer to excuse him.

On the morning of March 29, 1849, Brown met Dr. Smith and the shopkeeper at the place that had been arranged for him to be packed into the crate. Several breathing holes were bored into the box, which measured only three feet, one inch in length, two feet in width, and two feet, six inches in height—a dangerously tight squeeze. Brown's only provision was a flask of water. "Being thus equipped for the battle of liberty," Brown wrote, "my friends nailed down the lid and had me conveyed to the Express Office, which was about a mile distant from the place where I was packed. I had no sooner arrived at the office than I was turned heels up, while some person nailed something on the end of the box." He would be at the mercy of careless cargo handlers throughout the arduous journey. During a transfer from train to steamboat at Potomac Creek, Virginia, he was left upside down.

"I felt my eyes swelling as if they would burst from their sockets," he wrote; "and the veins on my temples were dreadfully distended with pressure of blood upon my head. In this position I attempted to lift my hand to my face but I had no power to move it; I felt a cold sweat coming over me which seemed to be a warning that death was about to terminate my earthly miseries, but as I feared even that, less than slavery, I resolved to submit to the will of God, and under the influence of that impression, I lifted my soul in prayer to God, who alone, was able to deliver me. My cry was soon heard, for I could hear a man saying to another, that he had traveled a long way and had been standing there two hours, and he would like to get somewhere to sit down; so perceiving my box, standing on end, he threw it down and then the two sat upon it. I was thus relieved from a state of agony which may be more easily imagined than described."

After twenty-seven hours, and several more mishaps, including being dropped on his head during a transfer in Washington, D.C., Henry Brown emerged in Philadelphia—but not quite a free man. The Fugitive Slave Act, passed in 1850, eventually forced him to escape once again, to Britain. It was a longer journey, but at least Brown didn't have to endure it as cargo.

# 4

~∕∕∕~

# Sneak Retreat

The Gallipoli campaign of World War I was an unmitigated disaster—except for its conclusion. It was then that one hundred and forty thousand Allied soldiers escaped almost certain slaughter in an epic ruse that completely fooled the Turkish foe.

The poorly planned offensive on Turkey's Gallipoli Peninsula, which tarnished for a time the reputation of its champion, First Lord of the Admiralty Winston Churchill, was intended to open a second front in the east to divert German strength from the stalemated western front, open a supply route to Russia, and facilitate the capture of Constantinople (now Istanbul) to immobilize the Turks. But the massive force that landed on the shores of Gallipoli in the spring of 1915 was immediately overwhelmed by enemy fire from the hills above the beaches. After several months, a staggering number of lives had been lost but little progress made. Churchill was called "the butcher of Gallipoli" amid cries for the feckless campaign to be abandoned. Opponents of withdrawal argued, however, that a retreat would result in a bloodbath if the soldiers left what little cover they had to make their way across the beaches to waiting evacuation ships.

A compromise was reached when it was decided that two of the three beachheads the Allies had managed to establish on Gallipoli would be abandoned. Lieutenant General Charles Monro was in charge of the evacuation, which required stealth and deception to succeed. His plan was to have hundreds of men slip away every night without the Turks noticing by making the beachheads appear unchanged. First the enemy had to be desensitized to the growing silence of the vanishing troops. For several days all sounds were muffled as much as possible. Soldiers held their fire. Blankets were spread in the trenches, and boots were wrapped in burlap. Then, on the night of December 10, 1915, the actual escape was set in motion. Flour marked trails from the camps to the shoreline where evacuation boats waited, and every night hundreds of men silently made their way to safety.

To maintain the illusion that the camps were still full, the remaining soldiers tended an unchanging number of campfires, set up dummy troops, drove empty supply wagons, and even played cricket to give the appearance of normalcy. A mechanism was also rigged to fire unmanned rifles at random intervals. "It's getting terribly lonely at night," an English soldier wrote in his diary. "Not a soul about. Only the excitement keeps us from getting tired."

The Turks were oblivious to the mass escape that was occurring right below them, and on December 20, the last soldiers slipped away after setting fire to huge piles of equipment and exploding mines that sent the bewildered enemy rushing to the beaches. Monro's deception was so successful that not one life was lost in the evacuation, which was repeated at the third beachhead several weeks later. Only Winston Churchill, who continued to stubbornly defend the Gallipoli campaign, seemed unimpressed, and wrote of Monro: "He came, he saw, he capitulated."

# 5

~~

# Out of Colditz

The primary duty of every prisoner of war is to try to escape. It was a responsibility the Allied officers held by the Nazis at Colditz Castle responded to with gusto throughout World War II. They were called *Deutschfeindlich,* anti-German troublemakers who had proven themselves to be high security risks at other POW camps, and they made Colditz a veritable escape factory. Though not all their attempts were successful—indeed only a handful actually made it out of Germany—even the failures were ingeniously plotted, and if nothing else they drove their captors to constant distraction.

Colditz Castle sits high on a rocky outcrop above the Mulde River in the heart of Germany. With its barred windows, floodlit courtyards, and precipitous drops, the towering edifice was deemed by the Nazis to be escape-proof. Even if a prisoner made it past the imposing walls and barbed wire, he would still have to contend with ever vigilant German citizens, especially the Hitler Youth, as he tried to get to the nearest neutral border hundreds of miles away. But the Nazis underestimated the tenacity and imagination of the British, French, Dutch, Belgian, Polish, and, later, American officers who spent their otherwise monotonous days and nights at Colditz looking for ways out. Escape was their sole preoccupation. They dug tunnels, created disguises, and even secretly built a glider in the castle's attic to fly off the roof.

The resourcefulness of the officers was extraordinary. Almost any available item became a tool of escape. Jelly from Red Cross parcels was used in a makeshift printing press to reproduce maps of Germany—then eaten. Blankets were refashioned into civilian overcoats. The prisoners even made a camera out of a cigar box and a pair of broken spectacles to take photographs for use on forged identity papers. And what couldn't be made or found at Colditz was smuggled in from the outside. The British War Office set up a special branch of the secret service called M19 for that very purpose. They sent parcels, called "naughty boxes," that contained all manner of escape apparatus—cheese wire for cutting bars concealed inside shoelaces, maps pressed into wax gramophone records, compasses hidden inside walnuts or bars of soap.

On one occasion, a German guard recorded the arrival of five dress uniforms for English officers, which were permitted, and the separate discovery of civilian clothes buttons hidden inside a board game. "What do they want with these buttons in a POW camp?" the guard wrote in his diary. "There has to be a connection between these and the dress uniforms! When we made another detailed search of the latter, we made the following discovery: when the front seam of the [uniform] collar was opened and the stiffening material pulled out, the collar immediately turned into a soft fold-over civilian collar. . . . Pockets and epaulets were only very lightly attached and could be pulled off easily. Within a minute the uniform turned into a civilian suit. A really clever piece of work, proving to us, in connection with all items we found hidden in things sent to the English, that there was an entire industry at work over there that produced escape items and sent them, masterfully hidden, to their POWs."

Although the British were forever devising new ways to escape, it was the French who first managed to get members of their ranks out of Colditz. One officer took a wild leap over a fence; another slipped into a house adjacent to the castle's exercise area and hid there until it was safe to steal away. The French were followed by the Dutch, who found a unique way out. In the exercise area was a large manhole cover secured by a heavy nut and bolt. Below it was a ten-foot-deep well. A Dutch officer managed to get the exact dimensions of the bolt and made a glass replica of it. The plan was to have a couple of officers slip into the well during the allotted exercise period and hide there until after dark. The glass bolt would make the cover look secure to the Germans, but would allow the men in the well to lift the cover and climb out. They would then sweep up the broken glass bolt and replace it with the real one so it would appear the cover had never been opened.

On the appointed day, the Dutch played a game of rugby as the guards watched. Using a scrummage as cover, they unfastened the bolt and the first man was quickly lowered into the well. Later in the game, he was followed by the second, with the real bolt in his pocket. The glass bolt was then applied. As the two officers were certain to be missed during a head count at the end of the exercise period, a third man created a dangerous diversion. He clipped a hole in the barbed wire fence around the enclosure and walked out into the surrounding woods. Having made no effort to conceal himself, he was quickly spotted by the guards. As they rushed toward him, guns leveled, he shouted into the woods, "Run! Discovered!" The tactic gave the Germans the impression that two others had gone out through the fence before him. Fortunately, he wasn't shot. While the surrounding area was scoured for the two phantom escapees, the real ones stood waiting in the well. They emerged later that night and commenced their adventurous trek across Germany to freedom. Two more Dutch officers were able to escape the same way a month later.

After thirty-five failed attempts, the British finally made their first "home run"[1] in early January 1941. Major Pat Reid, the British officer in charge of escapes, discovered a passage out of the castle beneath the stage where prisoners put on plays and musical revues. It was an incredibly risky route, though, because an escaper would have to walk right through a room full of guards. Airey Neave, a British officer with a demonstrated knack for making realistic German uniforms, was chosen to make the first run. He was paired with

---

1. A successful escape out of Colditz, and then out of Germany itself, was considered a "home run."

Tony Luteyn, a Dutch officer who spoke perfect German. Because of his fluency, which was vital to the success of the venture, Luteyn was to pose as a senior German officer. Neave's impersonation of a junior officer, however, needed a little work.

"Normally Airey walked with his hands in his pockets, like most of the British officers at Colditz, slouching around," Luteyn later recalled in an interview with author Henry Chancellor. "I had to train him to be subordinate to me, so we spent a week walking in the courtyard, up and down, him walking on my left-hand side, because I was a superior, and when I turned, he had to turn around me. I'm not sure Airey liked pretending to be an upstanding, well-dressed German lieutenant, walking around with his captain."

On the night of January 5, right after a performance by the camp orchestra, Airey Neave and Tony Luteyn disappeared beneath the stage. They quickly removed their outer garments, beneath which they wore civilian outfits, then put on their homemade German uniforms. After sneaking through a series of passages, they approached the guardroom. "We heard voices and knew the guards were inside," Luteyn recalled. "Now if an officer comes into a room everybody has to jump up and stand to attention. So when we went in a guard shouted very loud, 'Attention!' And all the guards sprang up, and we walked in, me first and then Airey—he had to keep the door open for me. And the sergeant of the guard opened the front door and let us out."

There were several harrowing moments as Neave and Luteyn walked across an outer courtyard toward a dry moat at the castle's perimeter, but they weren't stopped. At one point a guard suddenly appeared out of the darkness, and the two startled escapers saluted him. The guard stopped and stared back at them. Luteyn had to think quick. "I remembered that this soldier had not returned my salute," he said, "so I turned around and scolded him in German. 'Why did you not salute your senior officer?' Then the soldier sprang to attention, and he marched away." Luteyn and Neave continued on the moat path, scaled a fence, and soon were away from Colditz. Two days later they crossed the Swiss border. Nine months after that, another pair of British and Dutch officers made an equally bold escape—through a hole cut into the wall of a German NCO's office.

—

One of the more audacious escape attempts from Colditz was an operation dubbed "Franz Josef," in which Lieutenant Mike Sinclair was to impersonate an older German officer named Rothenberger, whom the prisoners called Franz Josef because his bushy white moustache made him look like the late Austrian emperor. Rothenberger made a nightly inspection of the sentries on the eastern terrace of the castle, then exited by a guarded gate. Sinclair, posing as Rothenberger, was to dismiss the guards around the terrace with the bogus announcement that an escape was in progress on the other side of the camp, then march up to the pair of sentries at the gate, replace them with two British officers dressed as Germans, and demand the gate key. If all went well, this would allow a few minutes for twenty British officers—perhaps more—to descend by rope from windows above the terrace and escape out the gate before the dismissed German guards found the real Rothenberger back at the guardhouse.

The operation required intense preparation. To transform Mike Sinclair into "Franz Josef," a false moustache was fashioned out of shaving brushes. The German's prominent Iron Cross was replicated by melting zinc taken from the castle roof and molding it with a broken-off table knife. His greatcoat was made from dyed blankets, and his leather holster from heavy cardboard buffed with boot polish. Sinclair spoke impeccable German and mastered Rothenberger's gait and mannerisms. But success still depended upon the darkness to obscure his features because he was thirty years younger than Rothenberger.

Identity papers and travel permits required of all German citizens also had to be forged for the large group of escapers. They were produced in an assembly line of sorts. "I suppose we worked union hours," Kenneth Lee, one of the chief forgers, told Henry Chancellor. "Every day we sat at a table opposite each other painstakingly copying the German Gothic script on the paper forms. We started in pencil then carefully went over the top of everything in india ink. The raw materials came from the canteen shop and I suppose it never occurred to the Germans that we might be able to use this for escaping purposes. They thought we were all drawing still lifes." A homemade typewriter was used to fill in the date and time of travel on the documents, and they were stamped with an insignia meticulously carved in a shoe heel.

Operation Franz Josef commenced on the night of September 4, 1943. Sinclair, in his Rothenberger disguise, crept out of a window accompanied by the two other officers posing as German guards. They approached the first sentry on the terrace, and when Sinclair announced that an escape was in progress, the guard dutifully marched off. So did the second and third when they were approached. Things were going well. The trio then came to the terrace gate. Sinclair climbed a catwalk above it, relieved the guard there, and replaced him with his own disguised man. But when he came to the other guard at the gate and demanded the key, the German balked. Sinclair shouted at him in Rothenberger's thick Saxon accent, but the guard still refused and asked to see the color-coded pass carried by all personnel at Colditz. When Sinclair produced his pass, lifted earlier from another guard, the German became more suspicious and rang an alarm bell. The pass color had apparently been changed that evening, so the one Sinclair carried had just expired. Relief officers rushed to the scene, and Sinclair was shot and wounded by one of them. Franz Josef had failed, but as one officer said earlier, when the plot was conceived, even if it did fail, "it would still make a damn good story."

The "faeries" that fooled the man behind Sherlock Holmes

# Part X

## GOTCHA!

*"Lord, What fools these mortals be!"*
—WILLIAM SHAKESPEARE,
*A Midsummer Night's Dream*

Not all deceptions are motivated by power or profit. Sometimes people fool other people just for the fun of it—to stand slightly above their fellow man and, like Puck or Alan Funt, watch him wiggle under the thumb of outrageous circumstance. What follows is a selection of history's greatest pranks.

# 1

≈

# No Shot, Sherlock:

# An Unlikely Fairy Tale

If Sir Arthur Conan Doyle had been half as rational as his fictitious detective, Sherlock Holmes, he might not have fallen for the clever deception perpetrated by two little girls. Instead, Doyle—an ardent believer in the occult, particularly in his declining years—wrote several breathless magazine articles and a book in which he gushed over the discovery that real "faeries" had been photographed in an English village called Cottingley Glen.

The series of pictures, taken in 1917 by fifteen-year-old Elsie Wright and her nine-year-old cousin Frances Griffiths, showed the girls posing with an assortment of winged sprites and gnomes who danced and pranced and tootled on flutes and such. Doyle, who made enduring celebrities of the young ladies, was enthralled by the pixie shots. "And what a joy is in the complete abandon of [the fairies'] little graceful figures as they let themselves go in the dance!" he rhapsodized. "They may have their shadows and trials [but] there is a great gladness manifest in this demonstration of their life." The writer also speculated at length on how certain people could tune in to "a race of beings which were constructed in material which threw out shorter or longer vibrations."

The Cottingley faeries became a national fascination, especially after several photography experts, including ones from the Kodak company, carefully examined the pictures and declared them free of superimposition, retouching, or other photographic tricks. It was all so much simpler than that. After denying their ruse for decades, the girls, by then old women, finally admitted in 1982 that they had simply posed with paper cutouts suspended by hatpins.

The episode did not exactly enhance Doyle's reputation among his contemporaries. "It has long seemed to me," observed G. K. Chesterton, "that Sir Arthur's mentality is much more that of Watson than it is of Holmes."

# 2

~~

# The Weirdest Thing
# You Ever Sawed

A retired carpenter known only as Lozier proved with a monu-mental hoax in 1824 that people can be almost unfathomably gullible. Lozier convinced folks in Manhattan that the island was in danger of snapping in half like a bread stick and sinking because of overbuilding on the lower end. If the situation were left unreme-died, he warned, the results would be catastrophic. Incredibly, Lozier convinced the city's honchos that the island had to be sawed in half and the lower end, known as the Battery, dragged out past Ellis Is-land, turned around, and reattached at the heavy end.

In a time of amazing industrial and scientific advances, few ap-parently doubted the feasibility of such an audacious undertaking. Hundreds of laborers were commissioned, some taking underwater breathing tests in preparation for steering the detached portion of Manhattan. Carpenters and blacksmiths adjourned to their shops to create the necessary tools, which included one-hundred-foot saws and gigantic anchors to prevent the separated island from slipping out to sea. To feed the workers, Lozier ordered five hundred cattle, five hundred hogs, and three thousand chickens assembled at the construction site, while barracks were hastily built to house the la-borers. It was reportedly a scene of bedlam, with hundreds of ani-mals clucking and rooting over the din of construction.

After several weeks of preparation, the big day arrived when

Manhattan would be dismembered and reattached, under the direction of Lozier. Hundreds came out to watch the spectacle, with musicians and a parade for entertainment. Several hours passed, however, with no sign of Lozier. A note from him was found, explaining that a sudden illness had forced him to leave town. Left to ponder their foolishness, the crowd turned irate and formed a posse to hunt down the deceptive carpenter. Lozier, though, was long gone. He apparently gained nothing from the venture, except a marvelous sense of accomplishment.

# 3

~~

# Home Delivery

Those frat boys and other lame pranksters who order one hundred pizzas delivered to a hapless victim achieve nothing more than a sorry imitation of a true original. It's called the Berners Street Hoax.

The English writer Theodore Hook apparently disliked his neighbor, a society lady named Mrs. Tottenham. Indeed, he disliked her intensely. His hostility reached a memorable climax in 1809, when he secretly arranged for half of London's merchants to arrive with their wares at Mrs. Tottenham's Berners Street address—all on the same day. Hook spent weeks issuing invitations and requests in his neighbor's name.

Chaos ensued as all manner of tradesmen came calling on the appointed day, and Berners Street became impassable. Reported the *Morning Post:* "Wagons laden with coals from the Paddington wharfs, upholsterers' goods in cart loads, organs, pianofortes, linens, jewelry, and every other description of furniture sufficient to have stocked the whole street, were lodged as near as possible to the door of 54, with anxious trades-people and a laughing mob." And that was just the beginning. "There were accoucheurs, tooth-drawers, miniature painters, artists of every description, auctioneers, . . . grocers, mercers, post-chaises, mourning-coaches, poultry, rabbits, pigeons, etc. In fact, the whole street was literally filled with the motley group."

Hook even got the lord mayor of London to make an appearance with a forged invitation. His lordship was not amused when he arrived at the scene in his carriage, with two livery servants, and discovered he had been tricked. And poor Mrs. Tottenham must have been horrified to find a coffin arrive at her door, built to her exact measurements, accompanied by an undertaker and hearse. As darkness fell, the street was still not clear. Hook had also sent out a call for servants seeking employment to arrive at five PM.

He reportedly savored the spectacle he had created from a window overlooking Berners Street, and though a reward was offered for the arrest of the culprit, Hook was never caught. Twenty years later he admitted what he had done in his autobiographical novel *Gilbert Gurney,* and offered the following bit of advice that all those pizza deliverers would do well to heed: "Copy the joke and it ceases to be one—any fool can imitate an example once set."

# 4

## A Ruse of One's Own

Virginia was a Woolf in sheik's clothing. In 1910 the young novelist-to-be and a group of her cohorts tricked the British navy into becoming fawning tour guides for imaginary Ethiopian royalty.

A telegram, purportedly from the London Foreign Office, was sent to the commander of the British flagship *Dreadnought,* announcing the arrival of the Ethiopian emperor and his entourage. Woolf and her gang then dressed in exotic garb from a local costume shop, complete with turbans, fake beards, and dark stage makeup. Virginia even cut her hair short for the occasion.

Arriving by train, they were met by a red carpet, saluting officers, and a barrier to keep curious onlookers at bay. The group was then taken aboard the *Dreadnought,* where they were received by the commander in chief of the home fleet, Admiral Sir William May. One member of the group spoke loudly in a mixture of basic Swahili, pig Latin, and distorted passages from Homer in Greek. "Bunga bunga!" the party exclaimed with delight as they toured the ship, with Woolf periodically chiming in, "Chuck-a-choi, chuck-a-choi."

The naval officers were delighted with the visitors' childlike reactions to such novelties as an electric light, and the ruse went off without a hitch, until it started to rain. With fake beards drooping and makeup starting to run, the entourage hastily excused itself and the grand tour was over. It wasn't until the next weekend, when the entire hoax was reported in the *Daily Express,* that the admiral realized he had been had. "Bunga, bunga!" became part of the English vocabulary.

# 5

~~

# Practically Indecent:
# Alan Abel and the Siege of Troy

The world has seen many great practical jokesters. One of the
contemporary greats is New Yorker Alan Abel. In 1959, with
rising comedian Buck Henry acting as his front man, Abel created a
bogus decency league ostensibly devoted to placing clothing on animals so their genitalia were not exposed. The press went nuts. In
the 1980s Abel got several newspapers and national magazines to
run stories about a supposed school for panhandlers. And once he
gulled *The New York Times* into running his own obituary. Compared with Hugh Troy, though, Abel is just some jerk in a loud suit
with a squirting lapel flower.

Hugh Troy was a smart aleck who spent much of his arguably
dissolute life perpetrating the most innovative of frauds. Perhaps his
greatest effort: One winter while a student at Cornell University in
the late 1920s, Troy got hold of a hideous old wastebasket with a
real rhinoceros foot as its base. He filled it with metal weights, tied
thirty feet of clothesline to either side of it, and with a friend late
one night carried it out onto the campus, suspended between them.
Every five feet or so, they would lower it into the snow, their own
footprints so far away as to raise no suspicions. Morning broke.
Someone noticed the prints. Learned professors with experience in
such matters were summoned. Gravely, they inspected the tracks.
"By Jove, Farnsworth!" they exclaimed. "It's a rhinoceros!"

Excitedly, the professors followed the tracks for hundreds of yards. Eventually they led out into the middle of Beebe Lake, which was the university's main reservoir. The lake was frozen over. The rhino tracks suddenly ended in . . . a gigantic hole. There didn't seem to be much anyone could do. The local newspapers wrote all about it. Half the population of Ithaca, New York, stopped drinking tap water. And for years, those who did swore it tasted like rhinoceros.

# 6

~~~~

# Plucking Pasta and
# Pulling Legs

No one knows for sure how April Fools' Day ever got started, but it's a lively tradition around the world, with many great tricks played in celebration of the occasion. One of the more entertaining of these annual gems of deception came from a most unlikely source—the veddy, *veddy* British Broadcasting Corporation. On April 1, 1957, Richard Dimbleby, one of Britain's most respected journalists, took viewers of the BBC news program *Panorama* on a tour of the spaghetti harvest in the Swiss town of Ticino.

"The last two weeks of March are an anxious time for the spaghetti farmer," Dimbleby earnestly reported, his narration accompanied by images of a cheerful Swiss family as they plucked strips of pasta off trees. "There's always the chance of a late frost which, while not entirely ruining the crop, generally impairs the flavor and makes it difficult for him to obtain top prices in world markets." Dimbleby then explained to viewers that spaghetti growing in Switzerland was a much smaller industry than in neighboring Italy. "Many of you, I'm sure, will have seen pictures of the vast spaghetti plantations in the Po valley," he intoned. "For the Swiss, however, it tends to be a family affair." And, he added, with the virtual disappearance of the spaghetti weevil, "the tiny creature whose depredations have caused much concern in the past," a bumper harvest was expected.

"After picking," Dimbleby's report continued, "the spaghetti is laid out to dry in the warm alpine sun. Many people are often puzzled by the fact that spaghetti is produced of such uniform length but this is the result of many years of patient endeavor by plant breeders who have succeeded in producing perfect spaghetti." The scene then switched to a celebration of the harvest, with revelers indulging in the tasty harvest. "For those who love this dish," the story concluded, "there's nothing like real, home-grown spaghetti."

After the report ran, the BBC was flooded with calls from people who wondered where they might obtain a spaghetti tree of their own. (The dish was relatively unknown in Britain at the time, and *Panorama* was a well-trusted news source.) The BBC reportedly responded to inquiries with the suggestion that callers might "place a sprig of spaghetti in a tin of tomato sauce and hope for the best."

# 7

~≈~

# Painting the Town Purple

Living in the nation's capital, the boys of Gonzaga College High School had a unique platform for the ingenious prank they pulled in 1969. And it all happened with the unwitting help of the United States government.

For years students at the Jesuit institution in the shadow of the U.S. Capitol had made a subversive art out of tagging some of the city's more prominent landmarks with purple signs (purple and white being the school colors) and the battle cry, "Go Gonzaga. Beat St. John's" (St. John's College High School being their long-time rival). But in an otherwise unsettled time for the school, struggling in a neighborhood scarred by the race riots of the previous year, emerged a masterpiece of adolescent exuberance that far surpassed all other displays of school spirit.

It was just days before the annual football showdown with St. John's. The plan was to cover the spotlights that illuminated the Washington Monument at night with a celluloid material colored purple. Obtaining permission to do so was almost too easy. "We convinced the [Department of the Interior] that we were doing a science project which tested the effects of casting light through a semipermeable membrane on a white oblique object," recalls Mark Smith, who orchestrated the caper during his junior year at Gonzaga and credits his older brother Michael with the idea. A forged letter on stationery snatched from the school's headmaster helped get the government on board.

The Mall in Washington was unusually busy on the night of November 11. Hundreds of thousands had converged for a massive antiwar rally and counterprotest. But at the Washington Monument, the U.S. Park Police were otherwise occupied. They cordoned off the area so the boys could conduct their "experiment" without interruption. As police stood by, the young conspirators drove a rented truck up to the monument and unloaded sixty-seven square yards of purple celluloid. Smith and his friends had made wooden frames for the material to fit over the gigantic spotlights, and as they went about placing them, the police helpfully kept the milling crowds on the Mall at bay.

At 7:05 PM, when the celluloid was slid into place, two sides of the monument instantly turned purple, and stayed that way for thirty-five minutes. The other two sides remained white. City residents were shocked to see a familiar landmark so oddly transformed. Switchboards lit up across Washington. Meanwhile, Smith and his buddies lay back in the grass and savored their handiwork. "We thought, this is the greatest moment of our lives," he remembers with joy barely diminished by time.

The *Washington Star* was impressed enough by the stunt to devote an entire page to it. Spiro Agnew, on the other hand, was decidedly less enthused. The soon-to-be-disgraced vice president fired off a scathing letter to Gonzaga's headmaster that condemned the defacement of a national monument. So did U.S. Park Police superintendent William Failor. "In the future," Failor warned, "any requests from your institution will of necessity be closely screened and documented." The Park Police had learned a bitter lesson and would not be burned again. Years later, a vigilant Major Bob Hines of the force declared to the *Washington Times* that "if anyone attempted that again we'd stop them once they did."

# *8*

~~~~

# Underhand Pitches

Some hoaxes are so successful they become enduring popular misconceptions. Such is the notion—often repeated in newspapers and scholarly journals as an example of situational linguistics—that Eskimos have more than two hundred words for different kinds of snow. Simply untrue. Snow is snow. The Eskimos have exactly two words for the stuff: *qanik,* which means snow in the air, and *aput,* which means snow on the ground.

One of the more persistent misconceptions resulting from a hoax is the entire notion of subliminal advertising. In the 1950s an amateur New York psychologist named James Vicary (rhymes with trickery) claimed to have conducted experiments with theatergoers proving that if you flashed a one-frame message such as "eat popcorn" every few minutes during the showing of a movie, popcorn sales would skyrocket. The message could not be read, he said, but it would subliminally imprint itself on the viewer's brain.

This bothered people. It seemed a little unnervingly Big Brotherish that people's behavior You loved this book! could be secretly conditioned and manipulated. And so the FCC investigated but could not duplicate the results. The Canadian Broadcasting Buy more copies! Corp. tried a similar experiment, subliminally urging people to phone the station; not one person phoned. It turns out Vicary never published his findings in any scholarly journal Farquhar is a genuis! and when asked to repeat his experiment in a theater setting, his equipment repeatedly malfunctioned, or the results came out Tell a friend! negative. That is because they were bogus. In 1962, Vicary finally admitted he had not done the research at all.

The fact is, subliminal advertising does not work, though unscrupulous merchants continue to try it from time to time.

# Appendix 1

## Ten Tricksters from Scripture

### 1. The Serpent (Genesis 3:1–24)

Adam and Eve had no sooner settled in the Garden of Eden, with all its abundant gifts, than the serpent slithered in and tricked them into defying God and precipitating mankind's fall by eating of the tree of knowledge of good and evil, which had been forbidden them. "You will not die," the serpent coaxed Eve. "For God knows that when you eat of it your eyes will be opened, and you will be like God, knowing good and evil."

Eve was enchanted by the serpent's lies and ate the forbidden fruit, which she shared with Adam. Both were banished from the garden and all its comforts. "In the sweat of your face you shall eat bread till you return to the ground," God said to Adam, "for out of it you were taken; you are dust, and to dust you shall return."

(The serpent, i.e., Satan, was up to his old tricks again in the New Testament when he tempted Jesus in the desert, but, unlike with Adam and Eve, his lies had no effect.)

### 2. Jacob and Rebecca (Genesis 27:1–29)

Isaac, son of Abraham, had grown old and his eyesight dimmed. As he prepared himself for death, he called his son Esau and instructed him, "Now then, take your weapons . . . and go out to the field, and hunt game for me, and prepare for me savory food, such as I love, and bring it to me that I may eat; that I may bless you before I die."

Isaac's wife, Rebecca, overheard the conversation. She wanted her son Jacob to have his blind father's blessing, not Esau, and told Jacob to fetch two goats so she could make a stew for him to present to his father and receive his blessing instead. But Jacob was reluctant. "Behold," he said to his mother, "my brother Esau is a hairy man, and I am a smooth man. Perhaps my father will feel me, and I shall seem to be mocking him, and bring a curse upon myself and not a blessing." Rebecca reassured Jacob, however, and dressed him in Esau's best garment. She also attached the skins of the goats she had used in the stew to Jacob's arms and neck, and told him to bring the food she had prepared to his father.

"How is it that you have found it so quickly, my son?" Isaac asked Jacob when, posing as Esau, he presented the stew.

"Because the Lord your God granted me success," Jacob responded.

But Isaac was not satisfied. "Come near," he ordered, "that I may feel you, my son, to know whether you are really my son Esau or not." Jacob then knelt before his father, who felt his hands. "The voice is Jacob's voice," Isaac said, "but the hands are the hands of Esau." He then asked, "Are you really my son Esau?" And Jacob answered, "I am." Isaac then bestowed his blessing on the son he had been made to believe was Esau.

### 3. Jacob's Sons (Genesis 37:1–36)

Just as Jacob had tricked his father, he was deceived in turn by his own sons. They were jealous of their brother Joseph for the favor Jacob had shown him—demonstrated by Jacob's gift to Joseph of a luxurious coat—and hated him even more when he told them of dreams he had in which they bowed down before him. One day Jacob sent Joseph to check on his brothers, who were tending their father's flock. When they saw Joseph approach from a distance, the brothers said to one another, "Here comes this dreamer. Come now, let us kill him and throw him into one of the pits; then we shall say that a wild beast has devoured him, and we shall see what will become of his dreams." But one brother, Reuben, counseled against killing Joseph. "Shed no blood," he said; "cast him into this pit here in the wilderness, but lay no hand upon him." When Joseph came to his brothers, they seized him and stripped him of the coat their father had given him, tossed him into the pit, and sat down to eat.

Soon a caravan of Ishmaelites approached bound for Egypt. Judah said to his brothers, "What profit is it if we slay our brother and conceal his blood? Come, let us sell him to the Ishmaelites, and let not our hands be upon him for he is our brother, our flesh." Joseph was taken away, after which his brothers killed a goat and dipped his rich coat in it. Then they took the bloody garment to their father and said, "This we have found; see now whether it is your son's robe or not." Jacob recognized the coat, and was overcome. "It is my son's robe," he cried; "a wild beast has devoured him; Joseph is without a doubt torn to pieces."

### 4. The Gibeahites (Joshua 9:1–27)

After many years wandering in the desert after the escape from Egypt, the Israelites were finally given permission by God to conquer the Promised Land and crush its inhabitants. Joshua subsequently destroyed the cities of Jericho and Ai. The people of Gibeah knew they would suffer the same fate because they lived in the land God had set aside for Israel. So they devised a ruse to trick Joshua into making peace with them. They pretended to live far away in another country, not right in the midst of the Promised Land, where God had forbidden the Israelites to make peace with any of its inhabitants.

The Gibeahites came before Joshua and the men of Israel. "We have come from a far country," they announced, "so now make a covenant with us." The men of Israel were suspicious, however. "Perhaps you live among us," they said, "then how can we make a covenant with you?" The Gibeahites had anticipated such skepticism and were prepared with props that suggested they had been on a long, arduous journey. "Here is our bread," they said, "it was still warm when we took it from our houses as our food for the journey, on the day we set forth to come to you, but now, behold, it is dry and moldy; these wineskins were new when we filled them, and behold, they are burst; and these garments and shoes of ours are worn out from the very long journey."

Joshua and the men of Israel were convinced, and made a sacred pact with the Gibeahites that could not be broken, even after they discovered they had been deceived. The Gibeahites were spared from slaughter, although they were reduced to servitude.

### 5. Ehud (Judges 3:15–30)

The people of Israel had long been subdued by Eglon, the king of Moab, and cried out to the Lord for deliverance. Ehud, the son of Gera the Benjaminite, was raised up for that purpose. Under the guise of presenting tribute to Eglon, Ehud went to the king with a sword hidden under his clothes. When the tribute had been presented, Ehud dismissed the men who had carried it. He approached the king and pretended to have a secret message for him. "Silence!" the king ordered, and sent away all his attendants. Ehud was now alone with Eglon. "I have a message from God for you," he said. As the king rose to receive it, Ehud suddenly drew his sword and thrust it into Eglon's enormous belly.

After he had killed the king, Ehud left his chamber and locked the doors behind him. When he had gone, the king's servants returned and found the door bolted. "He is only relieving himself in the closet of the cool chamber," they thought. But when Eglon failed to emerge after a reasonable time, they unlocked the chamber and found him dead on the floor. Ehud, meanwhile, had plenty of time to escape and rally the people of Israel. The Moabs were crushed in a single day.

### 6. Gideon (Judges 7:15–23)

Gideon used an illusion to trick the Midianites into believing his tiny force was much larger. (See Part III, Chapter 4.)

### 7. Delilah (Judges 16:4–30)

Samson had long been a bane to the Philistines, and they were eager to learn the secret of the tremendous physical power he used to repeatedly defeat them. They approached Delilah, the woman Samson loved. "Entice him," the lords of the Philistines said to her, "and see wherein his great strength lies, and by what means we may overpower him, that we may bind and subdue him; and we will each give you eleven hundred pieces of silver."

So Delilah went to Samson and asked him to tell her the secret of how he might be bound and subdued. He told her seven fresh bowstrings that had not been dried would make him weak. The Philistine leaders brought the bowstrings to Delilah, and she bound Samson with them as several men lay hidden in wait. "The Philistines are upon you, Samson!" she shouted, and Samson easily snapped the bowstrings. "Behold," Delilah said, "you have mocked me and told me lies; please tell me how you might be bound."

Twice more Samson fabricated the secret to make him weak, and twice more Delilah unsuccessfully tested it. At last she said to him, "How can you say, 'I love you,' when your heart is not with me? You have mocked me these three times, and you have not told me wherein your great strength lies."

Samson finally told Delilah the truth: he would lose all his strength if his hair was ever cut. She then lulled Samson to sleep on her lap, after which the Philistines shaved his head. When he awoke, his strength was gone, and the Philistines seized him, gouged out his eyes, and took him away. It was only when his hair grew back that Samson was able to exact his revenge and bring down the temple upon his enemies—and himself.

### 8. Amnon (2 Samuel 13:1–14)

King David's son Amnon lusted after his half sister Tamar, but he believed she was unobtainable. When he told his friend Jonadab how tormented he was by desire, Jonadab, a very crafty man, said to him, "Lie down on your bed, and pretend to be ill; and when your father comes to see you, say to him, 'Let my sister Tamar come and give me bread to eat, and prepare the food in my sight, that I may see it, and eat it from her hand.'"

Amnon did as Jonadab had instructed. He feigned illness and his father sent Tamar to him. After she prepared the food, Amnon sent everyone in the house away, and said to her, "Bring the food into the chamber, that I may eat it from your hand." Tamar did as she was told, but when she approached Amnon, he grabbed her and said, "Come, lie with me, my sister." Tamar protested, but Amnon was stronger and took her by force.

### 9. Solomon (1 Kings 3:16–28)

King Solomon, in his great wisdom, used a trick to elicit the truth in a dispute between two women. "Oh, my lord," the first woman said to the king, "this woman and I dwell in the same house; and I gave birth to a child while she was in the house. Then on the third day after I was delivered, this woman also gave birth; and we were alone; there was no one else with us in the house. . . . And this woman's son died in the night, because she lay on it. And she arose at midnight, and took my son from beside me, while our maidservant slept, and laid it in her bosom, and laid her dead son in my bosom." The second woman claimed the opposite; that the living child was hers.

Solomon listened, then said, "Bring me a sword." A sword was brought forth, and the king said, "Divide the living child in two, and give half to the one, and half to the other." The first woman was distressed by the judgment. "Oh, my lord," she cried, "give her the living child, and by no means slay it." But the other woman said, "It shall be neither mine nor yours; divide it." The king knew the true mother of the living child would rather have lost it than to see it slaughtered. "Give the living child to the first woman," he commanded, "and by no means slay it; she is its mother."

### 10. Jezebel (1 Kings 21:1–16)

Ahab, king of Samaria, coveted the vineyard next to his palace that belonged to Naboth the Jezreelite. He said to Naboth, "Give me your vineyard, that I may have it for a vegetable garden, because it is near my house; and I will give you a better vineyard for it; or, if it seems good to you, I will give you its value in money." But Naboth refused the offer because legal and religious custom required that ancestral land remain in the family. "The Lord forbid that I should give you the land of my fathers," Naboth said.

The king, depressed by Naboth's refusal, took to his bed, turned away his face, and refused to eat. His wife Jezebel came to him. "Why is your spirit so vexed that you eat no food?" she asked. When the king told her, Jezebel replied, "Do you now govern Israel? Arise, and eat bread, and let your heart be cheerful; I will give you that vineyard of Naboth the Jezreelite." She then proceeded to write letters in King Ahab's name to the elders and nobles of Jezreel. "Proclaim a fast," she instructed, "and set Naboth on high among the people; and set two base fellows opposite him, and let them bring a charge against him, saying 'You have cursed God and the king.' Then take him out and stone him to death." Jezebel then sealed the letters with the king's seal and sent them off.

The elders and nobles did as they were instructed, and Naboth was denounced and killed. When Jezebel received the news, she said to Ahab, "Arise, take possession of the vineyard of Naboth the Jezreelite, which he refused to give you for money; for Naboth is not alive, but dead."

# Appendix 11

—

# Ten Great Liars in Literature

**1. Iago,** the antihero of Shakespeare's *Othello,* is perhaps the most skilled and nuanced dissembler in all of literature—"the most perfect evildom," Swinburne called him, "the most potent demi-devil." Passed over for promotion by Othello, Iago is determined to ruin him by an intricate tapestry of lies—rich in detail, lethal in application—that suggest to Othello his devoted wife, Desdemona, is unfaithful. "He holds me well; the better shall my purpose work on him," Iago says of Othello as he masterfully draws him into his web of deceit until Othello, crazed by jealousy, kills Desdemona and then, after he realizes Iago's treachery, himself.

**2. Claggart,** the wicked sergeant at arms in Melville's *Billy Budd,* is simultaneously attracted to the young hero's good looks and repelled by his virtue. After feigning friendliness toward Billy, Claggart crushes him with a false accusation of sedition aboard the H.M.S. *Bellipotent.* Billy is so stunned by the charge that he is rendered speechless and thus unable to defend himself. In his fury, he attacks Claggart and accidentally kills him—a crime for which he must hang.

**3. Becky Sharp,** the scheming, albeit resourceful vixen of Thackeray's *Vanity Fair,* lies, connives, steals, and flatters in her relentless quest for social status. And, in the process, she manages to outshine all the novel's other duplicitous and hypocritical characters—no mean feat. At one point, Thackeray compares her to a siren: "They look pretty enough when they sit upon a rock, twanging their harps and combing their hair, and sing, and beckon you to come and hold the looking glass; but when they sink into their native element, depend on it those mermaids are about no good, and we had best not examine the fiendish marine cannibals, reveling and feasting on their wretched and pickled victims."

**4. Tom Sawyer**, Mark Twain's perfect embodiment of boyhood, deftly manipulates his pals into whitewashing his aunt's fence—and paying for the privilege—by making the task appear to be a unique form of fun that would ordinarily be forbidden. "He had discovered a great law of human action," Twain writes, "namely, that in order to make a man or a boy covet a thing, it is only necessary to make the thing difficult to attain."

**5. Mephistophilis,** the servant of Lucifer in Marlowe's *Doctor Faustus,* did not tempt the play's protagonist to sign away his soul—Faustus did that on his own accord—but was ready with a lie whenever he wavered. "When I behold the heavens, then I repent," says Faustus, "And curse thee wicked Mephistophilis, Because thou hast deprived me of those joys." Mephistophilis reminds him that the choice was his, and adds, "But think'st thou heaven is such a glorious thing? I tell thee, Faustus, it is not half so fair As thou, or any man that breathes on earth."

**6. Bob Ewell,** the drunken bigot in Harper Lee's *To Kill a Mockingbird,* falsely accuses Tom Robinson, a black man, of raping his daughter Mayella. Atticus Finch ably defends Robinson and discredits Ewell, but it's for naught. Ewell's lies resonate with the all-white jury, which is unwilling to believe a black man over a white man—even one as mean and ignorant as Ewell. "I don't know," answers Atticus when his son, Jem, asks him how the jury could convict against all contrary evidence, "but they did it. They've done it before and they did it tonight and they'll do it again and when they do it—seems that only children weep. Good night."

**7. Uriah Heep,** the unctuous clerk in Dickens's *David Copperfield,* is the ultimate literary phony. He maliciously plots to undermine his boss, Mr. Wickfield, and gain control over his fortune, all the while maintaining a mask of perfect politeness and humility. Heep's "umble" pretense is on vivid display when the novel's hero, whom he hates, offers to teach him Latin: "Oh, indeed you must excuse me, Master Copperfield! I am greatly obliged, and I should like it of all things, I assure you; but I am far too umble. There are people enough to tread upon me in my lowly state, without my doing outrage to their feelings by possessing learning. Learning ain't for me. A person like myself had better not aspire. If he is to get on in life, he must get on umbly, Master Copperfield!"

**8. Smerdyakov,** the bitter illegitimate son of Fyodor in Dostoyevsky's *The Brothers Karamazov,* kills his loathsome father, but sets up the murder in such a way as to make one of his half brothers, Dmitri, appear to be guilty of the crime, and another, Ivan, complicit in it. "You murdered him," Smerdyakov later says to Ivan, "you are the real murderer; I was only your instrument, your faithful servant, and it was following your words I did it."

**9. Jay Gatsby,** the wealthy, worldly bootlegger desperate to win back the love of Daisy Buchanan in Fitzgerald's *The Great Gatsby,* is actually a false identity constructed by James Gatz when he was a young midwestern dreamer eager to escape the monotony of his ordinary existence. "I suppose he'd had the name [Jay Gatsby] ready for a long time, even then," relates the narrator, Nick Carraway. "His parents were shiftless and unsuccessful farm people—his imagination had never really accepted them as his parents at all. The truth was that Jay Gatsby of West Egg, Long Island, sprang from his Platonic conception of himself. He was a son of God—a phrase which, if it means anything, means just that—and he must be about His Father's business, the service of a vast, vulgar, and meretricious beauty. So he invented just the sort of Jay Gatsby that a seventeen-year-old boy would be likely to invent, and to this conception he was faithful to the end."

**10. Pinocchio,** created by Carlo Collodi and one of the best-known liars in children's literature, suffers a terrible consequence each time he fails to tell the Fairy the truth about the gold pieces hidden in his pocket: his wooden nose grows longer. The marionette is filled with shame and despairs over the length of his nose, but "The Fairy showed no pity toward him, as she was trying to teach him a good lesson, so that he would stop telling lies, the worst habit any boy may acquire." She finally relents, and a thousand woodpeckers fly into the window and peck Pinocchio's nose back to normal.

# Appendix III

*Ten Classic Deceptions from Greek Mythology*

1. Cronus, lord of the universe, knew a son would someday supplant him, just as he had usurped his own father, Uranus. To avoid such a fate, Cronus swallowed each of his children as soon as his wife Rhea delivered them. They lived inside him, and there could do him no harm. Rhea was distressed by what Cronus did to their children, however. Five had already been swallowed, and she didn't want to lose another. So when the sixth, named Zeus, was born, Rhea was ready. She wrapped a stone in swaddling clothes and gave it to Cronus. The great god swallowed the deception, while the baby god Zeus was spirited away and hidden in a cave on the island of Crete.

When Zeus grew to be a young man, he sought to defeat his father. But his wife Metis, goddess of prudence, warned him that he could not conquer Cronus alone; he needed allies. So Metis went to Cronus and tricked him into eating an herb that she said would make him invincible to all enemies. Instead, it made him so violently ill that he vomited up not only the stone he thought was Zeus, but his five other children as well. They were the gods Poseidon and Hades, and the goddesses Hestia, Demeter, and Hera. The divine siblings united against Cronus, who fled, and Zeus became lord of the universe.

2. Zeus married his sister Hera, who became queen of the gods. She was a jealous spouse who hated all of Zeus's other wives. Indeed,

she had refused to marry him because of the other women, but the great god won her with a sly ruse. He created a thunderstorm and transformed himself into a little bird in distress. Hera took pity on the poor little creature when it flew into her arms for comfort during the storm and held it close to give it warmth. It was then that Zeus—who used similar tricks to win other women—reverted to himself, and Hera found herself snuggling her mighty brother.

Zeus went to great lengths to hide his other wives from Hera's jealous rages, but she usually saw through his deceptions. Once she spotted a storm cloud inside of which she suspected Zeus harbored one of his wives. She raced into the cloud and found her husband. With him, however, was not a woman but a beautiful cow. Hera wasn't fooled, though she pretended to be, and asked Zeus to give her the cow. He could not deny such a simple request without betraying himself, so he acquiesced. Hera then took possession of the cow, who was really Zeus's wife Io, and tormented her mercilessly.

Hera also hated Zeus's wife Semele, the mortal mother of Dionysus, god of wine. One day she appeared before Semele disguised as an old crone and pretended to be friendly. She asked Semele who her husband was, and what kind of man he might be. Semele proudly answered that he was none other than the great thunder god. Hera feigned skepticism, and suggested he might not be who he claimed. She then suggested that Semele ask Zeus to reveal himself in all his glory to prove that he really was lord of the universe. So when Zeus returned to her, Semele asked him to grant her a wish. He swore a sacred oath that he would give her anything, but was then horrified to learn what she wanted. No mortal could withstand the spectacle of Zeus in his full radiance, hundreds of times brighter than the sun. He begged Semele to change her mind, but the seed of doubt Hera had planted made her adamant. Distraught, but bound by his sacred promise, Zeus reluctantly revealed himself and Semele was instantly reduced to ashes.

3. Zeus had many children, seven of whom shared his glory atop Mount Olympus. His son Hermes, god of thieves and others who lived by their wits, was the cleverest. When just a day old, he

sneaked into the pasture of his brother Apollo, god of light and music, and selected fifty of Apollo's best cows to steal. He wrapped the hoofs of the cows with bark to disguise their prints, and tied brooms to their tails so they would erase their own tracks. Hermes hid the cows in a grove, after sacrificing two of them to the gods, then raced back to his mother and pretended to be asleep. But Apollo wasn't fooled. An oracle revealed to him who had stolen the cows, and he confronted Hermes. The baby god denied it, claiming to be too young to know what a cow was, let alone how to steal one. Enraged, Apollo chased Hermes up to Olympus, where their father, Zeus, benevolently told his younger son to give the cows back. Apollo was satisfied, until he realized two cows were missing. To quell his brother's renewed fury, Hermes produced a lyre he had created by stringing the entrails of the sacrificed cows across the shell of a tortoise. Mesmerized by the music, Apollo offered Hermes his whole herd in exchange for the instrument. Hermes agreed, and harmony between the two divine brothers was restored.

4. Sisyphus, king of Corinth, was clever enough to fool the gods. He had angered Zeus by revealing to the river-god Asopus where Zeus had taken Asopus's daughter to elope. In his fury, Zeus asked his brother Hades, lord of the underworld, to take Sisyphus away to his dark realm and punish him for his insolence. But when Hades came to Sisyphus, the king asked him why Hermes, whose job it was to lead souls to the underworld, hadn't come to fetch him. As Hades searched for an appropriate answer, Sisyphus deftly wound a chain around him and kept him prisoner. With Hades thus bound, the world was thrown into chaos. No one could die. It was only when the gods threatened to make Sisyphus's life miserable that he let Hades go. Order was restored, and people could die as the Fates decreed.

The first person to be claimed was, of course, Sisyphus. But the king was prepared with another trick when Hermes came for him. He told his wife not to hold a funeral or put a coin under his tongue to pay for passage across the river Styx into the underworld. Hades was shocked when Sisyphus arrived the way a poor beggar would. His wife had to be punished for her neglect, or a bad precedent might be set. So Hades sent Sisyphus back to the living world to teach his wife respect. This was just what Sisyphus wanted, and he was able to spend many more happy years with his wife. Hades had been fooled once again. In the end, though, the king, like all mortals, had to die. When he reached the underworld for the second time, he was given a task that would leave him little time to come up with any more tricks. He was made to push a boulder up a steep hill, but each time he neared the top, the boulder would slip from his hands and roll back down. And so it went for eternity.

5. Heracles, a mortal son of Zeus, was the strongest man who ever lived. But because he was the son of one of Zeus's other wives, Hera hated him and made him insane. Out of his mind, Heracles mistook his own children for wild beasts and killed them. He was horrified by his crime when his senses returned, and sought to atone by performing twelve tasks for his cousin Eurystheus, king of Mycene. Hera helped Eurystheus devise the most difficult tasks imaginable, one of which was to find the secret garden of the Hesperides and bring the king three golden apples from a tree that grew there. On the way to the garden, Heracles came across Prometheus, who had been chained to a mountain by Zeus as punishment for having given mankind fire. Heracles took pity on him and broke his chains, after which the grateful god warned him that only an immortal could pick the golden apples.

Near the garden, the titan Atlas bore the sky on his shoulders. Heracles asked the god to pick the apples for him, which Atlas agreed to do, provided Heracles take the sky while he performed the task. Heracles did, but when Atlas returned he refused to take back the heavy burden. Heracles, known for his strength, not his brains, nevertheless managed to outwit the god. He feigned resignation, and asked that Atlas just hold up the sky briefly while he adjusted the padding on his shoulders to make the weight more bearable. Atlas found this reasonable enough, but when he took back the sky for what he thought would be a moment, Heracles triumphantly walked away with the apples.

6. Heracles tricked Atlas, but later fell victim himself to a deadly deception. He married a princess from Caledonia named Deianira, and they made a happy couple. One day as they traveled, Heracles and Deianira came across a swollen stream. Heracles forded it easily, but Deianira was afraid. A centaur named Nessus came along and politely offered to carry her across. Now like all centaurs—creatures that were half men and half horse—Nessus was lustful and vulgar, and as he arrived with Deianira on the other shore he decided to carry her off. As he galloped away, Heracles shot him with a poisonous arrow and he fell to the ground. Before he died, Nessus told Deianira to collect some of his blood and save it. If she ever felt she was losing her husband's love, he said, all she had to do was rub some of the blood on his tunic and his ardor would be restored.

Some time later, after Heracles won a great victory while away at war, he sent a messenger home to pick up his best tunic for a victory celebration. Deianira believed, however, that Heracles wanted the garment to impress another woman. So before she sent it to him she coated it with some of the dead centaur's blood. When Heracles put on the tunic he was overcome by a burning agony, for the centaur's blood had extremely toxic poison in it from the arrow Heracles shot into him. And though he was too strong to succumb to the poison outright, the agony was so great that Heracles ordered his men to build a pyre and burn him upon it. As the flames grew around him, Zeus drew him up to Olympus to live with the gods forever.

7. Daedalus was a marvelously skilled architect and inventor who built the great palace of Cnossus for King Minos of Crete. Underneath the palace Daedalus designed a labyrinth from which escape was impossible. There lived the Minotaur, a monstrous creature, half man and half bull, that ate only human flesh. Every nine years fourteen Athenian youths were sent to Crete and sacrificed to the Minotaur as a tribute to King Minos to prevent him from attacking Athens. One year a young hero named Theseus, vowing to slay the Minotaur, volunteered to go to Crete in place of one of the sacrificial youths. But when Ariadne, the beautiful daughter of King Minos,

saw Theseus she despaired. She hated to see the handsome hero devoured by the monster and begged Daedalus to help him. The inventor gave Theseus a magic ball of thread that led him through the maze and to the Minotaur's lair. There Theseus surprised the monster and killed it with his bare hands. He then freed the other Athenians and escaped from Crete with Ariadne.

King Minos was enraged when he discovered his daughter had fled with the Athenians and imprisoned Daedalus. But the clever inventor fashioned wings from feathers and beeswax and escaped with his son Icarus (who flew too high and fell back to earth). Minos pursued Daedalus to Sicily, where the local king denied that he harbored the escaped man. Unconvinced, Minos devised a scheme to prove that Daedalus was at the king's palace. He sent the king of Sicily a conch shell and offered a sack of gold to anyone who could wind a thread through the shell's passages. The king enlisted the help of Daedalus, who after some thought found a solution. He tied the thread to the leg of an ant and placed the tiny creature at one end of the shell. On the other end he left a dab of honey. The ant smelled the honey and wound its way through the shell to get to it. When the king of Sicily claimed the gold, Minos had his proof that Daedalus was in the palace and demanded his surrender. No one else could have figured a way to thread the shell. Seeming to acquiesce, the king of Sicily invited Minos to dinner, after which he promised to deliver Daedalus. But as Minos bathed before the feast, as was customary, Daedalus sent boiling hot water through the faucet and scalded him to death.

8. The beautiful sorceress Medea helped her love Jason through many perils in his quest for the Golden Fleece. But a trick she used to protect him from his uncle, King Pelias of Iolcus, earned her the wrath of the gods. The king had promised Jason his throne if he could obtain the fleece and bring it to him. Yet when he returned with the prize, Jason learned that Pelias had killed his father and meant to kill him as well. Medea intervened. Disguised as an old witch, she entered Iolcus and announced that she had

magic herbs which could restore youth. When King Pelias insisted that she prove her claim, Medea took an old ram, cut it into pieces, put the pieces in a cauldron of boiling water, and sprinkled in her herbs.

Pelias was amazed to see a young lamb emerge from the pot, and asked Medea to make him young again, too. The sorceress demurred. She told the king only his daughters could perform the necessary ritual. So the daughters of Pelias reluctantly cut their father to pieces, and put him in the boiling water. When they turned to Medea for the magic herbs, however, they were horrified to discover she was gone. The gods disdained Medea's cruel trick and turned from her. Then, after all she had done for him, she eventually lost Jason's love as well. To avenge herself, she sent Jason's new wife a beautiful robe as a wedding present. It was tainted, and when the bride put it on she was consumed by flames. With her anger still aroused, Medea killed the two sons she had with Jason, and, as he cursed her, flew off in a chariot driven by dragons.

9. The gods gathered for the wedding of Peleus, the king of Thessaly, and the sea-nymph Thetis. Only Eris, goddess of strife, wasn't invited, and in her fury she threw a golden apple of discord among the wedding guests with the announcement that the fairest goddess should have it. Hera, Athena (goddess of wisdom), and Aphrodite (goddess of love) all fought over the apple, and the dispute became so heated that Zeus decided Paris, a handsome prince of Troy, should settle it by awarding the apple to the one he thought was the fairest. Each goddess made extravagant promises to Paris if he would select her, but the prince settled on Aphrodite because she promised him the hand of the most beautiful woman in the world.

Now it so happened that Helen of Troy was the most beautiful, but she was already married to Menelaus, king of Sparta—one of many who had sought Helen's hand. All of her suitors had vowed to her father that they would abide by his decision as to who would marry her, and to help the victor defend her if anyone should ever

try to take her away. So, when Paris came to Sparta and took Helen—
after Aphrodite's son Eros helpfully shot an arrow of love into her
heart—her previous suitors were bound by their oath to help
Menelaus reclaim her. Most came forward immediately when
called, except Odysseus, who was happily married to Helen's cousin
Penelope and had no wish to engage in such a troublesome affair.
He pretended to be insane when a Greek leader named Palamedes
was sent for him. He yoked an ass and an ox to his plough and began to sow salt. Palamedes saw through the deception, however, and
tested Odysseus by placing his infant son in the path of the plough.
When Odysseus swerved to avoid his child, he showed he wasn't
mad and thus could no longer escape his vow.

Achilles was another reluctant warrior. His mother, Thetis, at
whose wedding Eris had tossed the apple of discord, warned him
that he would be killed if he joined the expedition against Troy and
hid him in the court of King Lycomedes disguised as a woman.
Odysseus, charged with finding Achilles, learned where he was and
came to the king's court dressed like a merchant. Among his wares
were beautiful ornaments for women, mixed in with various arms
of war. While the women of the court were enthralled by the ornaments, Achilles handled the arms and thereby betrayed himself.
Odysseus then persuaded him to do his duty.

10. The Olympian gods actively took sides in the epic clash between the Greeks and Trojans that followed the abduction of Helen.
Hera and Athena, for example, favored the Greeks, while Zeus was
sympathetic to the Trojans. The immortals used deception in a
number of instances, sometimes against one another, to assist
whichever side they championed.

As Poseidon, lord of the seas, assisted the Greeks—against the
will of Zeus—Hera sought to distract her husband from the battle.
Her plan was to seduce him and then make him sleep. She went to
Aphrodite, who favored the Trojans, and tricked her into lending
her a girdle that made anyone who wore it irresistible. She told the
goddess of love she was going to use it to help reconcile two other
gods who had been feuding, when in truth she wanted to dazzle

Zeus. Thus armed, she appeared before her husband, who was monitoring the battle from Mount Ida. Zeus found Hera enchanting, like when he first fell in love with her, and they had sex, after which Hera enlisted Morpheus to put him into a deep sleep. As the great thunder god dozed, Poseidon led the Greeks to victory.

# *Appendix IV*

~~

## Ten Egregious Examples of Modern American Doublespeak

1. President Nixon's press secretary Ron Ziegler in 1974 on whether a certain batch of Watergate tapes was still intact: "I would feel that most of the conversations that took place in those areas of the White House that did have the recording system would in almost their entirety be in existence, but the special prosecutor, the court, and, I think, the American people are sufficiently familiar with the recording system to know where the recording devices existed and to know the situation in terms of the recording process, but I feel, although the process has not been undertaken yet in preparation of the material to abide by the court decision, really, what the answer to that question is."

2. NASA official on whether shuttle performance had improved after the 1986 Challenger explosion: "I think our performance in terms of the orbital performance, we knew more about the envelope we were operating under, and we have been pretty accurately staying in that. . . . I think we have been able to characterize the performance more as a function of our launch experience as opposed to it improving as a function of time."

   NASA also euphemistically described the shuttle explosion as "an anomaly," the bodies of the astronauts as "recovered components," and the astronauts' coffins as "crew transfer containers."

3. State Department spokesperson Christine Shelley when asked in 1994 if the mass killing of ethnic Tutsis in Rwanda was a genocide: "The use of the term 'genocide' has a very precise legal meaning, although it's not strictly a legal determination. There are other factors in there as well."

A decade earlier, the State Department announced it would no longer use the word "killing" in official reports on the status of human rights in other countries, but would replace "killing" with the phrase "unlawful or arbitrary deprivation of life."

4. James Johnston, chairman and chief executive officer of R. J. Reynolds Tobacco Company, testifying at a congressional hearing in 1994: "The allegation that smoking cigarettes is addictive is part of a growing and disturbing trend that has destroyed the meaning of the term by characterizing virtually any enjoyable activity as addictive, whether it's eating sweets, drinking coffee, playing video games, or watching TV. This defies common sense."

William Campbell, president and chief executive officer of Philip Morris, USA, at the same hearing: "Cigarettes contain nicotine because it occurs naturally in tobacco. Nicotine contributes to the taste of cigarettes and the pleasures of smoking. The presence of nicotine, however, does not make cigarettes a drug or smoking addiction. Coffee, Mr. Chairman, contains caffeine and few people seem to enjoy coffee that does not. Does that make coffee a drug? Are coffee drinkers drug addicts? I think not."

5. U.S. Air Force press officer, Colonel David H. E. Opferin, to reporters after a 1973 bombing raid in Cambodia: "You always write it's bombing, bombing, bombing. It's *not* bombing! It's air support!"

The war in Vietnam produced other such euphemistic expressions as:

> Collateral damage (killing innocent civilians)
> Removal with extreme prejudice (assassination)
> Energetic disassembly (nuclear explosion)
> Limited duration protective reaction air strikes (bombing villages in Vietnam)

Incontinent ordnance (bombs which hit schools and hospitals
  by mistake)
Active defense (invasion)

6. President Jimmy Carter on the failed military rescue of the American hostages in Iran in 1980: an "incomplete success."

7. Central Intelligence Agency term for mercenaries hired to carry out raids in Nicaragua in 1984: "Unilaterally controlled Latino assets."

8. President Bill Clinton, in 1993, on how his proposed health-care plan would be financed: a "wage-based premium."

The Reagan administration had also previously avoided the word tax by substituting the term "revenue enhancement."

9. White House spokesman Marlin Fitzwater in 1988, after a U.S. Navy fighter fired two missiles at an Iranian passenger jet: "At this point I will not confirm any part of the incident." Fitzwater did say, however, that President Reagan had been informed "soon after the incident happened." As to what incident: "The incident that I'm not confirming."

10. Secretary of State Alexander Haig testifying before the House Foreign Affairs Committee on the 1980 rape and murder of three nuns and a religious lay worker in El Salvador: "I'd like to suggest to you that some of the investigations would lead one to believe that perhaps the vehicle that the nuns were riding in may have tried to run a roadblock, or may accidentally have been perceived to have been doing so, and there'd been an exchange of fire and then perhaps those who inflicted the casualties sought to cover it up. And this could have been at a very low level of both competence and motivation in the context of the issue itself. But the facts on this are not clear for anyone to draw a definitive conclusion."

Haig, the next day before the Senate Foreign Relations Committee, when asked if his previous statement was meant to suggest that the nuns might have run a roadblock: "You mean that they tried to violate . . . ? Not at all, no, not at all. My heavens! The dear nuns who raised me in my parochial schooling would forever isolate me from their affections and respect."

And in response to a question from Senator Claiborne Pell on whether his previous phrase "exchange of gunfire" meant to imply that the nuns had shot at the soldiers: "I haven't met any pistol-packing nuns in my day, Senator. What I meant was that if one fellow starts shooting, then the next thing you know they all panic."

# Select Bibliography

## Books

Ambrose, Stephen E. *Eisenhower: The President*. New York: Simon & Schuster, 1984.

Barstow, Anne Llewellyn. *Witchcraze: A New History of the European Witch Hunts*. San Francisco: Pandora, 1995.

Behr, Edward. *Kiss the Hand You Cannot Bite*. New York: Villard, 1991.

Bradlee, Ben. *A Good Life: Newspapering and Other Adventures*. New York: Simon & Schuster, 1995.

Brown, Anthony Cave. *Bodyguard of Lies: The Classic History of the War of Deception That Kept D-day Secret from Hitler and Sealed the Allied Victory*. New York: Quill/William Morrow, 1975.

Cadbury, Deborah. *The Lost King of France: How DNA Solved the Mystery of the Murdered Son of Louis XVI and Marie-Antoinette*. New York: St. Martin's/ Griffin, 2002.

Chancellor, Henry. *Colditz: The Untold Story of World War II's Great Escapes*. New York: William Morrow, 2001.

Cheesman, Clive, and Jonathan Williams. *Rebels, Pretenders and Imposters*. New York: St. Martin's Press, 2000.

Cohn, Norman. *Warrant for Genocide: The Myth of the Jewish World Conspiracy and the Protocols of the Elders of Zion*. London: Serif, 1996.

Collins, Paul S. *Banvard's Folly: Thirteen Tales of People Who Didn't Change the World*. New York: Picador, 2002.

Dallek, Robert. *Flawed Giant: Lyndon Johnson and His Times 1961–1973*. New York and Oxford: Oxford University Press, 1998.

DeCerteau, Michel. *The Possession at Loudun*. Translated by Michael B. Smith. Chicago and London: The University of Chicago Press, 2000.

Dundes, Alan, ed. *The Blood Libel Legend: A Casebook in Anti-Semitic Folklore.* Madison and London: The University of Wisconsin Press, 1991.

Elton, G. R. *England under the Tudors.* London: Methuen & Co. Ltd., 1967.

Fay, Stephen, Lewis Chester, and Magnus Linklater. *Hoax: The Inside Story of the Howard Hughes–Clifford Irving Affair.* New York: Viking Press, 1972.

Fedler, Fred. *Media Hoaxes.* Ames, Iowa: Iowa State University Press, 1989.

Gallagher, Hugh Gregory. *FDR's Splendid Deception: The Moving Story of Roosevelt's Massive Disability—And the Intensive Efforts to Conceal It from the Public.* Arlington, Virginia: Vandamere Press, 1999.

Harris, Neil. *Humbug: The Art of P. T. Barnum.* Chicago and London: The University of Chicago Press, 1973.

Heckscher, August. *Woodrow Wilson: A Biography.* New York: Scribner's, 1991.

Hoving, Thomas. *False Impressions: The Hunt for Big-time Art Fakes.* New York: Touchstone Books, 1997.

Hurst, Jack. *Nathan Bedford Forrest: A Biography.* New York: Alfred A. Knopf, 1993.

Hynd, Alan. *Professors of Perfidy.* New York: A. S. Barnes and Company, Inc., 1963.

Kurth, Peter. *Anastasia: The Riddle of Anna Anderson.* Boston, Toronto, and London: Little, Brown, 1983.

Ludwig, Emil (translated by Eden and Cedar Paul). *Bismarck: The Story of a Fighter.* London: George Allen and Unwin Ltd., 1927.

MacMahon, Edward B., M.D., and Leonard Curry. *Medical Cover-up in the White House.* Washington, DC: Farragut Publishing Company, 1987.

Massie, Robert K. *The Romanovs: The Final Chapter.* New York: Random House, 1995.

McGuigan, Dorothy Gies. *The Habsburgs.* New York: Doubleday, 1966.

Nickell, Joe. *Inquest on the Shroud of Turin.* Amherst, New York: Prometheus Books, 1983.

Pacepa, Ion Mihai. *Red Horizons: The True Story of Nicolae and Elena Ceausescus' Crimes, Lifestyle, and Corruption.* Washington, DC: Regnery, 1990.

Palmer, Alan. *Bismarck.* New York: Scribner's, 1976.

Pickover, Clifford A. *The Girl Who Gave Birth to Rabbits: A True Medical Mystery.* Amherst, New York: Prometheus Books, 2000.

Pollard, A. F. *Henry VIII.* London, New York, and Toronto: Longmans, Green and Co. Ltd., 1905.

Rayner, Richard. *Drake's Fortune: The Fabulous True Story of the World's Greatest Confidence Artist.* New York: Doubleday, 2002.

Ridley, Jasper. *Henry VIII: The Politics of Tyranny.* New York: Viking, 1984.

Shirer, William L. *The Rise and Fall of the Third Reich.* New York: Simon & Schuster, 1959.

Sillitoe, Linda and Allen Roberts. *Salamander: The Story of the Mormon Forgery Murders*. Salt Lake City, Utah: Signature Books, 1989.

Time-Life Books. *Library of Curious and Unusual Facts: Hoaxes and Deceptions*. Alexandria, Virginia: Time-Life Books, 1991.

Volkogonov, Dmitri. *Stalin: Triumph and Tragedy*. Translated and edited by Harold Shukman. New York: Grove Weidenfeld, 1991.

Walker, Barbara G. *The Crone: Women of Age, Wisdom, and Power*. New York: Harper & Row, 1985.

Walsh, John Evangelist. *Unraveling Piltdown: The Science Fraud of the Century and Its Solution*. New York: Random House, 1996.

## Periodicals

Arthur, Billy. "The Queen Imposter." *The State,* February 1991.

Carlson, Peter. "Sins of the Son: Kim Jong Il's North Korea Is in Ruins, but Why Should That Spoil His Fun?" *The Washington Post,* May 11, 2003.

Green, Bill. "Janet's World: The Story of a Child Who Never Existed—How and Why It Came to Be Published." *The Washington Post,* April 19, 1981.

Haines, J. D. "The King of Quacks: Albert Abrams, MD." *Skeptical Inquirer,* May/June 2002.

Kaiser, Robert G. "Cambodia Story a Hoax, Reports *New York Times*." *The Washington Post,* February 23, 1982.

Kurtz, Howard. "Unrepentant Blair Taunts 'Idiot' Editors." *The Washington Post,* May 21, 2003.

———. "*N.Y. Times* Uncovers Dozens of Faked Stories by Reporter." *The Washington Post,* May 11, 2003.

Powell, Michael. "Mob Boss Admits Insanity Was a Ruse." *The Washington Post,* April 8, 2003.

Wert, Jeffry D. "The Civil War Gold Hoax." *American History Illustrated,* January 1980.

# Acknowledgments

A number of good people contributed their ideas, time, and talent to the creation of this book. I want to thank my agent Jenny Bent, and my editor Caroline White, along with all the folks at Penguin. Also, Patterson Clark, Manus Cooney, Tom and Mollie Dodd, Nick Galifianakis, Kristin Inglesby, Regina Koehler, Ann Marie Lynch, Eileen Monahan, Kevin Murphy, Mike Pate of F.I.B.C., Boyce Rensberger, Rose Mary Sheldon of the Virginia Military Institute, Mark Smith, David Steward of Hillsdale College, Anthony Tambasco of Georgetown University, Lyndsey Tate of the National Council of Teachers of English, John Ziolkowski of George Washington University, and my colleagues at *The Washington Post:* Madonna Lebling, Peter Masley, Scott Moore, Eddy Palanzo, David Von Drehle, Rick Weiss, and Gene Weingarten, the generous genius to whom I owe so much.